EL PASO'S MUCKRAKER

EL PASO'S MUCKRAKER

THE LIFE OF OWEN PAYNE WHITE

GARNA L. CHRISTIAN

UNIVERSITY OF NEW MEXICO PRESS | ALBUQUERQUE

© 2015 by the University of New Mexico Press
All rights reserved. Published 2015
Printed in the United States of America
20 19 18 17 16 15   1 2 3 4 5 6

Library of Congress Cataloging-in-Publication Data

Christian, Garna L.
  El Paso's muckraker : the life of Owen Payne White / Garna L. Christian.
      pages cm
  Includes bibliographical references and index.
  ISBN 978-0-8263-5545-4 (cloth : alk. paper) — ISBN 978-0-8263-5546-1 (electronic)
  1. White, Owen P. (Owen Payne), 1879–1946. 2. Journalists—United States—Biography.
      3. Authors, American—20th century—Biography. I. Title.
  PN4874.W5165C58 2014
  070.92—dc23
  [B]

                                2014017333

Cover illustration: Photo of Owen Payne White courtesy the University of Texas at
El Paso Library, Special Collections Department, Owen Payne White Papers, MS112.

Jacket designed by Catherine Leonardo
Typeset by Felicia Cedillos
Composed in Adobe Caslon 11/15
Display fonts ITC Caslon 224 and Helvetica Neue

Contents

PREFACE   vii

   1. The Making of Owen Payne White   1

   2. "You know I'm not going to get hurt in this war"   15

   3. Launching a National Career   49

   4. The Muck and the Rake   75

   5. "Like a terrier in a barnful of rats"   99

   6. "Dammit Sis, I've got to finish this book"   133

NOTES   153

BIBLIOGRAPHY   173

INDEX   183

Preface

In July 1893 the historian Frederick Jackson Turner presented a paper, "The Significance of the Frontier in American History," to an assemblage of the American Historical Association at the World's Columbian Exposition in Chicago. His findings still debated well over a century later, Turner feared for the future with the official closing of what he considered the incubator of American democracy. Owen Payne White, whose writing career lay ahead of him, was fourteen years old. He had already seen railroads penetrate the most western reach of Texas, Indian attacks against his family, and classic gunfights of the century in or near his native El Paso, Texas. Young Owen had also developed a moral code based on the rightness of action and character that he believed to be inherent in that frontier society. While Turner despaired for democracy, Owen White considered the passing of his personal frontier, and by extension the transformation of the entire West from village to modern, progressive city, a tragic morality play.

Amid roles ranging from high school honor student, college law student, medical corpsman in World War I France, banker, jewelry clerk, feed store owner, rancher, farmer, and sometime poet and newspaper columnist, the man-about-town White had passed his fortieth birthday when he finally accepted the challenge of writing a history of El Paso. The resulting *Out of the Desert* separated itself from the sterile fate of other local histories when the publisher sent copies to two of the nation's top publications, *American Mercury* and the *New York Times*. Each followed with surprising positive reviews, giving the book and author national prominence and White a professional writing career. White received assignments from both periodicals, undertook a lifelong friendship with the salacious *Mercury* editor H. L. Mencken, and moved to New York City with his wife, "Mike," the erstwhile Hazel Harvey. From his Long Island residence and for Manhattan publishers, White wrote eight books on the Old West, an autobiography, and dozens of articles as a staff editor at *Collier's: The National Weekly*, one of the two most widely circulated magazines in the country. Often traveling to the site of a favored story, he uncovered hypocrisy, heroism, and crime, earning national recognition, the ire of political leaders, death threats, and a million-dollar lawsuit against him and the magazine that employed him. Utilizing his knowledge of Mexico and the Spanish language, he followed leads or inclinations into the neighboring country, where he once concocted a financial scheme, was wined and dined by prominent natives, covered snatches of the Mexican Revolution, and was forced to flee the country. Through it all, White never lost his sardonic wit, scrupulous directness, and independence from any organized faction.

Owen White brought local history to center stage, intrigued readers nationally with tales of the Old West, and spotlighted corruption in high and low places. Yet by the early twenty-first century his best-selling books were out of print and his name was seldom voiced in the genre of western histories and muckraking, to which he signally contributed. Only a few pages of scholarly research have described his vital career. Here follows the first full-length biography of an articulate man born and raised during the fascinating transition of this country's most appealing region. It is based primarily on the Owen White Papers in the C. L. Sonnichsen Special Collections Department of the University of Texas at El Paso Library, Owen White materials at the El Paso County Historical Society, and personal collections of relatives of White. These materials have been supplemented by vertical files at the Dolph Briscoe Center for American History at the University of Texas at Austin, existing brief biographical essays, and books and articles by White.

The author is heavily indebted to Laura K. Hollingsed, Claudia A. Rivers, Anne Allis, and the staff of the UTEP Special Collections; Patricia H. Worthington, curator of the El Paso County Historical

Society; Don Carleton, curator of the Dolph Briscoe Center for American History, University of Texas at Austin; Mr. and Mrs. Oliver Osborn of Lake Jackson, Texas; and Mr. and Mrs. James M. Shatto of Houston. Any errors are, of course, the property of the author.

Garna L. Christian
Sugar Land, Texas

CHAPTER I

The Making of Owen Payne White

In unequal parts, muckraking, libertarianism, and late nineteenth-century El Paso contributed to the singularity of Texas-born writer Owen Payne White. White's name is seldom linked with muckrakers Ida Tarbell, David Graham Phillips, or Upton Sinclair; indeed, in the twenty-first century his name is seldom invoked at all. The occasional reference is more than likely to his role as a local historian and author of a half-dozen books on notorious Western gunmen, now collectors' items. Yet in his heyday, from the 1920s through the mid-1940s, his acerbic wit and perseverance were the bane of malefactors and others whom White deemed unworthy of their positions.

At once contentious and compassionate, Owen White was born June 9, 1879, in El Paso, Texas. In 1923, already a war veteran and an established local speaker and poet, he wrote the classic history of his hometown, *Out of the Desert: The Historical Romance of El Paso*. Through an unusual combination of the author's bravado and good fortune, the book attained national prominence and the support of legendary newsman H. L. Mencken and the *New York Times*. Although conservative and libertarian by nature, White began engaging the power structure with wit and criticism at the prestigious Manhattan newspaper and increased the readership at *Collier's*. As a contributing editor of the journal for fifteen years, White enhanced that organ's visibility with popular articles on the Old West and crusading investigations that produced death threats for the author and lawsuits for him and the magazine. A series of books on the nineteenth-century frontier brought additional fame to his native El Paso, which White physically neglected for a life and career in New York. During World War II, despite failing health, White threw himself into the war effort on the home front against the Fascists, whom he detested. Even at that patriotic task, he shocked readers of his autobiography with the comment that he welcomed the Japanese attack on Pearl Harbor as a unifying force. White had neared completion of a never-published history of western exploration when he died of heart failure on December 7, 1946.[1]

The term "muckraker" burst forth in 1906 when President Theodore Roosevelt mounted his bully pulpit on at least three occasions to assess the new investigative journalists who defiantly took on corporate and political greed. While the renowned trust-buster grudgingly acknowledged "as a benefactor every writer or speaker . . . who . . . with merciless severity makes such attack," he warned "that the attack is of use only if it is absolutely truthful." Casting suspicion on the veracity of the upstart newspaper, magazine, and novel writers, Roosevelt compared them to "the Man with the Muck-rake" in John Bunyan's *Pilgrim's Progress*, "who could look no way but downward with the muck-rake in his hands; who would neither look up nor regard the crown he was offered, but continued to rake to himself the filth on the floor." Thus "muckraker" entered the nation's vocabulary, and in future years observers of Owen Payne White could address him by an alternative to the sobriquet "Rattlesnake Pete."[2]

The protest tradition, to which White adhered, originated well before the prime of the muckrakers, whose pinnacle approximated the period of 1902 to 1912. Much distinguished and popular writing of the post–Civil War period had celebrated the unification of the previously warring sections of the nation, albeit at the expense of the abandoned freed slaves and the rise of unregulated industry based on American creativity and social Darwinism. Newspapers and magazines often reflected in their outlook the increasing amount of advertising by corporate giants, even though they maintained some diversity in rapidly expanding readerships. Critics of the status quo steadily gained public attention, however, as economic panics rocked the nation in 1873 and 1893; farm prices, beset by high costs and overproduction, dropped to ground level. Violent strikes erupted along the rail lines in 1877, at Cyrus McCormick's Chicago plant in 1886, at Andrew Carnegie's Homestead steel company in 1892, and at George M. Pullman's company town near Chicago in 1894. These events only highlighted the day-to-day struggles of farmers, labor unions, and immigrants for survival.[3]

Organizers and sympathetic writers began to demand changes to the status quo in the last third of the nineteenth century. The idealistic labor unions, the National Labor Union and the Knights of Labor, which sought reform through enlightenment and persuasion, gave way to the more practical American Federation of Labor, which threatened and employed economic pressure on reluctant owners. Elizabeth Cady Stanton and Susan B. Anthony stood in the forefront of the women's suffrage movement, reinvigorated after the granting of the franchise to freedmen. The Women's Christian Temperance Union and National Prohibition Party strengthened support for another post–Civil War prohibition campaign. The Greenback Party, advocating inflation to elevate farm prices, and the Populist Party and American Socialist Party, demanding political and economic democracy, captured the votes of many farmers and laborers. The more drastic anarchists appealed to a lesser number of radicals. The Social Gospel religious movement, led by Washington Gladden and Walter Rauschenbusch, emphasized the need for reform in this world, rather than a wait for divine reward in the next.[4]

Literature, to which White contributed in addition to journalism, buttressed these challenges to the system. Edward Bellamy attacked social Darwinism and advocated nationalization of industries as business corporations demolished competition. Cosmopolitan, naturalist, and realist novels depicted the individual in a complicated web of interior and exterior forces. In this collective deterministic view, Stephen Crane, Jack London, Frank Norris, Theodore Dreiser, and Upton Sinclair described the lower classes as helpless pawns of uncontrollable economic and social currents. Newly addressed themes of divorce, sex, poverty, and crime frustrated the lives of the characters. William Dean Howells, often considered the leading American realist, criticized the nation's economic conditions. Not even rural and small-town America escaped the authors' scrutiny. Hamlin Garland shocked his readership with descriptions of poverty among midwestern farmers and villagers.[5]

Nonfiction writers preceded White in questioning society, as well as their own fields of interest. Jacob Riis exposed the extent of widespread poverty in American life. Henry George attributed the widening disparity between rich and poor to unearned increment in the value of land. Thorstein Veblen denounced the conspicuous consumption of the wealthy. Sociologist Lester Frank Ward reinterpreted Darwinism as a justification of government regulation. Economist Richard Ely envisioned an improved economic climate through employment of government policies. Frederick Jackson Turner and Charles Beard, in their studies of democracy, moved historical thinking in new directions. Future muckraker Henry Demarest Lloyd attacked the practices of John D. Rockefeller's Standard Oil trust a dozen years before Roosevelt designated it a monopoly.[6]

Lloyd, commonly cited as the first investigative reporter, epitomized the role of muckraker. Born in New York City in 1847 to a Dutch Reformed minister, Lloyd had well-to-do relatives who paid for his college and law degrees. Before moving to Chicago in his twenties, he participated in the Liberal Republican anti-Grant movement and the opposition to Mayor William "Boss" Tweed that resulted in the latter's downfall. Lloyd wrote for the *Chicago Tribune* and married the daughter of a wealthy stockholder, though his subsequent exposés of big business severed the newspaper connection and caused his father-in-law to disinherit Lloyd's wife. As a freelance journalist, he gained fame and notoriety by denouncing Standard Oil in an *Atlantic Monthly* series in 1881 and by the expansion of his research in *Wealth against Commonwealth* thirteen years later. Although not an ideologue, Lloyd supported reform movements, including protection of workers' rights, women's suffrage, and limiting working hours of women and children in industry. He was a close friend of Jane Addams and reform governor John Peter Altgeld.[7]

Other popular writers, many with the same genteel and nonradical backgrounds, joined the ranks of White's forbears. Lincoln Steffens investigated political bosses and corruption in state and local governments in a magazine series and later in book form as *Shame of the Cities* (1904). David Graham Phillips's article "The Treason of the Senate" infuriated President Roosevelt to the point that he labeled the group "muckrakers," but it also strengthened the movement toward direct election of federal senators. Ray Stannard Baker reported on the little-publicized plight of African Americans in *Following the Color Line* (1908), and in magazine pieces he alleged malfeasance of railroads. Samuel Hopkins Adams aroused public concern at the state of public health and the contents of patent medicine in his "The Great American Fraud" series, assisting in the passage of the Pure Food and Drug Act. Ida Tarbell, the best-known female investigative reporter, also wrote articles on Standard Oil and published *The History of the Standard Oil Company* in 1904. In possibly the most influential book of the genre, Upton Sinclair uncovered the unsanitary conditions within the meatpacking industry while writing sympathetically about recently arrived immigrants in *The Jungle* (1906). The book is widely regarded as influencing the passage of the Meat Inspection Act, which Roosevelt signed into law that same year. Charles Edward Russell, like Sinclair a moderate Socialist, wrote of widening class divisions in "Growth of Caste in America." Many of the muckrakers were trained in newspaper journalism and wrote novels and serial fiction. Russell won a Pulitzer Prize for a biography of conductor Theodore Thomas, founder of the Chicago Symphony Orchestra, in 1927.[8]

McClure's Magazine, the pacesetter of the investigative journals, was established in Boston by college classmates Samuel McClure and John Sanborn Phillips in 1893. McClure, an Irish immigrant, had already worked himself out of childhood poverty and established the first newspaper syndicate in the United States. Seeking wide readership through low costs, the coeditors sold copies for fifteen cents each and signed up leading popular writers, such as Rudyard Kipling, Jack London, and Arthur Conan Doyle, serializing novels in progress. McClure moved the publication in its famous direction in January 1903 by running exposé articles by Tarbell, Steffens, and Baker in the same edition. McClure's creativity, receptiveness to ideas, and casual work environment earned him popularity with a stable of investigative writers, but the same directionless approach and flamboyant lifestyle brought the magazine financial ruin and ultimately alienated McClure's colleagues. After three years of successful but hectic existence, McClure's leading contributors left with assistant editor Phillips to create *American Magazine*, a nonmuckraking publication. *McClure's* suffered a loss of readership and increasing debt, forcing the sale of the magazine to creditors in 1911. Reorganized as a women's journal, minus the original leadership, in 1921, *McClure's* published its last issue at the end of the decade. *The Smart Set*, a literary magazine edited by H. L. Mencken, absorbed the historic trendsetting publication. Although McClure lived to age ninety-two and received the Order of Merit of the National Institute of Arts and Letters in 1944, he never regained his earlier place in crusading journalism.[9]

Other magazines vied with *McClure's* to satisfy the reading public's fascination with corruption and power. *Atlantic Monthly*, where Lloyd's first exposé appeared, predated *McClure's* by a generation. Established publisher Moses Dresser Phillips founded the organ in 1857—ironically, the birth year of Samuel McClure. James Russell Lowell, the first editor, set its direction toward literary and cultural commentary, bolstered by a coterie of writers that included Harriet Beecher Stowe, Ralph Waldo Emerson, Henry Wadsworth Longfellow, and John Greenleaf Whittier. Lloyd wrote his report on Standard Oil under the editorship of William Dean Howells, who enticed realists Mark Twain, Henry James, and Edith Wharton into the journal's ranks. Nevertheless, the journal largely continued with its original format until after the success of *McClure's*. Unlike most of its contemporaries, the *Atlantic*, under its later title, adjusted to changing readerships and remains one of the leading venues of opinion in the twenty-first century.[10]

More strident than *Atlantic Monthly* and also older than *McClure's*, *Collier's Once a Week* was the creation of Peter Fenelon Collier in 1888. Like McClure, Collier hailed from Ireland and developed into a successful American publisher. He steered his vessel of fiction, wit, and news toward muckraking under the editorship of journalist Norman Hapgood in 1903. A reformist in his own right, the legally trained Hapgood acquired the talents of Ida Tarbell, David Graham Phillips, Ray Stannard Baker, Jack London, Upton Sinclair, and Samuel Hopkins Adams. Circulation doubled to one million sales under Hapgood's tutelage, but he moved on to *Harper's* in 1912, three years after Collier's death. *Collier's Weekly*, as it had become known, continued to attract top-line writers after the muckraking era and competed with *Saturday Evening Post* as the nation's best-selling magazine before its demise in 1957. Hapgood's legacy influenced Owen Payne White's decision to join *Collier's* in the 1920s.[11]

Second only to *Scientific American* as the oldest continuously published magazine in the United States, the originally titled *Harper's New Monthly Magazine* dated to 1850, introduced by Harper & Brothers of New York City. The journal boasted that it anticipated the muckraking movement by decades with its publication of Thomas Nast's exposé of William "Boss" Tweed and Tammany Hall in 1868. Ida Tarbell, David Graham Phillips, Ray Stannard Baker, and Lincoln Steffens, among others, wrote for *Harper's* in the early 1900s. In similar fashion, White subsequently took up his pen against deviant political and business leaders.[12]

Perhaps the most zealous of the investigative magazines, the relatively short-lived *Arena* offered a didactic approach to literature under the guidance of founder Benjamin Flower. The Illinois-born journalist, influenced by the writings and philosophies of Edward Bellamy and Henry George, started the magazine in 1889, left it for a time, and then returned to its editorship in 1904. The heavy emphasis on social reform failed financially, and the publication succumbed to poor sales five years later.[13]

The muckraking era fell into decline only a few years afterward. This partly owed to the legislative success of many of the writers' causes. Roosevelt's administration strengthened the Interstate Commerce Commission in the Hepburn Act and the Sherman Antitrust Act and prosecuted the Northern Securities organization. His presidency saw the passage of the Meat Inspection Act and the Pure Food and Drug Act. The following term of William Howard Taft witnessed the passage of the Sixteenth and Seventeenth Amendments, fulfilling reformers' goals of direct election of U.S. senators and of a graduated income tax. Banking reform, federal aid to schools and roads, and another antitrust act followed during the tenure of Woodrow Wilson. While critics lamented the incomplete nature and enforcement of many of the reforms, the Progressive middle-class agenda of the muckrakers largely had passed into law. This apparent success coincided with a resurgence of corporate power within the media to shape policy through bestowal or denial of precious advertising.[14]

At first sight, Owen Payne White appeared an unlikely member of the muckraker genre. An avowed antireformer, he railed against modernity, particularly Progressivism's legacy of prohibition. Geography and time seemed to conspire against his inclusion: a Far West Texan writing after the demise or decline of most of the literary vehicles. Yet *Colliers*, Owen's pulpit of the

1920s and 1930s, formed a direct link to the tradition of investigative reporting under the editorship of William Ludlow Chenery. Indeed, Tarbell, Sinclair, Steffens, and Baker all lived into at least the 1930s and 1940s. White's libertarianism held targets of the political right as worthy as those of the left and his deeply felt convictions of right and wrong made him an intransigent foe. In common with many of the muckraking magazines and writers, his interests beyond the moment enabled him to diversify his literary production with poetry, history, and personal reminiscences.[15]

Libertarianism, a core principle of White's, dated from at least the late Enlightenment of the eighteenth century; in its various forms it promulgated the maximization of individual liberty in thought and action. Its basic premise is that each individual should be free to do as he or she pleases as long as the action does not harm others. Libertarians, who agree on full self-ownership, range in belief from the minimal state to anarchy, exhibiting a "left" wing that claims the right of each person to a share of natural resources and some sort of income redistribution and a "right" wing that focuses mainly on economic freedom. Among early European exponents of self-independence, William Belsham argued for free will in 1789 and Joseph Dejacque wrote from an anarchist communist position in 1857. Pointedly, the left wing dominated libertarian thought for much of the following century. Its hands-off position for government allied with free traders of the laissez-faire school of economics, melding with liberal economic and political theory. The success, if not the application, of Adam Smith's *Wealth of Nations* after 1776 fashioned liberal capitalism in the United States, though the mercantilist-oriented programs of Alexander Hamilton to build up fledgling business and banking dominated early economic policy.[16]

Thomas Jefferson and the Democratic-Republican Party built their political philosophy around the preference for a small and unobtrusive national government, in opposition to Hamilton's Federalist Party. In the name of "Jeffersonian Reform," the minimalists pursued a passivity of government that would allow agriculture to remain supreme at the expense of incipient industry. The Sedition Act, passed under Federalist president John Adams, sparked a conflict that elevated freedom of thought to the level of minimal statism among the political opposition. Jefferson and James Madison, railing against government suppression of free speech in the Virginia and Kentucky Resolutions, posited the right of states to nullify unconstitutional federal encroachments. Although proclaimed in order to protect civil liberties of individuals, the doctrine of nullification later reappeared under the vestige of states' rights to protect slavery and racial segregation. For most of the remainder of the nineteenth century, American liberals attempted reform under the banner of limited government, in contrast to a Hamiltonian model that perceptively protected business interests through government power. The surge of corporate power after the American Civil War placed reformers in a quandary. The Grangers, among the first of the embattled agricultural and small-town groups fighting the political and economic preponderance of railroads, held fast to their Jeffersonian model. The more radical Farmers' Alliance movement, which culminated in the Populist movement, departed from reform tradition by exhorting the national government to rescue the common man from the claws of the corporate monster. The People's Party, by the 1890s, demanded government ownership of railroads and other corporations, while issuing a slate of political reforms, including term limitations and direct election of U.S. senators. The Democratic Party, long the champion of free trade, co-opted the movement in 1896, with William Jennings Bryan running a pale version of the agenda, essentially centered on currency expansion, in an effort he lost to orthodox Republican William McKinley.[17]

Progressive writer Herbert Croly provided a rationale for the role of government in reform by disassociating political liberalism from the minimalist Jeffersonian state in *Promise of American Life* (1909). He boldly summoned Hamiltonian measures to achieve Jeffersonian goals of democracy. As political liberalism, during the Progressive and New Deal periods of the twentieth century, increasingly identified with a strong and interventionist government, libertarians emphasized classic economic liberalism, establishing a cleavage between liberal economics and liberal politics. Nevertheless, proponents of the minimal state and of the active state often found common ground in endorsement of individual rights of speech, press, association, and, in the second half of the twentieth century, a noninterventionist foreign policy.[18]

Henry George (1839–1897), perhaps the most similar predecessor of Owen White, afforded an example of the ability to combine two apparently dissimilar movements, muckraking and libertarianism, in the same person. The author of *Progress and Poverty* (1879) and the most conspicuous advocate of the "single tax" on land, the Philadelphia-born George pursued a variety of occupations, limited by a brief formal education. He spent fourteen months at sea as a foremast boy, turned to apprentice typesetting, failed at gold prospecting, and then returned to the printing trade. George practiced reporting, editing, and, eventually, management as the owner of a San Francisco newspaper in the 1870s. Politically, he first favored the Republican Party under Lincoln but converted to the Democrats, eventually losing a campaign for the California Legislature. As a newsman, George attacked railroad and mining interests, corrupt politicians, land speculators, and labor contractors in a strong muckraking spirit.[19]

According to George, he conceived the idea of the single tax while horseback riding near San Francisco Bay. A chance remark by a resident on the price of land and the sight of cows grazing on a distant lot convinced him that the growth of population pushed up the value of land, creating greater overhead for operators and advancing both wealth and poverty. A visit to New York City reassured him that the poor in that metropolis suffered more than their counterparts in less-developed California. The resultant *Progress and Poverty* appealed to a reading public mystified by the contradictions of the industrial growth the nation had experienced since the Civil War, selling over three million copies. The author postulated that landholders and monopolists controlled a large portion of the wealth created by social and technological progress in a free-market economy because of economic rent. This unearned wealth also largely produced poverty. Private profit stemming from the restriction of access to natural resources burdened productive activity with heavy taxes, creating a system equivalent to slavery, or wage slavery. George noted that California railroad construction in particular increased land values and rents as fast or faster than wages rose. He based his solution, the single tax, on his belief that unearned profits on land should be shared by society. Although this might be accomplished by nationalizing land and then leasing it to private parties, George favored a substantial land value tax to cause the value of land titles to decrease. He opposed tariffs as a form of revenue, due to their protection of corporations, and in later years extolled free trade, a staple of libertarianism.[20]

George's economic theory, Georgism, attracted a wide and persistent following among libertarians. A tax on unused land did not arouse their opposition to taxes on productive wealth, and many agreed with the socialization of natural resources. Revenue attained from the single tax, for example, could be used to fund the state, redistributed to citizens as a pension or basic income, or divided between those two options. The first option could preclude further taxation, as George intended, guaranteeing a minimal state. Georgism's antimonopolistic and antiprivilege implications, combined with advocacy of democratic political machinery, melded into the Populist and Progressive movements and inspired local support for property taxation. Over a hundred years after George's death in 1897 liberals and neoclassical conservatives on several continents vied for his heritage.[21]

Unquestionably, the sparse and rugged American West deeply influenced the libertarian Texan White, providing, in his mind, an example of frontier individualism. Historians have debated the veracity of the popular notion of the independent and free westerner, popularized by the penny press, Hollywood silent and talking movies, and, more recently, the Marlborough Man. Frederick Jackson Turner concluded that westerners relied on government as much as their own instincts for survival. El Paso, Texas, still raw and gritty at the time of White's birth in 1878, provided his imaginative youthful mind bountiful examples of giants walking the land.[22]

In only one sense was El Paso young at White's birth. The railroad-created hub lay far in the distance for first-generation residents of the mountain pass. The Jumano and other Native Americans had roamed the area for thousands of years before the Spanish began to take note of it in the sixteenth century. Two Spanish parties, led by Álvar Núñez Cabeza de Vaca and Francisco Vásquez de Coronado, possibly traversed the site in the 1530s and '40s, respectively. The Rodríguez-Sánchez expedition documented the pass in 1581, and Juan de Oñate celebrated Thanksgiving a short distance downriver from the present site in 1598, claiming the entire area drained by the Rio Grande for his sovereign. A half-century later Spanish missionaries established an outpost in what is now Ciudad Juárez, across the Rio Grande from present-day El Paso, and in 1680 Spanish and Tigua survivors of the Pueblo Revolt in northern New

Mexico founded Ysleta, a present-day suburb. By the middle of the eighteenth century approximately five thousand Spanish, mestizos, and Indians lived in a chain of communities bordering the south bank of the shifting great river.[23]

Three events in the early 1800s shaped the future of the area, vividly documented by its later historian, White. The Mexican independence movement culminated in 1821, transferring the region to the new nation. Eight years later recurring floods carved a river channel south of the towns of Ysleta, San Elizario, and Socorro, placing them on the north bank. Two decades later, a war between Mexico and the United States (1846–1848) ended with the Treaty of Guadalupe Hidalgo, forging American sovereignty over the north bank of the Rio Grande. The U.S. Department of War placed Fort Bliss in the first of its several locations, at the Pass of the North, assuring permanence of the Far West Texas town. Immigrants from the United States began trickling in even before the war, attracted by the Chihuahua trade and other perceived opportunities under Mexican rule.[24]

Two Kentuckians, Hugh Stephenson and James Wiley Magoffin, arrived in El Paso during the Mexican period. Aside from their identical origins, the two men shared other striking similarities. Born within two years of each other, 1798 and 1799, Stephenson and Magoffin married Hispanic women, attained success in business enterprises, acquired landholdings that housed Fort Bliss at different times, supported the Confederacy during the Civil War, and died within two years of each other. Another Kentuckian, Ben Dowell, arrived after the Mexican War, in which he fought, and he followed a similar path. A proprietor and landowner of note, he also married a local Hispanic woman, absorbed himself with both societies, and advocated southern secession. Dowell directed his ambitions toward politics, being elected El Paso's first mayor and serving as alderman and county commissioner. The social assimilation of the three men into Hispanic culture, while they maintained political and economic domination in an overwhelmingly Hispanic society, set a model for leadership in El Paso in its early American period.[25]

El Paso notched signs of progress in the immediate postwar period, but nothing compared to what occurred after the arrival of the railroads in 1881, a scant two years after White's birth. As the railheads of four companies drew nearer, transients and future residents filed into the town, multiplying its population. The immigrants included future town leaders, political and business, whose names adorned buildings and street signs in future years. Zach White, O. T. Bassett, Charles R. Morehead, and a fortunate quantity of others fit this description. Logically, the newcomers also included hangers-on and lawless adventurers of the type that fascinated young Owen White. Saloons and bordellos bloomed from the desert, with Tillie Howard and the Great Western (Sarah Bourgett), attaining legendary status as proprietors of the latter establishments. Dowell's bar, gambling den, and meeting center stood out in popularity among hundreds of competing saloons. The gunslingers who put El Paso on the map and in the headlines frequented both types of establishments, indiscriminately distributing their victims as chance arose.[26]

Among the legends who lived by the gun and attained immortality in White's writings, Dallas Stoudenmire, John Selman, and John Wesley Hardin appeared in the late nineteenth century. Stoudenmire, from Alabama, served as a Confederate soldier, a Texas Ranger, and a New Mexico marshal before accepting an appointment as town marshal in El Paso in 1881. Only three days later he participated in the sensational "Four Dead in Five Seconds" gunfight in downtown El Paso. Stoudenmire feuded with the Texas Rangers, local politicians, the press, and local bar owners George, Frank, and James Manning. The brothers killed the thirty-seven-year-old Stoudenmire, by then a U.S. deputy marshal, in 1882 but escaped conviction.[27]

John Selman, known to young White and others as "Uncle John," hailed from Arkansas and followed a crime-ridden trail to El Paso in 1893. Already in his maturity, the fifty-four-year-old Selman had lived a desperate life, replete with Confederate service and desertion, cattle rustling, gambling, murder, and rape. He had also pinned a deputy sheriff badge to his vest and married and lost a wife along the way. At the Pass of the North Selman gambled and held the post of city constable, once killing a former Texas Ranger in a brawl at Tillie Howard's establishment. Selman earned his greatest notoriety by fatally shooting John Wesley Hardin in a saloon in 1895. Although Hardin took three bullets in his back, a hung jury failed to convict Selman. Deputy Marshall George Scarborough, in turn, gunned down Selman after an altercation in a local bar.[28]

John Wesley Hardin, Selman's victim, accumulated one of the most violent records of any outlaw, en route from his native Bonham, Texas, to El Paso. The son of a Methodist preacher, Hardin inaugurated his killing career while still a youth, bringing down the wrath of the Union army, Reconstruction government, and Texas Rangers. Captured in Pensacola, Florida, after being accused of the murder of a Texas deputy sheriff, Hardin was returned for trial to Comanche, Texas, in 1878 and sentenced to twenty-five years in prison. Alternately seeking to escape and studying theology and the law, Hardin wrote his autobiography while in prison and was pardoned and admitted to the bar in 1894. The following year the forty-two-year-old lawyer opened a practice in El Paso but could not escape his past or habits. He took as a mistress the wife of one of his clients and may have had the protesting cuckold killed. Selman, perhaps a participant in the shooting, then turned on Hardin, as noted, and shot to death El Paso's most famous personality of the time. At his death John Wesley Hardin had carved at least thirty notches on his pistol.[29]

Muckraking, libertarianism, and frontier El Paso consciously and unconsciously mingled to form the outlook of Owen Payne White, but his mountain and desert home, where stolid individuals appeared to make their own peace and future, outpaced the others.

CHAPTER 2

"You know I'm not going to get hurt in this war"

Owen Payne White, whose prolific writing made him a staple of New York publishing firms, preserved his first conscious memory, of staring at his pair of beaded Indian moccasins as he trailed behind his father on a hunting expedition in an isolated patch of the Arizona Territory. It was the late nineteenth century, some time and distance after June 9, 1879, Owen's birth date in El Paso, Texas. Later White would consider the adobe hut at Arivaca to be in poorer condition than a similar one in the less tiny and more interesting settlement at the Pass of the North.[1]

Certainly, central Arizona offered little to settlers aside from mountain men, prospectors, traders, trappers, and government officials, such as Owen's father and companion in food gathering, Dr. Alward White. Not organized as a territory until midway through the Civil War, Arizona was best known to many as a gateway to California, with stagecoaches under constant threat of Apache attacks and known copper and gold reserves. The census counted fewer than ten thousand souls in 1870, with little indication of migrant growth.[2]

The White family, consisting of Dr. White, Kathryn (Payne) White, and children Alward, Owen, and Leigh, appeared as unlikely as any of the sparse residents. Kathryn (also Cathrine Josephine Payne) was born to landholder David Hamilton Payne and Eliza Ann Pace in Petersburg, Virginia, on November 24, 1845. Kathryn was educated at the Female Academy of Williamsburg, acquiring a love for literature that she later carried to the frontier. Her father served the Confederacy as a member of the home guard, slipping through Northern lines to report troop movements and delivering supplies and messages. The family, consisting of the two parents, four sons, and three daughters, lost their home in the path of Union cannonading, fleeing first to a relative's home and then to Abington, Virginia. At that location Payne and two of his sons operated a hotel for two years before the family moved to Colorado, according to Owen, financed by the money Kathryn had earned from teaching. While sharing with the family the management of a hotel at Evans, the young lady met her future husband.[3]

Alward McKeel White, born September 3, 1847, also traversed much of the American continent to reach the frontier West. A native of Talbot County, a slaveholding area in eastern Maryland that produced abolitionist Frederick Douglass, White descended from three generations of physicians. Named for his father, Alward was described by Owen as small, redheaded, and prone to stammering. White graduated from the precursor to the University of Maryland and later from Bellevue in New York. Alward joined the U.S. Army as a contract surgeon in 1869, on condition that the military dispatch him to the Apachería. There is an account of a "Doc White," apparently Alward, as a member of a posse in or near Lavaca County, in southeast Texas, in late 1870. He is credited with shooting Henry Kelly, a member of the Sutton outlaw gang, from his saddle in a major shootout. In any case, Alward was not disappointed with his military orders. The assignment took his cavalry detachment through the village of El Paso on his mission northward, subjecting the unit to fierce Indian assaults.[4]

Despite White's initial enthusiasm for the task, several years of service in the Colorado Territory turned him to the more promising pursuit of ranching on the Platte River. The loneliness of the work, even with a partner, provided the opportunity to read the several boxes of books that had joined him from back east. In the best romantic tradition, one day Alward rode into Evans, fifty miles distant, and met Kathryn. They were married on April 8, 1875, and moved into the ranch house. Her eastern background notwithstanding, the bride, under the tutelage of Alward, was soon riding, shooting, and chasing buffalo. Soon the Indians' fascination with the ranch and its stock overwhelmed their livelihood, but Kathryn insisted they persevere until their first son, Alward, was born in 1877.[5]

Having depleted their savings through loss of cattle and Apache depredations, the Whites were at loose ends until the senior Alward learned of a possible customs position at El Paso. Considering the discomfort of his passage through the area en route to Colorado, he surprisingly retained a favorable image of the town. He got the job and sent for the family; the seven-hundred-mile trek by Concord coach featured a lynching outside their hotel window at an overnight stop and the constant threat of an Indian ambush or a detour into a deep ravine. For all their trouble reaching El Paso, the Whites resided there only a little longer than it took to make an addition to the family. Little Owen remembered nothing personally from his first brief tenure at the Pass, but his mother's vivid description of the residence remained etched in his mind. He liked to remind twentieth-century readers that his hometown lay six hundred miles from the nearest rail station and that only a half mile of sand and river guaranteed him American citizenship. He would also argue, mostly unsuccessfully, against the myth that he was the first white man born in El Paso. The White family's one-room, one-story adobe hut boasted a substantial dirt floor, a roof of the same origin, and a single door and glassless window. But it was the story of the roof that intrigued White: a centipede frequently wriggled inside the earthen ceiling and dangled above the bed of the mother and child. Kathryn silently watched and wondered which of them the insect would land on when it fell. Being the larger, she wagered successfully that she would be the target, thereby sparing baby Owen the trauma.[6]

Prerailroad El Paso in 1878 harbored, as yet, more dreams and transients than actual settlers and commodities. The next census, two years later, would show only 736 residents. In retrospect, Owen calculated a population of half that amount, about 90 percent of Mexican origin, scattered over the two settlements, Magoffinville and Franklin, separated by a mile of desert. Yet the young family shared in the general conviction that an economic boom was approaching along the nearing cross-ties. They enjoyed their life, not dwelling on the dark side, in which Alward made himself a human target by taking on cattle-rustling bands. Kathryn, by necessity and for some amusement, shot the heads off trespassing rattle-snakes. About six months into Owen's young life, the U.S. government ordered his father's transfer to Silver City, New Mexico, a hamlet with even a tougher reputation and fewer comforts than El Paso. Alward pronounced his new workplace unsuitable for his loved ones and placed them on a stage for Colorado. Suffering a horrendous experience, Kathryn and the small boys were spared a scalping party only by the last-minute intercession of the U.S. cavalry. The rescue dissuaded Kathryn from passing to her children and herself the cyanide tablets that she always carried in the locket of a necklace for the worst contingency.[7]

Circumstances, and Alward's superiors, forced the Whites to spend a few years in territorial limbo before returning to their adopted home at the Pass of the North. Owen, still in his precognitive stage of infancy, would learn later that his parents had somehow uncovered a comparative palace at rough-hewn Silver City. The four-roomed, wooden-floored, glass-windowed house, built by Alward, provided a warm contrast to life outside its walls for a year. Constructed in the heart of the Apachería, Silver City was still enjoying an ore boom in the 1870s, but the danger remained. Founder John Bullard filled the town's first grave site, a victim of the Plains Indians. Billy the Kid (William Bonney) added his presence in that decade, forging a pre–Lincoln County notoriety. Then the expected but dreaded telegram arrived from Washington: Alward received the order to take control of the customshouse at Arivaca, Arizona. Owen's awareness developed at an ironic time; unable to appreciate the comforts of the Silver City residence, he fully apprehended the conditions on the new frontier. The one-room hut in Arivaca bore no windows, although it boasted two doors, and sat on the edge of a malarial swamp. The remains of two captured and scalped prisoners of the Apaches along a trail improved no one's disposition. Kathryn took to leveling a shotgun at the door on nights when Alward was on duty. Owen later calculated the eleven months at Arivaca to be the low point of his mother's frontier experience. Young Alward and Owen both contracted malaria in their outdoor wanderings, though they avoided a worse fate. Living among Mexican families, the impressionable Owen quickly learned Spanish, an asset for his future years on the border. When Apache raids forced out many of the families, Alward closed the customshouse on his own initiative and moved it to Tucson.[8]

The former territorial capital and still the largest town, Tucson had reached about seven thousand in population when the Southern Pacific arrived in 1880. This modern stroke, along with the varying quality of the new residents, presented the southern Arizona center parallels to the immediate future of El Paso. Lawman Wyatt Earp, dispatched to curb the sporting and shooting element, set off the Arizona War by killing Frank Stilwell, whom he accused of murdering his brother, Morgan Earp. The increased and cheaper imports and contributions to culture fostered by the railroad more than offset the seamy side of progress for the Whites. They enjoyed living in a five-room structure with real wooden floors, despite the cracked dirt roof and its location as the last house in town, drawing inebriated passersby prone to shooting out lights. Kathryn resolved the first problem by tacking muslin to the insect-infected ceiling and ameliorated the second by drawing the curtains tightly after nightfall.[9]

The drawn curtains enclosed affectionate family affairs, the first actual opportunities to share each other's company. Apparently few books had survived the travels, but the parents maintained a storehouse of knowledge and talents to provide the eager boys with a taste of their eastern educations. Young Alward and Owen absorbed Shakespearian lines and were soon acting out plays for the pleased parents, who fabricated the costumes. Because the same trains that dropped off desperados also brought in touring companies, Tucson provided the boys the ability to view real plays. Unfortunately for Kathryn, the variety-theater venue repelled ladies of class and she was limited to hearing descriptions of *Richard III* from her male family members. Years later, Owen recalled his first play as a highlight of his life. Still, the real world intruded. Justice continued to flow from a gun barrel, and on one occasion the boys were caught up in a cattle stampede, narrowly avoiding death. Duty called the father away much of the time, and in most encounters the other party was an armed cattle rustler.[10]

The most memorable event of the family's Tucson chapter was the birth of Leigh, the youngest child and only daughter, on November 19, 1884. A microcosm of the civilizing of the West through the settlement of women, her birth represented to the family the dawn of a new age for the

Arizona Territory. Almost simultaneously an Episcopalian minister appeared, preaching in private homes in the absence of churches; he christened both Leigh and Owen. Young Alward had received the sacrament at the age of two weeks, back in Evans, Colorado. Playfully describing the process to Owen as akin to branding cattle, Alward so unnerved his little brother that Owen bit the hand of the minister. A miraculous new ice factory that delivered its product to the very door of its customers surely sealed the frontier. Accordingly, as Tucson appeared to be entering the modern age, the Bureau of Customs terminated the employment of Alward White, probably the act of a spiteful superior.[11]

With El Paso the preferred family destination, Alward first had to return to Silver City to sell the house and land. Owen entered public school, excelled at reading because of familial preparedness, lost his first schoolyard fight, and cheered the apprehension and public display of Apache prisoners. Young White's contempt for the Plains Indians, quite in keeping with the times, came naturally to him. His father and, indeed, his mother fought off Indians, or expected an attack, on virtually any journey. Alward's introduction to El Paso featured a pitched battle between Apaches and his cavalry troop. In Colorado Indians pursued their cattle and in Arizona their lives. Granted that much of this history took place before Owen's birth or in his infancy. White's popular accounts of the Wild West in the 1920s and '30s showed little compassion for the Natives, though his poetry sometimes reflected a dignified respect. Nearer the end of his life, Owen sympathized with Indians as victims of whites' avarice, as their stoic and independent existence came to represent to him the freedom that his libertarian instincts treasured.[12]

After several months in the mining town, the Whites returned to El Paso and the father resumed medical practice as the town's first doctor. It was 1887, Owen was nine years old, and he would spend more than half his life at the mountain pass. The boy engaged in his expected share of adolescent pranks, subject to opportunities, by helping himself to the mayor's watermelon and cantaloupe patch and commandeering with a friend the mule-driven El Paso–Juárez streetcar. In more constructive veins, however, Owen renewed his public school education, really enjoying it for the first time. He felt comfortable in the undemanding Episcopal Church and regularly attended Sunday school. His parents continued to supplement his instruction with examples of their own, his father subsidizing the child's education by customarily offering him a quarter to learn a poem by the end of the day. The tutelage demonstrably succeeded: at age thirteen Owen delivered an address that received coverage in the local press, and he graduated from Central High School as the class valedictorian in 1896, speaking extemporaneously on Julius Caesar from his vast storehouse of readings. The scheduling of commencement at Myar's Opera House signaled the growth of public education in a growing community of homes and churches. The 1900 census showed a population in excess of fifteen thousand, reflecting a 50 percent gain over the past ten years. El Paso was transforming into a transportation, mining, trade, and cattle center, with a brick skyline rising appropriately, fueled by immigration from the United States, Mexico, and Europe.[13]

Indeed, El Paso enjoyed solid growth between the Whites' return in 1887 and the turn of the century. In typical newspaper boosterism, the *El Paso Herald* proclaimed the family's first full year at the Pass one of healthy growth and the following year one in which the community led every southwestern town in progress of wealth and population. In this instance, however, the figures matched the praise. By early 1893 a $10-million-dollar dam and irrigation company was operative—though that endeavor would later draw its measure of criticism from Owen and others—the citizenry approved a quarter-million-dollar waterworks system, and a new railroad promised entry. At the following new year, El Paso boasted four newspapers, three banks, three international streetcar lines, two electric light companies, two large waterworks, a $3-million-dollar dam and reservoir, eighteen hardware stores, ten restaurants, "and five hundred Chinamen," the latter having contributed the labor for the transforming railroads. As a reward for their successes, city fathers demolished Chinese businesses in preparation for the construction of a downtown brick building. The national depression of the 1890s braked the economy in El Paso as elsewhere, but in 1898 real estate sales surged with investments of nearly a half-million dollars. Seven months later the *Herald* trumpeted the absence of idle people and vacant dwellings. New structures included a copper and lead smelter, with an adjacent community, Smelter Town, of the American Smelter and Refining Company (ASARCO) on the west side near the river. In 1900 the police chief, acting on numerous complaints, prohibited boys from playing baseball in the streets because of horse and buggy traffic. Concurrently, the International Light and Power Company introduced arc lights and the city cleared adobe *tiendas* to make room for a two-story brick structure. An Austin financier, already holding $30,000 in local municipal bonds, sought an additional sum of $156,000, while a survey noted the growth of 654 buildings within the previous two years.[14]

El Pasoans seized the opportunity to enjoy more entertainment than offered by the saloons and gambling dens. Myar's Opera House, which had certified Owen's public education, brought to its stage the likes of Edwin Booth, Sarah Bernhardt, and Lily Langtry between 1887 and 1905, when it burned to the ground. Its spirit continued in Chopin Hall, a competitor for fine music since 1896. Touring companies held no monopoly on the arts, particularly music, as locals in the nineties offered up melodies for virtually every taste, from the El Paso Symphony Orchestra to the mirthful McGinty Club, which featured musicians in long, dark coats and high hats who ended sessions with fireworks and cannon fire. In between, amateur theatricals performed the works of Gilbert and Sullivan, and the Fort Bliss band, El Paso Cornet Band, and *típica* orchestras played to enthusiastic audiences. Virtually every civic or social occasion included music, even the arrival of visitors by train. The Cactus Club emerged as a serious debating society in the eighties, the El Paso Woman's Club sponsored a centennial ball in 1900, and two years later the tony Toltec Club and El Paso Country Club, both of which enlisted Owen White, made their appearances. The prominent women in society included Mrs. White virtually from the time the family arrived. In later writings and interviews, Leigh confirmed the developing genteel side of the frontier community. She recounted the evolution of El Paso from a hamlet of dusty streets to a turn-of-the-century city in which kid-gloved suitors called for their young ladies in hired hacks after sending calling cards. Meanwhile, unspoiled ladies of the house visited the poorer neighborhoods, nursing the sick and attending to newborns. After Owen attained success with his gun-barrel Western histories, his younger sister frequently chided him for neglecting El Paso's cultural advances in his writings.[15]

El Paso became a sporting town beyond the familiar horse races and gaming places during the last decades of the century. Athletic young men applied themselves to baseball, eventuating in the formidable El Paso Browns, a regional contender, although perhaps the best-remembered event concerned the El Paso Fats, who in 1892 journeyed to Deming, New Mexico, to defeat a hefty team and inspire fighting among fans on the return train. A natatorium and skating rink provided family recreation, while the more dedicated joined the Border Wheelmen and the Sporting and Athletic Club. The most publicized sporting event of the period was the one that got away. Heavyweight boxing champion Jim Corbett vacated his title to the winner of a projected Bob Fitzsimmons-Peter Maher match. Since most states had outlawed boxing, including a hasty action under Texas governor Charles Culberson, the venue posed a real problem. Nevertheless, El Paso sportsmen succeeded in landing the fight, planning to stage it in the neighboring Juárez bullring. When the Mexican governor closed off that venue, only the famous Judge Roy Bean of Langtry could save the situation. He held the contest barely on the Mexican side of the Rio Grande one week after Valentine's Day in 1896, while hundreds of rail-delivered spectators looked on and Texas Rangers glowered from the American bank. Owen, though initially caught up in the excitement, deigned to splurge his meager resources on the trip after his father, who medically advised Maher, confided that the fighter's poor physical condition would betray him after one punch. Dr. White nearly predicted the outcome, as Fitzsimmons dispatched his Irish-born opponent in barely over a minute.[16]

Unfortunately for the city builders, the old, unruly El Paso refused to quietly move away. A curious and gregarious young man such as Owen could hardly avoid it, given its media-documented notoriety and the fact that his father healed not only the genteel folk but also the denizens of the border. Dr. White, having returned to medical practice, had scrupulously upheld the law in his former position of customs officer by angrily denouncing an attempt to bribe him and lecturing Owen on the rascality of the famed gunmen. However, he considered not all the customers of the bars and bordellos nor the providers of those services bad people. Indeed, he occasionally sent Owen into the south side on errands to familiarize himself with conditions there, a supplement to the lad's own investigations. When a renowned madam died, Alward unabashedly wept in Owen's presence. Dr. White, who had witnessed a share of hypocrisy in his careers, may also have intended a lesson in morality for his son, who viewed some of the leading civic and political lights in an entirely different role in the tenderloin area. If so, Owen's later observations on local society proved it a lesson well learned. Owen's first bout of intoxication as an adolescent alarmed his mother more than his father. The young man learned another lesson and never indulged in the presence of Kathryn. As it turned out, that lesson carried a price tag. Winning $800 in a saloon poker game with appropriate stimulants, Owen succumbed to the invitation of a kind stranger to check into a hotel in order to avoid his mother. He awoke to find his new friend and his money gone, etching another notch of skepticism in the young man's mind.[17]

Owen stated that his father, as far back as Tucson, had instilled in him a thorough contempt for pistol-brandishing outlaws. In El Paso, Dr. White's profession brought him in even closer contact with the most notorious. Alward treated John Selman after the latter suffered a wound while gunning down Baz Outlaw, a former Texas Ranger. Outlaw had killed a Ranger in Tillie Howard's establishment, perhaps facilitating Selman's jury acquittal. White examined the bullet-riddled body of Martin M'Rose (also Morose, Mrose, and Mroz), probably ordered killed by John Wesley Hardin or Selman. As the El Paso health physician, White certified seven penetrating wounds in the chest and abdomen, two directly through the heart. Alward also prepared the medical report on Hardin, shot to death by Selman, possibly as a spillover from the M'Rose incident, in the most sensational killing of the time. The subsequent wounding of Selden by Deputy U.S. Marshall George Scarborough raised the alarm for White to rush to the scene. On first examination the doctor found only a neck wound and sent the man home for a more thorough examination. Two colleagues agreed that Dr. Howard Thompson should remove a bullet pressing on the spine, but the steadily weakening Selman died at Sisters Hospital. Whether sardonically referring to the murder rate or to the number of gamblers who despaired at their losses, a local newspaper declared El Paso a mecca for suicides. Alward suffered knowledge of at least one grim example when a woman whom he had diagnosed as pregnant sent him her suicide note.[18]

Despite the harsh demonstrations of a gunman's fate, there is no gainsaying that the proximity of the protagonists of penny dreadfuls aroused curiosity in young Owen. Eventually he thought of them as exhibiting an individualism, albeit in a skewed form, that complimented his libertarian world view. White personally viewed or was knowledgeable about the mythical figures who trod the stage of El Paso on one side of the law or the other—John Selman, Dallas Stoudenmire, the Manning brothers, and John Wesley Hardin among them. Owen liked to recount how he had exchanged pleasantries on the street with "Uncle John" Selman just before he gunned down Hardin on a summer night in the Acme Saloon. The bullet in the back of the most infamous killer in the west necessitated a trial, which the boy followed at first hand. Albert B. Fall, prior to becoming a U.S. senator or secretary of interior, came in from New Mexico to defend Selman in court. White noted that the long frock coat that Fall habitually wore covered not only his thin frame but also a hole in his pants. The tattered clothing did not detract from the brilliance of Fall's argument of self-defense, however. He convinced the jury that Hardin saw Selman's entry into the saloon through the wall mirror and actually drew before Selman. For his verbal footwork, the attorney attracted a misfired bullet, which, if it had been successful, White later wrote, might have saved the nation from the Teapot Dome scandal.[19]

Owen's graduation from high school did not immediately take him from the Pass of the North. Respectable, yet not wealthy, the young man spent the next two years enriching his experiences in a town on the make. He witnessed his first evangelical revival, which, stated minimally, made a lasting impression on him. Accustomed to collecting bills for his father among all classes of his patients, Owen landed a job selling and collecting for a jewelry store. Life sent him another lesson when he spied the expensive brooch purchased by a married civic leader adorning a young lady in the church choir. An after-hours robbery of the store, which posed no danger for White, proved the high moment of his employment, when townspeople showered him with attention and requests for information. Meanwhile, he read voraciously, finally concluding that he could not stay even with the volumes rolling from the presses. Impressed by his diligence, Dr. White banked on Owen's learning capacity by sending him to the University of Texas to study law. He found college study comfortable and the Austin social scene even more so, but the death of his father aborted his academic career and returned Owen to El Paso.[20]

The unexpected passing of Dr. White on March 7, 1898, plunged the entire community into mourning. Widely regarded as one of the most prominent medical doctors in the Southwest and one of the most popular local citizens for his charitable deeds and unpaid services, Dr. White's record of service earned him the affectionate title of "the Beloved Physician." He had taken ill a few days earlier with what appeared to be a slight attack of grippe; however, the ailment developed into fatal pneumonia. The medical community of nineteen doctors met to express their respect for their colleague, drawing up a resolution of praise. The family, now intact with Owen home from Austin and Alward returned from the School of Mines at Golden, Colorado, scheduled services for St. Clements Episcopal Church, with burial at Evergreen Cemetery. Throngs of admirers sadly watched Dr. White's white horse pull the carriage at the head of the funeral procession.[21]

Owen personally viewed the local reform movement that transformed El Paso and, according to later statements, he abhorred it. Clearly, many people felt the city was in need of reform, but neither the moral condition of El Paso nor the wish to convert it approached uniqueness. Every despicable or loveable trait resulted from its history as part of Mexico, the United States, Texas, and the West. From its beginnings as a male-dominated Spanish colony, typically few women accompanied the conquistadores. Mexico, in turn, imposed few restraints on sexual liaisons, prostitution, gambling, and drinking. Although preaching morality and enforcing religious conformity, the Roman Catholic Church tolerated human frailties more than many of the Protestant sects north of their country. Even so, the United States harbored more vice than later moral reformers would acknowledge in their pleas to return the nation to its religious origins. Camp followers, a minority of whom were involved in illicit activities, and lotteries supported the Continental Army during the Revolution. John Adams's morning cider symbolized the alcoholic thirst of the new people. Thomas Jefferson, another author of the Declaration of Independence, famously made wine at his Monticello domicile. Nineteenth-century urbanites might satisfy their lusts at parlor houses, or perhaps concert houses if financially endowed or at the cheaper but lively bawdy houses if not. Public condemnation, at least from the more whole-some segments of society, in tandem with alarming rates of intemperance and sexually transmitted diseases, brought faltering efforts from the U.S. government. Congress passed legislation prohibiting the immigration of persons of immoral character, the transport of women into the country as prostitutes, and the distribution of lewd materials through the mail. Future suffragettes found a haven in the temperance movement. Nevertheless, the corner saloon, and sometimes more, remained a staple of working Americans, enough girls of the street plied their trade to influence realist writers in the last decades of the century, and stores sold narcotics openly.[22]

Unlike the federal government, state and local officials dealt with the issues at close hand. That usually meant tolerating the status quo as long as possible, as these officials were needful of protecting their own safety, the economy that sin subsidized, and often, the business interests of civic leaders. Loathe to squeeze a commodity that the citizenry by its partici-pation supported, the establishment frequently limited its reform to seg-regating all the vice in a single location and warning decent people to stay away. Commonly called red light districts, the most famous of these, Storyville, contributed to the legendary status of New Orleans and its improvisational music.[23]

The frontier West built a history of sin of mythic proportions. In one isolated village one might find as many of the seven sins in such combi-nation as one could afford. Spawned by the mining booms of the early 1800s, lacking genteel women and ways, encouraged by the vastness of the underpoliced territories, and enriched by the commerce carried by the iron horse, dusty hamlets from New Mexico to Arizona to Colorado, as Owen saw, matched or topped any lurid experience in the Lone Star state. Towns sporting names drawn from death or dying, with boot hills for cemeteries, burned brightly and passed into dime-novel fiction or into civilized society, to the dismay of journalistic sentimentalists.[24]

Although not the worst of the lot, Owen White's Texas, devoid of mining boomtowns and territorial status, possessed an aura among its nineteenth-century contemporaries. Before and after Texan indepen-dence from Mexico in 1836, fledgling towns generally sported saloons, gambling halls, and attendant ladies of pleasure before erecting any churches. Houston fit that description at the time the new Republic of

Texas designated it as the national capital, and Waco, later the state center of Baptist Christianity, earned the epithet "Six-Gun Junction." Trends dimmed only slightly after Texas joined the United States in 1845, as signs stating "Gone to Texas" dotted the eastern premises of desperate men. San Antonio and Fort Worth, astride the Chisholm Trail following the Civil War, catered to the influx of cowhands, the latter town carving out Hell's Half Acre, the state's most notorious district. The expulsion of most of the Plains Indians by the U.S. Army, Texas Rangers, and buffalo hunters in the early 1880s made West Texas safe for frontier towns, while rails created others from work camps. By the end of the century many of the state's cities vied with Fort Worth's vice reservation: Galveston's Post Office Street, San Antonio's Sporting District, Houston's Happy Hollow, Dallas's Frogtown, and El Paso's Utah Street. Despite the illegality of the zoned activities, local governments as a matter of course licensed houses of prostitution and taxed the residents.[25]

As elsewhere, reform winds blew sporadically on Texas, the earliest gusts directed against hard drinking. The fact that the momentum chiefly emanated from religious and women's groups, absent at the towns' creation, stoked the disapproval of saloon owners, their habitués, and individualistic males. Indeed, saloons in the early days acted as civic halls, Houston's Round Tent Saloon hosting government leaders, officially and unofficially, and Judge Roy Bean holding trials in his famous establishment. Nevertheless, advocates regarded the saloon as the lynchpin of other vices, such as gambling, brawling, and prostitution. The Sons of Temperance, organized in the 1840s in New York, immediately set down roots in Texas, supported by reformed drinker Sam Houston and three thousand others impatient with public debauchery and familial abuse. Thirty-five of forty-one counties enacted laws in the next decade prohibiting the sale of liquor in amounts smaller than a quart, but a state court overturned the measure before implementation. Prohibitionists managed to introduce local option into the Constitution of 1876 and six years later the Women's Christian Temperance Union joined the fray. Texas men defeated a prohibition amendment to the constitution in 1887, as women lacked the franchise. Nevertheless, reformers drove saloons out of most of North and West Texas by county local option by the 1890s, and the issue bitterly divided the dominant Democratic Party.[26]

Moral reformers inevitably arrived at the Pass of the North. Simeon Harrison Newman's newspaper, the *Lone Star*, unleashed attacks on the city administration's tolerance for vice and, by reliable accounts, initiated the reform movement in 1883. Born in 1846 in Lexington, Kentucky, Newman trekked to New Mexico at age twenty to teach school. Five years later he bought the *Las Vegas Weekly Mall* and for a decade editorialized against graft. In the epic year 1881 several El Paso businessmen offered Newman a thousand dollars to move the newspaper to the Pass and re-name it the *Lone Star*. The scrappy editor, who once engaged in a fistfight with a rival editor in New Mexico, brought down the wrath of the very businessmen who solicited him as he exposed corruption. Withdrawn financial support caused Newman to cease publication in 1886, although he remained in El Paso as a businessman.[27]

As the city's premier reformer, Newman, in July 1883, inspired forty or fifty like-minded residents to organize the Citizen's Reform League and push for reform of the city council under Mayor Joseph Magoffin, the son of James Wiley Magoffin and one of El Paso's leading landowners and businessmen. When the Magoffin administration failed to impress Newman, the *Lone Star* attacked him also. However, enthusiasm was building among the reformers that carried into successive administrations. The Law and Order League, a segment of the local Democratic Party, got behind the council, which passed an ordinance raising the license fee on gamblers virtually to prohibitive levels after 1890. A revived council, spurred by Juan Hart's *Times*, pressed police to arrest prostitutes; J. A. Smith's *Herald* focused its ink on the gamblers. Landlords who rented rooms to prostitutes off the reservation faced arrest in their own right, and orders went out to close gambling dens. Constable John Selman, now operating on the side of the angels, made a list of all the gamblers in town and ran them out or put them in jail. A lone defiant gambler received a beating for his independence. The local historian Cleofas Calleros believed that El Paso had shed its hard shell by 1896–1897. Skeptics, perhaps including Owen, doubtless noticed that Uncle John merely sent two civic leaders across the river to sober up when they engaged in roughhousing.[28]

The reform movement peaked in the mid-nineties. According to one chronicler, a few months of reform was all El Paso could stand at one time. The presence of Ciudad Juárez across the river made real reform difficult in any case. Interestingly, unlike in most of Texas, here the question of prohibition had not even entered the arguments about gaming and whoring. Apparently enough outcasts sneaked back from exile to affect the municipal elections in 1895, as the stalwarts returned to power and reversed the cleanup. Shootouts, the deaths of Hardin and Selman, and the relocated Fitzsimmons-Maher fight appeared to absorb public attention. Faltering steps toward reform in the new century, cheered by *Herald* editor Hughes Decoursy Slater, forced gambling dens upstairs and closed saloon doors on Sundays. A native Virginian and New York resident, Slater came to the Pass for the healing climate and immediately engaged the establishment. The eventual owner of the *Herald* and the *Times*, he also advocated for public parks, scenic drives, public charities, and slum eradication. Through public pressure rather than the ballot box, reformers claimed victory in 1904. Conservative mayor Charles R. Morehead, for decades a defender of the status quo, closed the dens, bordellos, and dance halls in the Utah Street district. A report stated that on the following day, 4,429 people crossed the bridge into Mexico, obviously more than the 600 known professional gamblers or the unestimated number of prostitutes. Mayor Morehead's decision to enforce all the state blue laws requiring Sunday closings for legitimate businesses further eroded support for reform. The outcasts discreetly retraced their steps and, at least, lived outside the public spotlight. The reform issue remained essentially in abeyance for another decade. Owen reserved comment until then.[29]

While Owen's brother returned to college, becoming a fifth-generation doctor, the younger sibling tried his hand at business. Part owner of a family enterprise, involving two uncles, in ranching, real estate, farming supplies, and machinery, Owen within two years bought out his partners. He formed his own partnership with William D. Wise, of approximately his own age. This success, coupled with eighteen months of experience in banking, augured well for the young man's future. Then, suddenly, White suffered the devastating loss of his mother on August 7, 1903. News accounts described the fifty-seven-year-old Mrs. White as succumbing to a lingering illness, surrounded by her immediate family. Hailed for her generosity and social leadership, Mrs. White particularly won admiration from the younger generation. Reverend Henry Easter conducted funeral services at St. Clements, which she regularly attended, with internment at Evergreen Cemetery.[30]

Kathryn's siblings, Frances Dunn McCutcheon, Jesse Bignal Payne, Frank Hamilton Payne, Ann Leigh Hughes, David Monroe Payne, and Walker Floyd Payne, also stood among the most respected citizens of El Paso. Walker Floyd, the youngest Payne, influenced the family move to El Paso and became a highly successful business and civic leader. He contributed to the formation or administration of important local organizations, the Franklin Club, Social Club, Country Club, Toltec Club, Athletic Club, and Border Wheelmen among them. As a Democrat, he served on the city council and was elected to the mayoralty when his predecessor resigned. For his assistance in obtaining a franchise for the electric streetcar in 1902, the city awarded him the old mule-driven streetcar, which he placed in his backyard as a playhouse for his daughter. All family members participated in the reform movement, with Floyd, as his name commonly appeared, and David playing particularly conspicuous roles. A brother-in-law, W. S. McCutcheon, ran several campaigns as a Republican and, with family members, influenced the construction of Elephant Butte Dam and agricultural development in the lower valley.[31]

Owen returned to his work after his mother's death, but his heart was not in it. Unable to regain the enthusiasm for his trades, he later quipped that he spent too much time reading and drinking. It was a matter of changing his goals in life from keeping accounts to exploring human nature. In the new mode White gregariously spoke in public and wrote numerous poems while delving into the lives of eccentrics, who have always gravitated to borderlands. He accepted an appointment as notary public from the governor and served on the committee opening the El Paso Country Club. Owen doubtless enjoyed the family affair of his brother and him ushering the wedding of a cousin, at which sister Leigh, "gowned in white liberty silk," acted as maid of honor. Several years later he and Alward enjoyed the pleasure of attending Leigh's marriage to engineer O. S. Osborn in Salt Lake City. Owen's contemplation of life provided him with a personal, though unexplained, religious philosophy. Nevertheless, neither respectability nor popularity could hold Owen. Fearing that the day of the adventurous had passed, and unreceptive to the forced orthodoxies of the new century, Owen decided that his hometown had become too nice. He sold his holdings, went to the train station without a clear destination in mind, and, on the suggestion of a friend, bought a ticket to Mexico City.[32]

Despite his fluency in Spanish, learned from infancy, and his familiarity with Mexican food, culture, and neighbors, White found himself in an unfamiliar situation. Never having lived in a town larger than El Paso, and having traveled little in any direction, Owen stepped down into one of the continent's largest cities, one with a social scene richer than any he had imagined. White did not allow his libertarian instincts about government to interfere with his enjoyment of the dictatorship of Porfirio Díaz. An iron-fisted ruler of Mexico, Díaz in 1907 was already courting the tumult that would shortly end his thirty-year reign, but his lavish treatment of foreign companies and citizens created a climate of intrigue and abandon that captivated Owen. Through his newly acquired contacts and his knowledge of the market, White concocted a plan to establish a Mexican stock exchange. He drew the support of almost everyone of standing in both Mexico City and New York, except for a prominent Mexican banker with intentions of his own. In attempting to outmaneuver his rival, Owen alienated some dignitaries and sought the comfort of El Paso until Latin tempers cooled.[33]

Owen found his town very much as he had left it, wearing reform on its sleeve but retaining its casual past in at least a chamber of its heart. He found his fascination for the inner workings of the society still active and his rhetorical skills and the demand for them intact. Owen continued to hone his poetry, the field in which he would first attain literary prominence. *Collier's*, ironically his future employer, judged a contribution to their verse competition on Theodore Roosevelt worthy of comment but lacking the potential for publication. The Toltec Club, where in White's view the leading men of the city preferred their drinking and gambling, seemed a second home and perhaps most reminiscent of his hobnobbing with the powerful and famous in Mexico City. Organized only in 1902, the Toltec Club had already become a local institution, with its fame stretching far beyond the Pass. The leading lights of El Paso applied for the charter on November 2—Britton Davis, J. A. Eddy, A. P. Coles, W. W. Turney, C. N. Tibbits, U. S. Stewart, Feliz Martinez, C. W. Kendrick, W. G. Choate, T. M. Wingo, J. G. Hitzinger, and

William H. Burges. Collectively they represented banking, the legal profession, ranching, realty, merchandising, publishing, and railroads. Davis, the first president, as a lieutenant had pursued Geronimo across the Southwest into Mexico and purportedly was the first white man to cross the Sierra Madre. Social functions required men to wear tuxedos, while resident members paid fifty dollars in annual dues. Over the years the club hosted Theodore Roosevelt, Porfirio Díaz, General John J. Pershing, and General Leonard Wood.[34]

Owen returned to El Paso when the club was in transition to a five-story building designed by Denver architect John James Huddart on Magoffin Avenue. Decorated with balconies, cornices, brackets, dentils, and hood molds, the triangular structure displayed Beaux-Arts and Renaissance Revival influences and had a restaurant on the ground floor and living quarters and club rooms on the upper floors. In the highlight of his speaking engagements, White accepted an invitation to speak to the U.S. senatorial committee studying the Elephant Butte Dam project. White opted to roast Senators Francis G. Newlands of Nevada, Francis Warren of Wyoming, Thomas Carter of Montana, and Wesley Jones of Washington. Owen's acerbic wit won the night, according to the outcome of the study. It was no small feat. Completed in 1916, the dam's immensity fashioned it second only to the Nile dam at Assouan, Egypt. It lay astride the Rio Grande in southern New Mexico, over five hundred meters long, creating two hundred miles of seashore and providing electrical power, flood control, and irrigation for the Southwest and West Texas.[35]

Despite his popularity and obvious enjoyment at deflating pretentiousness, White embarked for Mexico City again in 1911. The timing was propitious for a lover of a good story. Owen believed that the stock exchange controversy that had chased him out of the country had cooled sufficiently for him to return to the high life, but actually Mexico was moving into the most heated chapter of its history. Francisco Madero, whose career Owen had followed with less than awe, was in the process of dislodging Díaz, one of the most powerful rulers in the world. The two figures stood in strong contrast to each other, and White saw no difficulty in supporting the senior man. World leaders, including the progressive Teddy Roosevelt, praised the octogenarian Díaz for raising his country to industrial heights and stabilizing the economy and the political system.

They didn't mind the openings for foreign capital, the cheap land and labor, and the honored position of Europeans and Americans, either. Non-Mexicans generally failed to observe the methods of *pan o palo* (bread or the stick), the use of bribery or force based on circumstance and individuals, that held the system in place. The special status of foreigners had turned even conservative businessmen into radicals, as they deemed themselves the stepchildren of Mexico. Madero, slight, philosophical, a vegetarian, a spiritualist, and a northern hacendado, appeared an unlikely revolutionary or the least likely victor over Díaz. His own options asunder as a result of the unrest, White went back to El Paso. He did not realize the Mexican Revolution would follow.[36]

El Paso began to view the future leading figures in the Mexican Revolution during the early twentieth century. The community's position as a gateway to the financial centers of the United States, a storehouse of monetary assets and munitions in its own right, and the home of a large and partisan Hispanic population predicted the importance of its role. Indeed, the poverty of recent immigrants in Chihuahita, below Second Street, inspired the premier novel of the revolution, *Los de abajo*, by Mariano Azuela. As early as 1905 Ricardo Flores Magón, publisher of the notoriously anti-Porfirian newspaper *Regeneración*, plotted an attack on Ciudad Juárez from the apparent safety of El Paso. The perception dissolved the following year when Mexican and American officials broke open the conspiracy, sending Flores Magón in flight to Los Angeles, where arrest awaited him. Perhaps hoping to discourage subsequent attempts, President Díaz arranged an invitation from President William Howard Taft to meet on the border on October 16, 1909. Locals breathed in the heady historical air of the first meeting between presidents of the two countries. A formal breakfast for the U.S. chief executive drew the mayor of El Paso and the governors of Texas and Chihuahua to the St. Regis Hotel, where well-heeled citizens paid twenty-five dollars per plate for the pleasure of attending. Díaz arrived shortly afterward and spent twenty nonpolitical minutes with his counterpart at the chamber of commerce building. Taft then established another precedent by leaving the country while in office, conferring with Díaz at the Juárez customshouse. The ensuing Mexican banquet even outshone the ambitious El Paso breakfast, displaying an ostentation that may not have had the effect on the Mexican peasants that Díaz had hoped. Taft then boarded a train for San Antonio to keep up public appearances in his own troubled administration, and Díaz returned to his seething capital. In a tantalizing sidelight, El Pasoans' lavish show of affection for Taft extracted a promise from him to give the Elephant Butte project, the raison d'être of Owen White's inspired speech to the U.S. senators, his personal attention.[37]

In a fall typical of dictatorships, the seemingly impregnable Díaz regime collapsed around itself in 1911, due largely to events in neighboring Ciudad Juárez. As the Madero revolt gained momentum across Mexico, adherents Abraham Gonzalez, Pascual Orozco, and Francisco "Pancho" Villa in January mounted onslaughts against the besieged city. Gonzalez established a junta in the heart of El Paso and arranged to purchase arms under the United States' pliant neutrality legislation. Journalists, secret agents, smugglers, curiosity seekers, and a wide assortment of freedom fighters, including Giuseppi Garibaldi, descended on the border. Madero, having sought refuge in Texas, arrived in El Paso in February and set up headquarters on the right bank of the Rio Grande.[38]

El Pasoans treated the warfare as a spectator sport, lining building roofs and other elevations to view the battle. A few onlookers unwillingly became participants, the victims of stray bullets. Unsympathetic to the instability wrought by the revolutionaries, Owen attributed his townsmen's fascination for the fray to the desire of primitives to see a good fight. The opposing sides declared a truce in April that stalled, prompting Orozco and Villa to overrun Juárez in May after three days of fighting. The battle of Juárez, concluded on May 10, chased Díaz and his government from office more than a thousand miles away and ushered in the short-lived Madero presidency.[39]

Madero's triumph inspired days of wild celebration across the Mexican nation, followed by rapid disillusionment and tragedy. El Paso joined in the praise, staging a victory banquet at the Toltec Club. There is no record of White addressing or attending the function, and his presence is doubtful. Owen believed that Madero's aristocratic family and friends considered the partially Indian Díaz an affront to their sensibilities and that their greed underlay the revolution. Although this view fails to acknowledge the multiple sources of a complicated power shift, allegations of corruption by this coterie soon stained the new administration. In the first moments of elation, El Paso businessmen took ads in the newspapers hailing the new chief, a lumber company emphasizing its product's name in Spanish, *madera*. In classic revolutionary sequence the moderate Madero could not hold the center, alienating both the stand-patters and the radicals. Orozco and Villa had tired of Madero's perceived timidity when they attacked Juárez on their own. Emiliano Zapata, the conscience of the revolution, broke with the president over his refusal to enact extensive land reform. However, the political right under General Victoriano Huerta delivered the fatal blow, overthrowing, arresting, and probably ordering the assassination of Madero and his vice president in February 1913. White might have experienced inner conflict over this: Huerta broadly represented the political philosophy of Díaz, which Owen respected, but he had also befriended Albert B. Fall, whom White detested.[40]

Events to the south kept El Paso churning with rumors, plots, and shifting alliances. Some businessmen opted to support rebel Bernardo Reyes, who attacked Juárez in 1911, and Orozco, who followed suit in 1912. Dissidents struggled to remove Huerta's forces from Juárez after he seized power. The persistent arms trade in El Paso, regardless of legal status, took on increased profitability when President Woodrow Wilson lifted the Taft-imposed embargo against the rebels to facilitate the defeat of Huerta. Wilson achieved his goal after much pressure and an invasion of Veracruz in April 1914 that resulted in Huerta's resignation in July. Federal lawmen arrested the deposed president a few months later for plotting in the United States, and the ailing Huerta spent his last days in El Paso. Still there was no peace. Venustiano Carranza, a former Coahuilan senator and a nonmilitary man, edged out his rivals for the presidency, but the armed competition continued. El Paso held several peace conferences between American generals and Mexican Revolutionary leaders; Fort Bliss swelled to new capacities, and war refugees flowed in from Juárez.[41]

Pancho Villa, prominent in taking down the Díaz dictatorship, placed El Paso at center stage of the revolution in its fifth year. Once a favorite of President Wilson, Villa's fortunes had declined precipitously in recent months as Carranza's general, Álvaro Obregón, routed his army at Celaya in 1915. The revolutionary suffered a loss of political support in Washington along with the stinging defeat, as Wilson now supported the victorious Carranza. Incensed at both leaders, Villa unleashed his wrath by executing sixteen innocent American mining engineers in Chihuahua and, three months later, attacking Columbus, New Mexico. Once admiring of Villa, many El Pasoans trained their anger on him and other Mexicans, threatening a racial war. Wilson ordered Fort Bliss commander General John J. Pershing across the border with six thousand troops in search of Villa, undertaking a frustrating nine-month mission. Villa remained at bay, but the American and Mexican armies fought pitched battles in northern Mexico, with slain U.S. soldiers receiving emotional and tense burials at El Paso. Chastened or discreet, Villa ensconced himself in the interior for a time and then invaded Juárez in 1919, again bringing out binoculars across the river. His historical moment had passed, however, and Carranza's former general, Obregón, took the presidential oath in 1920 and enjoyed a raucous public reception and a formal banquet attended by Texas governor William P. Hobby in El Paso. Retired to his considerable holdings in Chihuahua, Villa met death, probably government inspired, at the hands of countrymen three years later.[42]

El Paso survived the Mexican Revolution with a certain air of confidence. The danger at its doorstep injected a large dose of adrenalin in the form of national publicity, enhanced security, and confidence in meeting challenges. Illicit trade and government appropriations helped balance the curtailment of legitimate commerce with Mexico. Fort Bliss grew from an insignificant infantry post, perhaps facing extinction, to a regimental cavalry base, second in the Southwest only to Fort Sam Houston at San Antonio. Indeed, the two cities carried on a newspaper war over which held the most importance to the larger region. It meant more than civil pride: construction, other government contracts, and payrolls constituted a major part of El Paso's economy. The number of troops in the area approximated the civilian population of the city, upwards of fifty thousand. The addition of National Guard units enriched the mix, while raising new problems of civilian-military relations. The fort also provided entertainment for concert, soccer, baseball, and polo enthusiasts. Civic boosters toed a fine line between presenting the case for Fort Bliss's expansion and not raising fears about security that might hinder desired relocations and business investment.[43]

A natural among the reporters and adventurers who gravitated to the Pass during the Mexican Revolution, White missed most of the early action. Considering that the profession's top correspondents, such as Jimmy Hare, John Reid, and Timothy Turner, descended on the Pass to cover the revolution, White's absence is remarkable. One can easily imagine a first-rate account of the epic emanating from Owen's curiosity, persistence, knowledge, and writing skill. By contrast, Leigh's collection of photographs of the Mexican Revolution constituted a major contribution to the University of Texas at El Paso archives more than half a century later. Lacking the enthrallment that others felt toward the momentous event, Owen leaped at the opportunity to pursue a legal career in New York. Shortly after the battle of Juárez, he received an offer to join a firm, though he lacked a law or a college degree. Owen's experiences in Mexico and discussions with Wall Street barons concerning a stock exchange undoubtedly shaped his attraction. He could obtain a legal degree with two years of study, follow the inner workings of the system up close, and resume the life of a New Yorker that he had previously enjoyed. Owen settled into a boardinghouse in Brooklyn, adopting a stray dog named Trouble whose winsome personality gained White status in his neighborhood. He soon found himself at sixes and sevens, enjoying the Brooklyn home life and growing sour on the Manhattan career. Assigned to research some cases involving large sums of money and even speaking at hearings, White could little differentiate the rightness of the law among greedy corporate heads, an arbitrary government, and chiseling con men. An investigation of a land swindle in Kentucky, in which he concealed his true identity to avoid bodily injury or worse, convinced Owen that the culprit possessed as many scruples as the grieving buyers who concocted their own resale scheme. To clear his mind, White visited his brother Alward, now practicing medicine in Shafter, Texas. Owen needed little persuasion to quit the legal profession and share with his sibling the purchase of a ranch in the Big Bend region of West Texas.[44]

The decision not only took Owen out of New York, though not permanently, but also transported him to the doorstep of the Mexican Revolution. Located 235 miles southeast of El Paso, Shafter dated to the discovery of silver ore in 1880 and the formation of the Presidio Mining Company two years later. It took its name from Colonel William R. Shafter, commander of nearby Fort Davis, who assayed the first ore and became a large landowner in the area. With the company town more than forty miles distant from the train station at Marfa, Owen managed a bumpy car ride from an old El Paso acquaintance turned local cattleman. Although no friend of the revolution, Owen relished the chance to follow the campaigns and, despite the sight of displaced persons and dusty saloons, considered the company town charming. He saw in Shafter a renewed El Paso of thirty years earlier. It was home to five or six hundred Mexican workers, about thirty Anglo officials, and Alward, the company physician. The proximity of the warfare, now against Huerta, and President Wilson's pronouncements against the usurper concentrated White's attention on the ongoing drama to the south. Owen's personal experiences in Mexico and new incidents in Shafter convinced him that Mexico was unready for the franchise, a view that had alienated him from Madero and now from Wilson, who insisted on free elections. White believed the Pershing expedition against Villa to be foolish and futile in the extreme, pronouncing it one of the most ill-conceived plans in American history. The vulnerability of the White ranch to attack convinced Owen and Alward to end their three-month venture in favor of buying a farm near El Paso.[45]

Owen's return to El Paso in 1914 marked his sixth change in career direction since his return from the University of Texas fifteen years earlier. In each endeavor—farm equipment sales, banking, stock trading, law, and ranching—he was successful or showed promise, but the activities could not contain his restlessness. Writing, his true profession, had so far inspired him as a release from necessary endeavors. White sporadically reported for the *El Paso Herald*, on one occasion covering a meeting of Ysleta and Socorro residents who hoped to merge the towns' school districts and improve facilities and teaching. In contrast to his later statements against reform, Owen lauded the plan, which required a tax increase: "The benefits to be derived from good schools will greatly outweigh the small cost; and yet, strange as it may seem to broad minded and progressive people, there is some opposition. . . . This opposition has not as yet caused the friends of better schools any uneasiness but it has caused us to marvel at the short sightedness of any person willing to go on record as an opponent of progress and better educational facilities." However, White harbored other visions of the good life and refused to commit himself to full-time local journalism.[46]

Farming also proved transient. Owen's dream of living laconically, sipping wine on his front porch while others worked for him, proved fortuitous. According to his memory, he acquired several dogs and horses and a house full of books and planted a thousand pear trees, six thousand grapevines, and a field of alfalfa. At that point of reverie, a reporter from the *New York Telegraph*, Tracy Hammond Lewis, visited at the instigation of his uncle, Alfred Henry Lewis, to gather material for a book on the borderlands. White claimed that the encounter changed his life. The elder Lewis's life virtually prophesied that of White: though an Ohioan by birth, he studied law, traveled to the West, including Texas and New Mexico, and wrote eighteen books on the frontier and a naturalistic novel on political corruption. Cognizant of Owen's knowledge about the borderlands, the uncle had recommended him as a source for what became *Along the Rio Grande*, published in 1916. In the course of their conversations, Tracy Lewis inveighed on White to show him a sampling of his poetry, asked permission to publish the pieces, and stated that Owen should be writing for a newspaper. When Lewis offered to find White a news position if he accompanied Lewis back to New York, Owen hastily agreed.[47]

Owen's professed third assault on New York, as with his endeavors at cracking Wall Street and the law, started with a full steam of enthusiasm and then waned. He completed assignments for *Cosmopolitan* and *Munsey's*, select magazines of the time, but by his own admission found the bohemian society of Greenwich Village simply too interesting. Cocktail discussions with the likes of literary lions Theodore Dreiser, Frank Harris, and Rex Beach eroded his routine but ultimately brought disillusionment. Owen concluded that people of ordinary backgrounds, even gamblers and stage drivers, possessed more knowledge and interest than the esteemed celebrities. As the dismally recurring disenchantment with his environment deepened, White lost his aptitude for the written word and sought relief in alcohol. After six to eight months on the New York scene, Owen abandoned journalism, vowed never to return to the city, and decided to visit relatives in Virginia en route to Texas. It was January 1, 1917, and events of that year would jettison the plans of White and millions of Americans.[48]

The fatal shots that a Serbian nationalist fired at Archduke Franz Ferdinand and his wife, Sofia, in Sarajevo in June 1914 reverberated around the world. Because Europe was an armed camp divided between the Central Powers of Germany, Austria-Hungary, and their partners and the Allies, led by England, France, and Russia, the assassination soon heralded a world war. President Wilson immediately declared the neutrality of the United States in the Great War but was unable to maintain that position indefinitely. The British and French sympathies of most Americans, including presidential advisors, the attraction of the English and French markets to industrialists and bankers, and the decision of the German high command to return to unrestricted submarine warfare over Wilson's protests pushed the United States into war against the Central Powers in April 1917. The far-reaching effects of the declaration shifted El Paso's scrutiny away from its immediate southern neighbor and riveted it on distant battles in obscure locations unvisited by most of its citizenry.[49]

Yet the news of U.S. entry in the war came not as a total surprise. The city's multiple newspapers had kept attentive readers informed of the European war for the past three years, and they followed the havoc rendered by German submarines on American shipping and lives. As elsewhere, speculation had run rife about how long the besieged President Wilson could stand on his assessment that Americans must remain neutral in thought as well as in deed in the face of political and editorial criticism. Local agitation had intensified with the disclosure of the Zimmermann telegram, which revealed Germany's plan to entice Mexico away from its neutrality. The note promised the return of territory lost to the United States in the War of 1846 if Mexico sided with Germany after a declaration of war from Berlin or Washington. President Carranza refused to act on the proposal, but many El Pasoans expressed anger at both Germany and Mexico. Across Texas and the nation, however, hatred of the Kaiser won out against suspicion of "the First Chief," Carranza. Thousands of El Pasoans enlisted or registered for the military, bought bonds, looked askance at locals of Teutonic origin, and supported the cancellation of German-language courses in the schools.[50]

Fort Bliss directly connected the Pass to the war and, in unexpected fashion, gave new spirit to the moral reformers. The winding down of the revolution had begun draining the base before the war news reached El Paso. The certainty of military personnel moving overseas created intense local interest in obtaining a National Guard training site to maintain a large troop presence. The Department of War announced its intention of establishing sixteen cantonments across the country, immediately inviting enthusiastic competition from cities desiring government payrolls. Even Houston, Fort Worth, and Waco, among Texas locations, vied for the prizes, despite having little or no history of accommodating soldiers. Each tried to woo the government by presenting the most attractive image of itself. Attractions touted included abundant and cheap or free land, a good water supply, transportation connections, and a welcoming attitude, all of which El Paso felt comfortable in offering. However, in a new element of the mix for a military town, Secretary of War Newton Baker insisted on a thorough eradication of saloons and prostitution, which posed a health threat to the inductees and threatened the nation's grain supply. Baker and his staff members bluntly cited El Paso's failings in providing the proper moral climate, thus reviving the sensitive reform issues that had rent the city in the 1890s and early 1900s.[51]

Although Owen White and other traditionalists insisted that reform had ruined El Paso, others were equally convinced that it had not gone far enough. The most conspicuous change had closed open gambling dens. Saloons remained ubiquitous, and efforts to end prostitution enjoyed only temporary success, scattering or driving the women and their customers into the streets. For the first time the federal government brought its considerable resources to the fight. The War Department established five-mile zones around military bases to keep liquor and licentious women away from the soldiers. Mayor Charles Davis threw his own resources into the fray. Combined, both entities met their match combating the deeply ingrained habits of a military town, the lack of support from much of the civilian and military populations, and the questions of what constituted a military base and how to distinguish sweetheart couples from business relationships. Patriotic El Pasoans bought drinks for soldiers, taxicabs featured false floors that served as liquor cabinets, servicemen dressed in civilian clothing and rented hotel rooms as bars, and Secretary Baker fumed. Abetted by the passage of state and federal prohibition laws, El Paso finally had the evils in hand, but not before the end of the war and the loss of the cantonment.[52]

Owen's own war experiences spared him the pain of watching El Paso morph into an even more reformist city. White's intended stopover in

Virginia developed into a prolonged delay. While visiting an uncle, and his former pet dog, in Prince William County, Virginia, he chanced to meet Ed Jenks, owner, publisher, and editor of the *Army and Navy Register* and the *United States Government Advertiser* of Washington, D.C. Born in St. John, New Brunswick, in 1866, John Edward Jenks entered publishing at age nineteen and assumed the editorship of the *Register* in 1898 and the *Advertiser* two years later. A regular press representative at the Navy Department Library, Jenks also contributed regularly to various magazines. Perhaps each saw a part of himself in the other, despite their dissimilar beginnings, for they immediately befriended each other. Jenks offered a position with the *Register* and Owen pushed away his plans to return to El Paso and farming. White found his second foray at professional writing much more to his satisfaction than the aborted attempt in New York. He hobnobbed with the Washington civilian and military elite, soliciting articles from foreign attachés, except the British, and surprisingly received a contribution from John D. Rockefeller Jr., who modestly apologized for a delay in the submission. A stern judge of human character, Owen granted a lifelong approval of the man, who increasingly dedicated himself to philanthropy, conservation, and fair employment practices. Others fared less fortunately: White noted the same inefficiencies and incompetence among generals and bureaucrats that had displeased him with lawyers, brokers, and other civil servants in New York and Mexico City. Jenks could not print some of White's revelations, but more secure sources picked up the threads, and Owen delighted in the transfer of some brass to field duty. Unceremoniously, White's actions presaged his later role as a muckraker. His success at the *Register* caught the attention of the El Paso press, with the *Herald* announcing in early 1918 Owen's promotion to the *Register*'s editorial department.[53]

Whereas the reality of his situation at the New York law firm had depressed him, in this case Owen balanced his skepticism with good humor. He relished the enthusiasm of the French and Italian attachés to provide interviews or articles. The first reacted so passionately to White's news of an Allied victory that the man planted a kiss on Owen, whereas the second remained on close terms. White even felt charitable toward Secretary of the Navy Josephus Daniels, who begrudgingly had ordered the naval invasion of Veracruz. The North Carolinian, born in 1862, spent his life as a newspaper publisher, sandwiched around his cabinet position and later ambassadorship to Mexico under President Franklin Delano Roosevelt, who assisted him in his cabinet position. Curiously, Daniels's sense of morality delighted rather than repelled the no- nonsense Texan. A soul mate of the straightlaced Secretary Baker, Daniels deemed knitted presents from women to sailors too intimate and regarded tattoos as prohibitive to enlistment. The latter edict inspired Owen to write another verse, though not with the seriousness with which he approached the Papago Indians, a semisedentary tribe in Sonora and Arizona, as "a part of His creation, of His eternal plan." White thoroughly disagreed with Daniels's notion as a practicing Christian that war was a national virtue and dying for one's country a noble expression. Drawing on his perception of the Mexican Revolution, Owen considered all wars immoral, including the present one, which he regarded as being for the benefit of Wall Street. Upon deciding to enlist anyway, White countered Daniels's argument with a prototype of General George Patton's famous words during World War II: he preferred to let the enemy soldier die for his country.[54]

Contrary to the typical doughboy, Owen harbored no illusions about paths of glory and thought the American Expeditionary Forces, commanded by former Fort Bliss commander John J. Pershing, a mercenary army of debt collectors. He communicated no hatred for the Germans nor any desire to kill or be killed. Still, breathing in the air of war for several months in the national capital had instilled in him an overriding curiosity. White must not allow the most important event of the century to elude him. Unwilling to present himself as a combat soldier, Owen enlisted in Base Hospital 45 at Richmond, Virginia, though his thirty-one years exceeded the draft age at the time. White's strong patriotism and sense of individual responsibility permitted him to set aside his skepticism at the moment of truth. He professed concern at the large number of men seeking military exemption and hoped for more volunteers from his Southwest. On the day before enlisting, Owen sketched a poem whose humor contained some personal convictions.

I'm a-going to join the army!
Tomorrow I set out.
I haven't been too hasty,

And I know what I'm about.
It's up to you; it's up to me,
To do our little part.
We won't feel right until we fight,
And now's the time to start.[55]

Reinforcing his suspicion of authority, White witnessed bullying non-commissioned officers, unmanageable recruits, arrogant commissioned officers, and inexplicable shortages in a first-rate medical unit. In later writing, he treated the situation in sardonic fashion, consistent with his adopted style, describing his immediate promotion to replace an offensive sergeant, winning over soldiers and officers with sage advice, and employing after-hours requisitions of needed supplies. Owen maintained the same confident attitude after the unit moved to France, persuading superiors with gifts of cognac and wine and once diverting a truckload of brooms destined for military headquarters. Placed in charge of record keeping, White acknowledged employing creative numbers in combination with lubricating an inspecting officer with liquor to earn his unit the award of returning to America among the first ranks.[56]

Owen exhibited the same air of control in a letter to his sister, Leigh, who was obviously concerned about his safety. While departing for Europe in July 1918, he comforted her: "I'm mailing this as I go up the gang-plank and aboard the ship. . . . From the time you receive it don't worry about me. You know I'm not going to get hurt in this war and [am] coming home when it is over to settle down and educate Owen." In December, after the end of the war, Owen wrote from Toul, France, expressing a satisfaction of some of the curiosity that had drawn him into the conflagration: "Traveling on French trains is delightful because it is so uncertain—we never know where a train is going or when it's going, in fact all we are sure of is two things—we know we are *not* going to pay fare and we are going to avoid all American M.P.s [military police]." Owen continued, explaining that the train left at 1:00 a.m., not 9:00 p.m., as scheduled, and he and his undisclosed traveling companion could not sit in a compartment until they neared Paris. They received permission to stay in the City of Light for twenty-four hours to see the sights. White thought the historical monuments "so much like their pictures that they are not particularly interesting." He drank coffee and cognac in a café as a parade honoring Presidents Wilson and Raymond Poincaré passed. White noted supporting two hefty French women on a small table in order for them to witness the celebration. "I was lucky to be there for that night," Owen wrote Leigh, "because three French officers told me the next day, Paris in all its history has never been as gay as it was that evening."[57]

The letters reveal much about Owen White, the confident attitude softened by wonder, the lack of hesitation in judging matters, and the ability to introduce humor, often self-deprecating, into a situation. Owen never believed in the stated causes of the war, but he felt compelled to experience it. His experiences usually justified his previous or first beliefs. He never exhibited any interest in returning to Europe after the war, his curiosity now sated. White's generally acerbic or offhanded remarks about World War I, however, could not have encompassed his entire range of emotions, as occasionally or briefly mentioned in his writing. In terms of human life and property destruction, the Great War surpassed all previous combat. Over sixty-five million troops mobilized, with nearly half suffering death or injury. The number of noncombatant casualties eluded statistics. Modern technology in weaponry, poison gas, and trench warfare skyrocketed injuries as the notorious Western Front chewed up both camps. France, where White served, offered up over 73 percent of its fighting men in dead or wounded, the third-highest share of any participant. By comparison, the United States' horrible 350,000 casualties, 8 percent of the American forces, appeared almost modest.[58]

White paints a brief but vivid picture of the reality of war in his autobiography, his emotions still taut more than twenty years later. Owen retained a pride in his war service, but not in Base Hospital 45, due to military inefficiency and insensitivity. Lack of basic supplies, even stretchers for the wounded, appalled him. The unit's death rate from lobar pneumonia hovered at twice as high as that of any hospital in the American Expeditionary Forces. The sight of men dying unnecessarily in the wards prompted him to seek information from nurses and another commanding officer, learning that superiors had banned morphine and other sedatives in the treatment of the illness. On one occasion Owen witnessed the transfer of a hundred blinded and gasping gassed victims, untended because the officers and nurses enjoyed a dance that night. Another time an orderly left his shell-shocked patients tied to their cots while he staged an all-night bender. A captain disappeared with the entire detachment payroll. An American soldier brought in under heavy guard proved to be a non-English speaking Mexican who finally had retaliated against hazing comrades. White, sometimes accused by literary critics of being insensitive to Hispanics, advised the distraught private in Spanish to pretend insanity until he reached home. The ploy worked, as Owen learned of the soldier's discharge and return to peaceful civilian life several years later.[59]

These narratives reveal more than a segment of Owen White's life. They show him as a sensitive, even idealistic, man who preferred the persona of a cold-hearted cynic, incapable of taking even himself seriously. His strong sense of justice, when later applied to journalism, produced the print crusades that stamped Owen with his adopted façade, "Rattlesnake Pete."

CHAPTER 3

Launching a National Career

After his much-anticipated return home, Owen Payne White experienced the same lack of direction that has plagued war veterans over the years. Still, his mild dissatisfaction with the range of current opportunities paled in comparison to the feelings of many of his counterparts. The government simply mustered out of service the 4.6 million servicemen, offering them little preparation for their conditions. Despite the entry of "shell-shocked" into wartime parlance, there existed as yet little knowledge about treatment of the emotionally disabled. Unemployed or, worse, disabled, veterans fended for themselves, with the later scandal-ridden Veterans Bureau not created until 1921, following a postwar recession in which joblessness reached 16 percent of the population. Veterans' benefits increased in the 1920s, reaching 20 percent of the federal budget, but inflation captured much of the gain. Congress, accordingly, voted in what became famously known as "the Bonus," with payment set for 1945. The Great Depression of the 1930s pushed many veterans to press for immediate payment. When President Herbert Hoover vetoed the measure, "Bonus Army" marchers camped in Washington, D.C., moving General Douglas MacArthur, under presidential directive, to disperse the veterans with troops, tanks, and tear gas. President Franklin Delano Roosevelt's Congress allocated the nearly $4 billion bonus in 1936, somewhat lifting the gloom of the bleak era.[1]

White's El Paso, where Owen remained until the publication of *Out of the Desert* in 1923, floundered during Prohibition. Although El Pasoans, like other Texans, had rejected the issue at the polls, the Eighteenth Amendment, prohibiting the manufacture, transportation, and sale of alcoholic beverages, became effective in January 1919. Abstinence advocates and opportunists cast their eyes toward neighboring Ciudad Juárez, one group in trepidation and the other with lust. To their combined dread and relief, Juárez indeed burst from a sleepy cocoon traditionally dwarfed by El Paso vice into a mecca for sin. Fueled by rum-running, tourism, and attendant delights, the population of the Mexican city doubled between 1920 and 1930 to almost forty thousand, though it remained little more than a quarter the size of its American counterpart. Even minus its saloons, El Paso enjoyed a building boom and expanding economy in the decade after the Great War. By 1925 the city boasted a population of one hundred thousand and sported new parks, swimming pools, a baseball stadium, truck lines, the world's largest custom smelter, homes supplied with natural gas, and a scenic drive along the rim of the mountain. Consistent with the boosterism stating that El Paso had arrived on the national scene, local newspapers ran stories about the quaintness of the town of the nineteenth century. Boarded-up bars and bordellos, however, failed to eclipse the antivice campaigns of resident and itinerant preachers, who railed at automobiles, dance halls, and movie theaters as shelters of sinfulness.[2]

The Ku Klux Klan, brandishing its new label of morality, captured the local school board, a remarkable achievement in a predominantly Hispanic and Roman Catholic community. Seemingly antithetical to the Klan's crusade against immigrants, Catholics, Jews, and African Americans, El Paso succumbed to the Klan's broad appeal to nationalism, law and order, religious fundamentalism, and traditional values, especially for enfranchised white voters. By the early 1920s the "new" KKK surged in Texas, as it did nationally, claiming perhaps two million adherents, a friendly or captured legislature, and an avowed member, Earle B. Mayfield, in the U.S. Senate. It confidently primed itself for higher offices before suffering a series of political defeats against opposition led by the *El Paso Times*, labor unions, and the non-Protestant, non-Anglo majority of El Paso in the mid-1920s. Bootleggers, preachers, and Klansmen all felt the sting of Owen White's sarcasm when he mounted his literary pulpit.[3]

Owen, the new civilian, had not yet centered on his writing career immediately after discharge, however. Reflecting that the world, not he, had changed, White pondered the widespread acceptance of what he considered an immoral war, fought on behalf of Wall Street profits, and the local adulation bestowed on him. In common with sensitive war veterans everywhere, Owen felt that he had not measured up to those he considered true heroes. Friends and neighbors, sometimes critical of Owen's free lifestyle in the past, now lauded him as the oldest living white man born in El Paso who had enlisted beyond the draft age for the war. He decided to relax and enjoy the back slaps and proffered toasts. Although still uncommitted to a full-time writing career, White sporadically accepted offers from local editors to put his thoughts into print. Mexico, which he had experienced and studied, was a favored topic. In October 1919 he reiterated in the *Times* his repudiation of President Wilson's mishandling of events of the Mexican Revolution, which included threatening but not enforcing demands on Huerta, embracing and then abandoning the unworthy Villa, thereby causing him to invade Columbus, New Mexico, and squandering over $200 million on the ill-fated Pershing expedition. While admiring many aspects of Mexico, Owen remained convinced that the people had not enjoyed sufficient time to pass from a state of barbarism to democracy. Notwithstanding that numerous historians have criticized Wilson's interventionist policies, even as they praised his reforms, most have not shared White's underlying assumptions and defense of Díaz. No issue from his critics dogged White more than a perception that he considered Mexicans unequal.[4]

White defined his noninterventionist, laissez faire instincts, exemplars of his frontier libertarianism, in an undated column for the *El Paso Herald*. He told a story of an early time in El Paso history when a Señor de Su O led an attack by Mexicans on the north bank against the south bank, capturing and holding the mayor for ransom, robbing stores, and confiscating wine and women. After several days of enjoying their captor roles, the invaders tired of their pleasures and returned home. "I know of no episode in all of El Paso's history that is more illuminating than that one.

There was no law on either side of the river, the river itself was more of an obstacle to traffic and pursuit than it was an international boundary line, and the people in El Paso and Paso del Norte were entirely indifferent to each other."[5]

Drawing on a signature theme, Owen described men "in those days" as "tough and hard" and oblivious to harmless deviltry. "It is more likely that Uncle Ben Dowell and his friends looked on at what happened much as they would have looked on at a cock fight or a horse race," White thought. "It was none of their business what the Mexicans did to one another, and the fact that the victors were El Pasoans was a source of congratulation and not condemnation." White passed on the story to his readership as a lesson on behavioral toleration rather than an engagement in racial stereotyping. Owen's laudatory account of the Toltecs, presented after he joined the *Herald* staff, clearly demonstrated his admiration for the Indian ancestors of Mexico.[6]

Considering White's penchant for and success with word crafting, it is curious that he declined to take up a literary career as soon as he returned to civilian life. In 1921 the House of McMath in El Paso published Owen's *Southwestern Ballads*, a compilation of poems previously printed in the *New York Morning Telegraph*, *Richmond (VA) Times-Dispatch*, and *Army and Navy Register*. Among the mixture of thirteen serious and humorous poems, White saluted "the Great Southwest, where hearts are strong and the take and give of the strenuous life makes a friend worth more than the untold wealth of Plutus' Store!" The following year the publication *Southwestern Milestones* depicted poems by White that captioned paintings by Edward Holslag adorning the walls of the banking room of the First National Bank of El Paso. White paid tribute to pioneers, Indians, the Ysleta Mission, the Rio Grande, smelters, buffalo, and even the burro. Owen subsequently confessed to a hesitation about his lack of a college education and dearth of subject material, concerns he quickly dispatched at the moment of resolution. For the time being, the new veteran bemusedly allowed himself to be honored by his mates and gravitated toward a number of business opportunities.[7]

His first lasting decision as a veteran was to enter into a lifelong marriage with Hazel Harvey, whom he always referred to as "Mike." White credited his uniform for capturing the gaze of the bank president's secretary, though they had worked in the same building for more than a year. After a seven-month courtship, Owen proposed and they married that same day, January 22, 1920. The *Herald*, White's occasional employer, covered the wedding prominently with a two-column headline on the society page. Dr. Floyd Poe, pastor of the First Presbyterian Church, officiated, with Owen's sister, Leigh, among those attending. The news story stated that the couple would divide their time between apartments at Palms Court and the groom's ranch in the lower valley. It described Mrs. White, who enjoyed a large circle of friends, as having resided for the past several years in El Paso and having formerly lived in Chicago. Before her present position, she had been assistant to the secretary of the chamber of commerce.[8]

Owen deemed the postnuptial months as the happiest and busiest of his life. Doubtless noting the expansion of fruit, chicken, and other farm production in that period, Owen and Mike settled into the comfort of the ranch. A disappointing performance from the fruit trees, however, steered Owen into the speculative oil business, where he promoted the sale of acreage to overly trusting investors. After receiving his share of the profits despite a series of dry wells, White enjoyed the bucolic life until an untimely frost forced another career shift. The continuing economic boom and a housing shortage at El Paso lulled the Whites into dependence on credit and banks until the bubble burst, several banks failed, and the couple's capital sank to a reported $4.30. The abruptness and depth of this personal financial crisis made a serious writer of Owen Payne White.[9]

White's writing efforts, heretofore restricted to recreational penmanship, an occasional news story, and three months staffing the *Army and Navy Register*, burst into a fulltime endeavor and remained such for the rest of his life. With a wife and a bevy of farm animals to support, Owen reached an agreement with the *Herald* to turn out a column at twenty-five cents an inch. To augment a salary of nine dollars or so a week, White produced a dozen or more articles on Mexican archeology, relying on his trained retentive memory of previous research. An article on the Toltecs in early 1923 demonstrated the depth of his research, his admiration for the ancient culture, and his sarcasm, which he honed to perfection. It also previewed Owen's flair for being dramatic while conveying the essence of his subject. Scorning the intolerance of Massachusetts Puritans, in the vein of H. L. Mencken's contemporary indictment of them, White favorably compared the Native Mexicans' worship of the peaceful Quetzalcoatl to the Calvinist religion that "set up a whipping post, put an incendiary torch under witchcraft as a profitable and healthy profession and in a general way planned the seeds of that fine Bostonian culture, with which we are all familiar." Consistent with his belief that an advanced culture required thousands of years of development, White surmised that the Toltecs must have been present at the time of Alexander the Great (323–356 BC) It is difficult to assess his estimate, as the people who established their civilization at Tula in central Mexico by the ninth century of the Common Era emerged from an obscure ancient past. White contrasted the industrious American society that worshipped the peaceful god Quetzalcoatl to the Spanish government that encountered them in the sixteenth century: "Charles V was a narrow minded, bigoted, devout churchman. He considered that he ruled by divine right. . . . The [Toltec] government of church and state . . . was more successful than it has been with other governments. . . . They existed as a ruling power for a period of time [approximately three hundred years] probably longer than the life of any government which is in existence in Europe today."[10]

William S. McMath, El Paso's leading printer, liked to relate the story of the circumstances that led to White's first successful book, *Out of the Desert: The Historical Romance of El Paso*. In the spring of 1923 a tall, lanky stranger came into his office to have a small book of poetry printed. The two struck up a conversation, which lengthened into tales by the gregarious Owen about early El Paso. With the ear of a publisher, McMath detected material for a history of their city and on one occasion conjectured that White could write that history. "I know damn well I can," Owen responded, little discerning the impact of his decision for his life and the future of El Paso. "That's how it started. Plans were made and the writing . . . was begun. Before Owen White had written a dozen pages I knew that he had told the truth," McMath recalled.[11]

T. F. Sharp, editor of the local *Post*, told a more whimsical version of the origins of the book. "I used to call Owen 'the laziest white man alive,'" Sharp recounted some years later, having persistently solicited White to write a brief daily column for his newspaper. Owen insisted he could not do good work on a tight schedule, preferring to laconically verbalize spellbinding stories of early El Paso in McMath's office. After delaying his contemplated history of the city for a dozen years, White leaped into action when it appeared that another writer's book on the subject was in preparation for publication. Sharp marveled that White, "a man who at middle-age had never been a newspaperman and had not written a line for a magazine," became "the most read writer of magazine articles and . . . one of the great reporters of today [1937]." As with most "overnight successes," however, Owen's career followed a less direct line than was publicly perceived.[12]

White's history of El Paso marked the first major effort to capture the city's past in over twenty years. William Wallace Mills authored the previous account, *Forty Years at El Paso*, in 1901. A controversial figure for most of his life, Mills was born in Thorntown, Indiana, in 1836 and accompanied his brother, Anson, to the West Texas village in 1858. Confirmed Unionists, both resisted the secessionist tide after the election of Abraham Lincoln and joined the U.S. Army at the start of the Civil War. William's arrest and escape from Confederates embittered him toward Texas secessionists, particularly Simeon Hart, whom he personally blamed for his captivity. Mills headed the local Republicans during Reconstruction as collector of customs, seizing Hart's property. Mills also prominently feuded with A. J. Fountain, a local Radical Republican leader. Mills's support of moderate A. J. Hamilton, whose daughter he married, earned him disfavor with the Radicals but failed to impress the Democrats, who ultimately controlled the state and city. His government and political career completed by the time he wrote El Paso's history, Mills, with his wife, moved to Austin in 1910, where he died three years later.[13]

Mills evidently underestimated the influence of his groundbreaking work. In the introduction he issued a "warning" that the account was "too rambling and egotistical," despite his best efforts at accuracy, to interest any reader unfamiliar with the subject or him. Mills acknowledged that he wrote almost entirely of topics connected to his life and omitted some history out of consideration for the living or their relatives. In a reprint more than sixty years later, historian Rex Strickland confirmed the inaccuracy of some of Mills's statements, drawn largely from the elderly man's memory many years after the events. Flawed by hearsay, prejudice, and the author's tendency to place himself at the center of the narrative, the book's considerable value lay in the "man's soul laid bare." Strickland considered it a complete account of the early days of the frontier town that needed only modest correction and clarification.[14]

Although it was the city's first formal history, *Forty Years at El Paso*, consistent with the book's title and Mills' acknowledgment, attempted no complete survey of the area's past. Clearly Mills experienced dramatic events during his four decades of residence in El Paso: secession and the Civil War, Reconstruction, the Salt War, the railroads' entrance from an initial distance of a thousand miles, legendary shootouts, and the reverberations of reform. Nevertheless, the book began with the author's arrival in 1858, without even a summary of the Spanish and Mexican periods. Mills's impressions of the citizenry on both banks of the Rio Grande were nostalgic, a criticism that later was sometimes leveled at White's writings. Mills also considered the armed pioneers of West Texas to be men of character, albeit not necessarily of good character. He praised the Mexicans of what was then El Paso del Norte (later Ciudad Juárez) for maintaining a 250-year-old dam, never asking assistance while still sharing the water generously with their northern neighbors. Indeed, the Spanish language and the Mexican silver dollar served as the coin of the realm on both sides of the river. However, Mills thought that those who entered El Paso after the completion of the railroads were of a decidedly inferior quality. Their propensity to sell votes to solicitous Anglo candidates equally tarnished the reputations of both.[15]

White accepted the challenge of an unnamed observer who dared anyone to write a truthful history of El Paso without denigrating the majority of its citizens. In contrast to Mills's account, Owen's stirring history transported El Paso's history back to the biblical flood! White, indeed, divided the city's past at a point between the scriptural inundation and the arrival of the railroads. For good measure, and for financial gain, Owen added biographical sketches of city fathers. In other respects Owen's history tracked that of Mills, despite White's expressed disdain for Mills's research as well as his actions following the Civil War. White judged Mills the most contentious voice during Reconstruction and deserving of his local unpopularity. Nevertheless, he shared with the late historian a respect for early El Pasoans, if not always support for their actions. Some critics also read in White's lines a dose of nostalgia and a propensity toward overstatement for emphasis. White's first public pronouncements on El Paso's reform periods appeared in *Out of the Desert*. By that time Owen had had years to fashion the events of those periods into a personal context and had also seen the beginnings of the prohibition era, which he heartily disliked.[16]

Considering the jibes he aimed at reformers in later years, White's comments on local reformers in 1923 seem quite bland. Perhaps he did not believe his history of the city to be a proper avenue for such personal opinion, or perhaps his perceptions of that time had not completely crystallized. He identified the *Herald*, which had covered his marriage generously, as the reform newspaper and the *Times*, which had denied coverage, as the status quo organ, without further comment. With Mills, White professed certain sympathy for the earlier gunmen, disdain for the gamblers and hangers-on, and an acceptance of inevitable reform. The first group, present until 1880, the last year before the railroads, he described as not actually outlaws but products of few laws and self-preservation. The rails brought in a lower type of society, gamblers and prostitutes, a class of border parasites. However, not everyone in the second wave fit that description; some were honest in accordance with the ethics of their profession and time. As long as this sporting element, good and bad, preyed on outsiders, the establishment allowed them to operate, over the objection of the churches. When the scalpers turned on locals in addition to strangers, according to White, the city fathers prosecuted them. Moral movements always won when they were properly directed.[17]

Owen's chief quarrel with modernity, at the middle stage of his life, lay in inefficiency, a theme on which he elaborated in later writings. In *Out of the Desert*, White stated that there had been less want and suffering in his hometown in the past, when neighbors donated to charities and sponsored celebrations, than in the present. He calculated that any civic accomplishment in the 1920s required four times the amount of time that had been needed during the administration of Joseph Magoffin in the late 1880s. Public schools, Owen maintained, had educated children more efficiently in the past and, somewhat whimsically, he contended that people were less critical and judgmental then. Some of the problems Owen also attributed to official timidity, once political parties with more strength emerged. In later writings White would decry an ordinance prohibiting bathing in the acequia as the beginning of El Paso's slide into progress. Even the usually responsible chamber of commerce wrongly supported an irrigation project in 1900 that led to a devastating boom rather than helping local farmers.[18]

The role of Spanish and Mexican influence on the frontier Southwest proved problematic for Texas historians of the time. Much of American history still coalesced around the negative image of the Black Legend, popularized by the English during Britain's colonial feud with Iberia. This interpretation described the Spanish conquistadors, government, and clergy as corrupt, ignorant, and fanatical, as in White's view of Charles V in his series on the Toltecs. The battle for Texan independence and the opening shots of the Mexican-American War on the banks of the Rio Grande in 1846 created a climate of bitterness between Anglos and Latinos. The Indian component of the mestizo culture struck fear and distrust in the minds of frontiersmen who had daily fought against the Apaches and Comanches at the time of Owen's birth. Prejudice against dark-skinned peoples, bolstered by the pseudoscience of social Darwinism, clouded the vision of many Americans into the twentieth century. Bias produced racial and cultural stereotypes of lazy, unambitious Mexicans, which adorned cartoons and magazine covers in the vein of insulting images that have been bestowed on minorities from the Irish to Asians to African Americans. Hollywood movies discovered the financial rewards of films about the Mexican Revolution, even while referring to the genre as "greaser" movies. Three years after the publication of *Out of the Desert*, a major oil company produced a pictorial history of Texas for grade school students that instructed the young with a one-dimensional and racist history for more than a generation.[19]

Owen enjoyed a closer relationship with Mexicans than many of his generation, who viewed them as loafers or outlaws. He grew up with the majority border population, played with his neighbors as a child, and learned the Spanish language and the delights of Mexican food while he was a small boy. Accompanying his father into the dark corners of El Paso strengthened Owen's insight into Mexican culture, though, unfortunately, he customarily encountered poor representatives of that society. White's voluminous reading and retentive mind made him an authority on Native American ancient civilizations, which he judged superior to

European ones. His several journeys to Mexico City increased his contempt for corrupt Mexican politicians and financiers, a scorn that White felt equally for their American counterparts. White bought into a strain of contemporary wisdom that held some cultures to be more highly evolved than others and penalized the perceived sluggishness of Mexico. Whereas other observers argued that a succession of dictators had stifled Mexican political maturity, Owen used a truncated time frame and emphasized a dark legacy of the savage side of Indian forebears. His retelling of the Su O incident, in which El Paso Hispanics raided their sister city, placed the motivation less on stereotypes than unstable conditions on the northern bank.[20]

Although blunting the edge of controversial issues, including secession, Civil War, and Reconstruction, and promising to reserve opinions on history, White wrote substantially from an expected Anglo viewpoint. Indeed, White's expressed theme stated the focus of his book to be the influences that created an American metropolis. Devoting less than a tenth of the text to the Spanish and Mexican periods, he credited Anglo leaders, merchants, lawyers, and doctors as responsible for El Paso's winning political supremacy over its rival communities. Still, the author plainly consulted Spanish sources, which his bilingualism facilitated, and noted brutalities on the part of both the conquistadors and the Plains Indians. Involving himself in a historical controversy still unsettled more than eighty years later, White placed Álvar Núñez Cabeza de Vaca as the first European in the El Paso area. As a gesture to the then-current cultural clash interpretation of Texas history, Owen described his ethnic group as less inclined to consider the lilies of the field than their Hispanic neighbors. His other ethnic judgments applied to specific segments or individuals from that society. He considered prerailroad county officials, mostly Mexican, to have been rendered useless as community members by their laziness, addiction to drink, and lack of sympathy for American law. White deplored the perfidious Father Antonio Borajo, who exhorted violence in the Salt War. Still, he placed more culpability for the fracas on Charles Howard, whose legal purchase of the salt flats instigated the response, than on the "ignorant and illiterate" Mexican parishioners. Owen reserved his most scathing comments for recent events involving the Mexican Revolution. El Pasoans caught up in the tidal wave he gauged as hungry for excitement. The assassinated Madero, a man he had previously labeled as corrupt and condescending, was described as an inept vegetarian. Owen's favorite target, Woodrow Wilson, was charged with poorly planning and extravagantly executing the Pershing expedition.[21]

Nevertheless, White maintained a sense of optimism about his native city. The citizenry, he believed, had reached a stage of maturity in rallying around the war effort, though Owen personally opposed the Great War. As White had done, El Pasoans succumbed to the postwar oil boom and lost their cooperative spirit, but they righted themselves. Publisher McMath volunteered that Owen reclaimed the spirit with his planning of the city's Fifty Year Jubilee. For his part, the author promised to distill an almost inexhaustible source of material into a book of anecdotes and reminiscences, a feat that he accomplished numerous times in later publications.[22]

Doubtless, *Out of the Desert* possessed the earmarks of a regional success in the form of lively prose, voluminous information, and the encapsulation of past and present community leaders in seventy-five pages of description, for a subscription of one hundred dollars per page. Writer and publisher, sharing profits equally, might have anticipated a nice nest egg or splurge and occupied the center of attention in the barber shops and grills. The history blanketed the front page of the *Herald*, quickly sold out three editions at three dollars a copy, and reportedly instigated more than a few quarrels and worse. Sales made it the number-one bestselling book in El Paso shortly after publication. Favorable reviews, even from distant locations, demonstrated the fortuitous combination of research and writing. The *New York Morning Telegram* called it "a comprehensive and well written volume"; the *Belfast Telegraph* predicted that "future generations will prize greatly the fact that the early days of El Paso had a painstaking historian."[23]

Indeed, except for a decision by McMath to draw national attention to the book, it and its author might have remained merely local favorites. White appeared comfortable with that prospect. In early 1924 Mrs. Lillian Hague Corcoran matched Owen's poetry with music for "An Evening with Owen White" at the McDowell Club. Several weeks later, White, writing anonymously, beat out ten competitors to win first place at the Writers' League contest for "The Man with the Black Box." That same year the McMath Company issued White's *Just Me and Other Poems*, which a local reviewer found "original and refreshing." The distant *Virginia Pilot* praised "a happy and original blending of Bret Harte pathos and sentiment, Artemus Ward humor, Robert Service's 'Open Spaces,' and James Whitcomb Riley whimsy. Not that Mr. White has imitated them."[24]

William McMath widened the circle immeasurably when he sent a review copy of *Out of the Desert* to H. L. Mencken, the owner of the prestigious *American Mercury* and a certified national caustic critic. Rarely lacking confidence, White felt his self-reliance crumble before the imagined attack by the literary lion. Mencken, the object of Owen's fears, had constructed a reputation based on a temperament that made even more hardened souls tremble. Born the son of a Baltimore cigar factory owner in 1880, Henry Lewis Mencken completed his formal education with a high school diploma and a night-school class in journalism. Having read Mark Twain's *Huckleberry Finn* at age nine, young Mencken fell to reading prodigiously and determined to become a writer. He undertook his successful career with a reporter's position on the *Baltimore Morning Herald* ten years later and moved to the *Baltimore Sun* in 1906. The *Sun* remained his full-time employer until his retirement forty-two years later. Between those dates the legendary acerbic gained national recognition, denouncing "boobs," "Puritans," sundry hypocrites, New Dealers, and others he deemed unworthy in a striking similarity to the later Owen White. Mencken would famously report on the Scopes "Monkey" Trial the next year and had already met his future wife, Sara Haardt, a professor of English at Goucher College in Baltimore, whose untimely death in 1935 devastated him.[25]

Incredibly to the apprehensive White, if not to the optimistic McMath, Mencken not only personally wrote and printed an *American Mercury* review, he liked the book. The great skeptic did not gush forth praise, but, considering Mencken's high toleration threshold, the review veritably shined. "It is a genuine pleasure to encounter such books. . . . Mr. White is no virtuoso of prose, but he tells the story of this struggle upward with considerable charm. . . . Why are there not more such books? I know of no American town so dull that its history would not make an interesting volume."[26]

Owen realized with relief that in Mencken he had found not only a champion but a soul mate who "had my number." Mencken's recognition of the author's and publisher's manipulation of local egos by charging for the city fathers' biographical sketches particularly pleased Owen. With a review in *American Mercury* guaranteeing national attention to his history, White received a further boost when Mencken asked him to write an article or two for his publication. True to his promise, the journal carried an article four months later in which White bemoaned the city ordinance of 1873 that prohibited swimming and bathing in the irrigation ditch and the plight of El Pasoans, who once lived naturally, now shaving and bathing daily, "changing their clothes by the clock," and playing golf.[27]

One stroke of good fortune, or appreciation of White's talent, deserved another. Prior to the exchange with Mencken, Owen had responded to a question by Arthur Sullivant Hoffman in his *Adventure* magazine. Hoffman, who once served on a board of directors with Theodore Roosevelt, the subject of an earlier White poem, and whose magazine inspired the Adventurers Club of New York, edited the foremost pulp fiction publication of his day. A crusader for authenticity in fiction writing, Hoffman often posed questions to his readership. His query on the credibility of Western fiction aroused in White a spirited twelve-page analysis. Hoffman suggested that Owen submit his critique to a magazine. Perhaps inspired by McMath to start at the top, White sent the paper to the *New York Times Sunday Magazine*. The prestigious publication promptly accepted it and asked for more. The welcome news, nevertheless, forced Owen to make some hard career decisions. Always more introspective than his confident exterior betrayed, Owen questioned his presence among the journalistic elite, his antecedents, his journalistic inexperience, and his lack of a college degree. White's ponderings led him to conclude that his western heritage at least equaled the backgrounds of those from the eastern seaboard, his encyclopedic knowledge of his subject was the equivalent of writing experience, and his individualistic education was superior to an instructed one. Furthermore, he reasoned that the public would prefer the red meat of a John Wesley Hardin story to the description of a Henry Adams ancestor.[28]

Lester Markel, the editor of the *New York Times Sunday Magazine*, had carved out a brilliant newspaper career by 1924. Born in New York City in 1894, Markel trained at Columbia University's School of Journalism. He effectively changed the nature of the Sunday newspaper when he introduced the concept of separate Sunday sections in 1923. Markel's direction of the *Sunday Magazine*, the *Book Review*, and the Arts and Leisure section brought a depth of information to the newspaper heretofore unknown. He subsequently formulated the News of the Week in Review section, for which he received a Pulitzer Prize, and became associate editor of the *Times*. Without having met White personally, Markel accepted his "Cattle Kings Pass with the Vivid West," the first of many positive transactions. The New Yorker praised the article as "better than I thought it could possibly be. Let us hear often from you." Contrasting the old and new West, Owen described the modern rancher as "look[ing] like his cattle. They are heavy, white-faced and sad-eyed, just as if they had always known, and they probably have, what their ultimate destiny is to be." The piece, plus one on El Paso for *American Mercury*, humanized the earthy inhabitants of frontier society and created a demand for similar material from other publications. His two articles that followed scored the abusive practices of Christian missionaries in the Sandwich Islands and described a one-act play, "The Mole," that challenged public tolerance with characters who appeared onstage nude. Owen White had clearly found his niche, although his editor declined White's request for a contract and continued their freelance agreement.[29]

Owen, never fond of politicians, found himself in the midst of two elections in 1924, one at his own instigation. Experiencing more success than aggrandizement and seeking a break from writing, White accepted an offer as publicity agent for the New Mexico Republican U.S. senator Holm Olaf Bursum, who faced a strong challenger for reelection. A native Iowan, Bursum had moved to the future southwestern state in 1881 at the age of fourteen. He later engaged in stock raising and, in succession, was elected to the Territorial Senate and Republican central committee, constitutional convention, and party national committee. When Owen's nemesis, Albert B. Fall, vacated his federal Senate seat to accept the office of secretary of interior, Bursum won the special election to replace him in 1921. Bursum's victorious opponent in 1924, Democrat Sam Gilbert Bratton, actually seemed a closer match in some respects to Owen. Born in Kosse, Texas, Limestone County, only a decade after

White, Bratton practiced law for five years in Farwell, West Texas, before migrating to Clovis, New Mexico, while still in his twenties. He held several judgeships, including associate justice of the state supreme court, before contesting Bursum. Monetary considerations aside, White's experiences with the legal system left him little respect for attorneys and judges. Owen developed disdain for both men's campaigns but was particularly impressed with a noncandidate, Bronson Murray Cutting, the subject of one of his future articles. Owen credited the powerful Santa Fe newspaper publisher with masterminding Bratton's victory and then reversing political positions four years later and delivering the state to Republican Herbert Hoover.[30]

Happily returning to El Paso "with the loot I had lied for," Owen soon had one of the most consequential assignments of his writing career drop in his lap. Miriam Amanda "Ma" Ferguson had just won the governorship of Texas and the *New York Times* asked him to cover the expected raucous inauguration. Indeed, anything connected with the Fergusons, already regional legends, promised nothing short of raucousness. James Edward Ferguson was born near Salado, Bell County, Texas, in 1871, the son of a preacher who died when Jim was four years old. Ferguson entered Salado College, a preparatory school, but was expelled for disobedience and left home at age sixteen to work his way at various physical labors through the American West. He eventually returned to Texas and took up the study of law, passing the bar, and married Miriam A. Wallace at her family home. Ferguson turned his attention to banking and helped establish the Temple State Bank while managing local political campaigns. Opting to run on his own for governor, the novice Ferguson defeated a wide array of opponents in 1914 on the issues of opposition to prohibition and championing of sharecroppers against rental exploitation. As "Farmer Jim," the new state leader saw his tenant legislation into law, and he popularly supported rural schools and highway construction in the spirit of the current Progressive movement. He won reelection, but his fortunes reversed when the Texas Supreme Court declared the Ferguson Farm Tenant Act unconstitutional and questionable personal loans from the brewery industry and other interests surfaced. Ferguson's feud with certain University of Texas professors and his subsequent veto of the university budget brought his administration to a crash, with threats of impeachment and charges of criminal offenses leveled against him. Impeached by the House of Representatives, Ferguson resigned in anticipation of a guilty vote by the Texas Senate in 1917. The ploy to remain eligible for future state office failed when a legal decision declared him actually removed from office. Following unsuccessful bids at federal offices not denied him by the state constitution, Ferguson persuaded his wife to seek the governorship in 1924.[31]

Miriam Ferguson, the new hopeful, also hailed from Bell County, born four years after James. She was educated at Salado College, also attended by her future husband, and Baylor Female College. The first-time gubernatorial candidate conflicted some Progressives, particularly women enthused by the prospect of the first woman governor in a male-dominated state and perhaps the first in the nation. Disappointing them, she ran on traditional issues, openly touted Jim as the actual contender, and adopted the slogan "Two governors for the price of one." The homey campaign, which reduced her given name, Miriam Amanda, to "Ma" by virtue of her initials, also profited from the notoriety of her chief opponent, Dallasite Felix D. Robertson, an unabashed Klan member. Although in retrospect the secret society had peaked several years earlier, its continued presence in a receptive state guaranteed an exciting primary. In a field of nine, Robertson, in fact, garnered over forty thousand votes more than the second-place Ferguson but failed to gain a majority of votes cast. The second, or run-off, primary, however, resulted in Ferguson overtaking Robertson by almost a hundred thousand votes. Minus the controversial nature of the Fergusons, Ma would have been home free in a state in which the Democratic primary winner suffered little or no Republican opposition.[32]

Ma Ferguson's nomination, hailed by many in the state and nation, frustrated the anti-Ferguson element, which atypically rallied around the Republican candidate, George C. Butte, in the general election. The challenger brought uncommon interest into the usually anticlimactic November election, as the dean of the law school at the University of Texas who had led the opposition to James Ferguson that led to his impeachment. Although Butte collected 41 per cent of the vote, ten times the Republican result in the 1922 campaign, Ferguson emerged triumphantly. In the only dampening effect on the Fergusons' celebration, the widow of the Wyoming governor took the oath of office to complete her husband's term two weeks before Ferguson's inauguration, depriving Ma of establishing herself as the first woman state governor in the United States.[33]

A close-second finish in the Democratic primary was sufficient to transform Miriam Amanda into a national figure. Several weeks after the election, Markel, representing the nation's most prestigious newspaper, asked Owen to write an article on the new governor's first week in office, "a character study" comparing "her regime with some others you have known in Texas—without, of course, drawing any editorial conclusions." The appended comment illustrated both the strengths and concerns for editors of Owen's spirited writing. Lest White somehow misunderstand the restraint, Markel wrote a few days later, "I do not want to dull your lively style but I think you will realize that in this particular article it is necessary to be quite reportorial." The redactor clearly regarded Owen as the favored writer for the assignment: he set a deadline of January 7, requesting approximately three thousand words, two or three exclusive photos, and "a little more [information] about yourself. . . . I have in mind a few more articles you might do for us up here." Although Owen later stated that he was pleased to draw the assignment for "the most spectacular thing since the fall of the Alamo," Markel obviously viewed him as reticent. Three weeks after first approaching White, the editor repeated his desires, moved the deadline back, and reiterated the *Times*'s intention of paying Owen's expenses in return for receipts. Almost apologetically, Markel volunteered that receipts were mandated by the newspaper's policy and "require[d] [of] all our correspondents." He again coaxed Owen to return to New York for two or three weeks "with the idea that you would get a new slant on us. What do you think of the plan?" Ten days later, Markel was still trying to get confirmation for the New York visit. Hoping not to allow a rejection of an article to spoil the plan, he implored the Texan to "not let that deter you in sending along anything else you may have."[34]

Whether by preoccupation or design, Owen lifted his silence, assuring his editor that the New York sojourn met with his complete approval and that he would be "subject to your orders just as soon as I get through with Mrs. Ferguson." He included a schedule in which he would stay in the Austin Hotel from January seventeenth until the twenty-fifth. A feeling of trepidation in the stoic-appearing Owen White would have been understandable. Although the *New York Times* continued to print his pieces on the deleterious effects of prohibition and other reforms on El Paso, past and present, the Ferguson story constituted his first major straight news report. The deferential treatment bestowed on Owen in Austin because of his association with the *Times* startled him, but he regained his composure quickly enough to write a colorful and well-received article on the inauguration. White did not tone down his visual verbiage for the stately "Gray Lady" of journalism. Describing the delirium of the crowd, he noted women happily crying aloud and a young lady, sporting a large cowboy hat, a broad smile, and chaps, emitting joyous yells, while "at the centre of it all, the one woman for whom all this disturbance was being created, was very calm, unruffled, and unmoved."[35]

White's gentle treatment of Ma Ferguson, in contrast to an easily attainable sarcastic account, held true for his further reportage on her. Doubtless he admired the Fergusons' stance against the Ku Klux Klan and agreed with Jim's opposition to prohibition. Owen remained so cynical about politicians that Jim's finagling in office could hardly have shocked or disappointed him. Only two months into Ma Ferguson's term, White reported in the *Times* that "the people of Texas have come to understand that the present Administration has a heart." He cited her granting an inmate permission to visit his ailing mother, though the warden considered him too dangerous; her veto of a bill allowing legislators and their kin unlimited rail passes; and her success in pressing the legislature to pass a much-publicized antimask law. "The Texas Legislature," White stated flatly, "is composed largely of Klansmen."[36]

Owen's self-confidence easily survived the challenge of his first major reporting assignment, but it wavered perceptibly when he received an assignment to write about the Texas Rangers. A telegram from Markel broke the enjoyment of his deferential treatment at the Austin Hotel when the editor instructed White to wire three thousand words on the fabled law-and-order group by the following afternoon. The sudden assignment and deadline cast Owen into a state of desperation. Throughout his early years he had become as accustomed to the Rangers' presence and heroics as the sheriffs and gunslingers who inhabited El Paso; yet aside from a vague admiration, he had formed no definite opinions about them.

Enforcement of prohibition, contrarily, had tarnished their image in his mind. After struggling with an acceptable theme for endless hours, White hit on the idea that civilization and moral reform had led to their downfall. He had tried it out in smaller-circulation venues and now found its appeal to blasé New Yorkers as well, judging from the editorial and public reaction. Owen's other writings had likewise gone well. That same year, 1925, Texas's best-known literary son, J. Frank Dobie, had saluted White's *Out of the Desert*, somewhat belatedly, as containing "the best description of border politics—the voting of Mexicans—that has been written so far as I know." Almost concurrently the Library Service of the Franklin Square Agency cited "A Glance at the Mexicans," published in Mencken's *American Mercury*, as one of the ten outstanding magazine articles for February. The distant *Denton (TX) Herald* picked up the news item near the end of the year. *Times* Sunday Editor Markel confirmed, "We have run all the articles you have sent us with the exception of the one on El Paso. If you have anything else send it along." Owen White's writing career, so long in the making, was rapidly accelerating.[37]

Isolated, prerailroad El Paso, into which Owen White was born, always remained for him a model society. Photo courtesy of University of Texas at El Paso Library Special Collections Department.

Urban El Paso of the 1920s, at the time White wrote *Out of the Desert*, had become too "civilized" for the frontier-born author. Photo courtesy of University of Texas at El Paso Library Special Collections Department.

Young White entered the University of Texas to study law, but the death of his father ended his college career. Photo courtesy of *Alcalde*.

Already a man-about-town, White (*middle right*) enjoyed the social life of early twentieth-century El Paso. Photo courtesy of University of Texas at El Paso Library Special Collections Department.

Although past draft age, White volunteered for service in World War I, serving in a hospital unit in France. Photo courtesy of University of Texas at El Paso Library Special Collections Department.

(*left*) White wrote as a reporter and columnist for the *El Paso Herald-Post* until the success of *Out of the Desert* in 1923. Photo courtesy of University of Texas at El Paso Library Special Collections Department.

(*right*) When New York publications beckoned, White made Long Island his home while writing nostalgically of Old El Paso. Photo courtesy of University of Texas at El Paso Library Special Collections Department.

(*left*) White contributed strongly to the circulation surge of *Collier's* before resigning from the editorial board in 1938. Photo courtesy of University of Texas at El Paso Library Special Collections Department.

(*right*) White won acclaim for civil defense activities during World War II after trying unsuccessfully to enlist. Photo courtesy of University of Texas at El Paso Library Special Collections Department.

CHAPTER 4

The Muck and the Rake

The spring of 1925 arrived in New York, almost simultaneously accompanied by Owen and Mike White. The El Pasoan had already lived in and left the city on several occasions, but this time, save for a few travels inland, White would live out his life in the metropolis and suburbs. His native West Texas, subject of many articles and books to come, would no longer hold him, except in his memory of sweeter days.

Despite *New York Times Sunday Magazine* editor Lester Markel's repeated invitations to White to come to New York, he hesitated until March to specify time and duration. "You have convinced me that you ought to come to New York," he wrote Owen in a curious selection of words. "I think we might try three weeks or a month of it but, before saying the final word, I should like to settle the financial end." He proposed paying travel costs from El Paso and back and asked White's preference of a fixed rate, though Markel had earlier repudiated the idea, or a piece rate for articles accepted. Owen expressed ignorance of both the customary pay "for my kind of work" and the cost of living for a transient in New York. White suggested $150 a week, from which he would pay all expenses except for travel and extraordinary costs for special assignments. Owen insisted that he simply wished to avoid losing money and would write additional articles for no payment if the *Times* made an unprofitable agreement. The epitome of conciliation, Owen stated that he would probably accept a dollar figure that Markel considered fair and even inquired, "Does it make any difference to you in what hotel I hang my hat? If so just indicate your favorite hostelry and I will register thereat."[1]

White's private uncertainty, as usual, contrasted sharply with his scrappy public stance. In a story carried by the *Sunday Magazine*, he told of a lady in 1894 El Paso who traveled to New York City to cure a serious illness and returned home in good health with the latest fashions. Enthused by men who followed her to the opulent shopping centers, even Owen bought a pair of yellow shoes that he died black after his father ridiculed them. After reciting the New York influence on El Paso's choices of food, types of clubs, and offices, the Texan stopped himself: "My eyes are dim with tears, and I can write no more."[2]

Having come to terms with the *Times*, the Whites moved into their new apartment on Long Island. Kew Gardens, the chosen location, lay a fifteen-minute train ride, according to the realty firm's advertising, from Manhattan offices and Owen's new world. A planned community, the hilly, one-square-mile, triangular neighborhood had rested only a few years earlier on a cornfield and golf course. Although Owen had convinced himself that he never again wanted to live in El Paso, his residence's interior harkened back to his roots. White's study sported Mexican handwoven rugs, drawings and etchings of border scenes, a serape, cactus, and wax and clay figurines. Indeed, White's articles on Old El Paso in the Old West and a published collection of his previous writings on that theme created a hungry national audience. The book, *Them Was the Days: From El Paso to Prohibition*, launched by a New York publisher, outlasted a field of sequels as White's all-time best seller. Fellow Texan Stanley Walker, whose New York newspaper background, criticism of Texas mores, political skepticism, and general conservatism mirrored facets of Owen, reviewed the book: "Packed with homely observation and grimly humorous anecdote, [it] is a tragedy recounted. The old Southwest is dead. . . . Perhaps Mr. White's book will bring [the advocates of "progress"] a proper sense of shame."[3]

Owen's first collection of his writings on the bygone frontier rang sympathetic notes with other reviewers as well. The *Dallas News* praised the basing of "his whole picture on clear, first hand observation. . . . The good men could be trusted anywhere and the bad ones could be identified at a glance." The reviewer approved the direct quote from White: "The games were straight, the liquor was unadulterated and the women were either openly professional or unapproachable. Everyone was happy—everything was on the square." The *St. Louis Post-Dispatch* considered it "the most thrilling Wild West book, and the best piece of near-literary art having to do with affairs of violence east or west of the Pecos, which this reviewer has read." A reviewer for the *New York Sun* detected a sardonic side to White's assessment of the gunmen's "Jehovah complex," by which they killed to satisfy their thirst for power and to prove their superiority over the law. "He makes a loud lament for a day that is done, yet the reader is compelled to feel that this lament has been penned with tongue in cheek and that the chief thrill for the author . . . lies in the security of recollection." The prestigious *Saturday Review of Literature* judged it "a delightful book . . . making no pretense to the 'literary' . . . with a natural grace of expression . . . supplied . . . by a sort of good-humored exasperation." The reviewer described White as "the oldest native of El Paso, Texas, of American parentage," a matter speculated on by Owen and quite distinct from the often-appearing erroneous statement, denied by Owen, that he was the first "white" child born in El Paso.[4]

Cheered by his successes, Owen uncharacteristically bragged to a friend back home, "How do you folks . . . like the advertising I am giving the old town? What has come has been pretty fair and there is more to follow of the same kind!"[5]

Perhaps the light humor carried over from the secret joke that White perpetrated on his editor, Markel. A mutual friend had playfully convinced the redactor, who was acquainted with White only through his writings, that the El Pasoan was a tobacco-chewing elderly mountain man who had never witnessed the bright lights of a big city. Owen's appearance at their first meeting dispelled the image but not Markel's belief in White's naiveté. White decided to continue the gag by pretending that he had never visited New York City, despite having lived there on several occasions. At one point, he wrote a whimsical story about his supposed introduction to the big city. "A few weeks ago, having grown tired of the dreary monotony of the open spaces and the wide-open places, I took off my spurs, pulled my pants down on the outside of my boots, changed my hat for one of a smaller caliber and much less capacity, put my gun in my suitcase and bought a ticket for New York," he began.[6]

Having heard of the wickedness of the place, White roamed the city in search of the well-known vices. To his pretended dismay, he found New York the victim of an undeserved reputation and lacking the open naughtiness of his hometown. Dismissing the high-priced speakeasies as inconvenient, White chortled, "We don't have to anchor a rum fleet thirteen miles offshore, in the middle of a stormy ocean, and dare the boys to 'come and get it.'" White's humor concealed more than prankishness; it allowed him to issue a denunciation of prohibition and other moral foibles under an innocent guise. Indeed, his distaste for faux morality would overtake his stories of the West in his later writings.[7]

Continuing his role as an awestruck observer, Owen penned an article on his wondrous excursions to Coney Island and Atlantic City, "where I was able to enjoy myself hugely. At Atlantic City I did all the daring, devilish things I saw everyone else do, except one. I ate, I danced, I even attended an auction sale, and I took a dignified ride on a sedate sky-chaser, but I wouldn't ride in a baby carriage. I have a weak heart."[8]

White's indignation began to emerge from its cover in later pieces. He acknowledged taking "a shot" at New York City mayor John F. Hylan "whenever I could," possibly hastening Owen's departure from the newspaper. Perhaps Hylan's association with Tammany Hall or his insistence on a municipally owned subway system rankled the libertarian, for the men shared certain commonalities. They both lived on Long Island, had attempted farming for a living, had studied law in New York, and fought corporate abuse. Although he was a crowd-pleaser elected to two mayoral terms, a reckless driving charge he received as a locomotive engineer and a blistering gubernatorial report that found the mayor complicit in thwarting the expansion of rapid transit showed his dark side. The report appeared all the more damaging as it emanated from the office of Alfred E. Smith, a political confederate. White attended several city council meetings and wrote acerbic accounts describing Hylan as a modern-day Ben Dowell that resulted in heavy editing by Markel and an editorial disclaimer unique in the newspaper's history.[9]

While both patronizing and frustrating his editor, Owen applied himself to several important stories during his brief tenure at the *Times*, and he also published some articles in the *American Mercury* and the *New Yorker*. He introduced non-Texan readers of the *Times* to the Santa Rita oil well in Reagan County that proved the worth of the Permian Basin of West Texas and placed the University of Texas atop a black goldmine. As early as the presidency of Mirabeau B. Lamar in 1839, the Republic of Texas established a public land endowment of fifty leagues (220,000 acres) for a projected "university of the first class." Buttressed by the confirmation of the state legislature in 1858, the construction of the university was delayed by the Civil War, which hastened the creation of the Agricultural and Manufacturing College of Texas through the Morrill Land Grant Act, in 1876. The University of Texas eventually opened in 1883 with a Texas public land endowment of two million acres, largely in nineteen West Texas counties. Little resulted from the later-lucrative Public University Fund until two El Pasoans, Haymon Krupp and Frank T. Pickrell, originally land promoters, organized the Texon Oil and Land Company, arranged funding, and drilled on the land themselves. They named the first site Santa Rita No. 1, for the saint of the impossible. After 646 days the well struck oil at a depth of nearly three thousand feet in May 1923. The spill from the gusher covered 250 adjacent feet and ushered in the area's oil boom. The university received one-eighth of the proceeds.[10]

Owen obviously relished publicizing the role of El Pasoans in his story and commended Governor Amanda Ferguson for not vetoing enabling legislation, as her political opponents had predicted. White could not resist poking fun at the legislature, which he had earlier pronounced a group of Klansmen, for mainly limiting the leased land to grazing: "In place of looking like a college of the first class, which it proudly claims to be," Owen teased the school he had once attended, "the University of Texas, when viewed by a stranger, looks like a second-class dairy farm."[11]

White's popular but individualistic writing style proved too much for Lester Markel's peace of mind. Even while encouraging Owen to write for the *Sunday Magazine* and to come to New York, the editor was wary of the Texan's self-management. He had frequently cautioned White not to stray from a straight report on Ma Ferguson's inauguration and had edited out unpleasing comments in Owen's articles on New York politics. After only a few weeks, Markel summoned Owen to his office and diplomatically released him on the pretext that the writer was worth far more than his salary and that the *Times* was empowering him to write for the more profitable magazines. Markel soothed the shocked White with the promise, even guarantee, that he would continue to buy articles from Owen during a generous transition period. On the street, recovering from the emotional jolt, White touched the letter of introduction in his pocket from Markel to *Collier's* editor William Ludlow Chenery. Although Owen continued to write for the *Times* for the next two months, his steps would take him to a virtual lifetime association with one of the best-selling and most influential magazines in the nation.[12]

More than the letter of introduction directed White to the offices of *Collier's Weekly.* An avid reader, the El Pasoan clearly recognized the prestigious history of the muckraking journal, which had been in decline in recent years. Owen admired the editorship of Norman Hapgood in the early 1900s and of the subsequent editor and social historian Mark Sullivan as well as the work of writers Julian Street and Samuel Hopkins Adams, who made the magazine the foremost muckraking vehicle of its time. White, in tune with many other *Collier's* fans, hoped for a comeback of "the brilliant writing" of a decade and more before. He hoped to rejuvenate the magazine and then ride the tide of its success. The most recent editor, after a succession of frustrated attempts, was the highly promising William Chenery.[13]

Chenery, the object of White's admiration, fully established himself as a leftist Progressive with his 1922 book *Industry and Human Welfare*, despite Owen's later grievance that the editor was prejudiced on behalf of the New Deal. "*Laissez-faireism* has been a doctrine useful to the owners and managers of industry," Chenery wrote. "It has seldom been appealed to as an argument to defeat the wishes of those who possessed property and political privileges. It has been chiefly a rein upon legislation designed to alleviate the conditions of the poor. The advocates . . . have seldom been aware that they were practicing social control in behalf of the owners of factories."[14]

Weighing possible career advancement against the chances of not impressing the *Collier's* editor, Owen procrastinated about arranging a meeting with Chenery. In the end he decided to lead with his strength, his encyclopedic and singular knowledge of the Old West's bad men. With a show of bravado, Owen persuaded Chenery that it would be a major failing not to strike an immediate accord. The editor agreed to judge a sample article and, if it was acceptable, to buy five others. White opted for the topic of Dallas Stoudenmire, El Paso's first marshal, which quickly sealed the deal with *Collier's*, and he committed to a boycott of the magazine's chief rivals, *Liberty* and the *Saturday Evening Post*.[15]

Owen's gamble on the ability of *Collier's* to rejuvenate itself appeared to be the correct bet. Management promised him job security and even listed him as an editor, despite White's later assertion that he never actually undertook that role. While vowing to release himself from his routine of Western writing, Owen's first eight articles for *Collier's* hewed to the line. Curiously, White opted to return to their source, El Paso, to clear his mind. At ground level the Texan realized the full impact of his success in the praise bestowed on him, despite criticisms of the modern city in his articles. When Owen and Mike returned to New York, late in 1925, he was pleased that the magazine had launched an effective campaign to regain and increase subscribers. Normally Owen would have objected to the serialization of a religious book by an author whom he detested, but he approved the resultant augmentation of southern readership. A balanced diet of Bible stories, Owen's gunmen, fiction, and bland editorials proved a route to success, as *Collier's* galloping circulation placed it within hailing distance of the pacesetting *Saturday Evening Post*.[16]

The magazine's prosperity presented Owen with the opportunity to broaden his range of topics. He persuaded Chenery to allow him to write a piece on the Anti-Saloon League, a powerful lobbying group that claimed credit for the passage of the Eighteenth Amendment. White's use of humor in demonstrating the ease in violating the law prompted a pugilistic challenge but delighted his readers. There followed a series of articles in which Owen proved his theme in locations across the nation. The threat of physical assault from a prohibitionist ranked among the least serious warnings to White in his transition to contemporary issues. His editors quashed an article on lawyers, whom Owen had come to despise during his law studies and later associations with them, when the legal staff pronounced it actionable. Owen barely escaped arrest when he bought quantities of machine guns to illustrate both the legality and ease of acquiring dangerous weapons that most of the public, including police, believed illegal. He credited his article and editors with inspiring gun laws across the country. White's piece on the origins of Palm Beach gambling impresarios John and Edward Bradley in nineteenth-century El Paso elicited death threats from the underworld. Owen later dismissed the danger as less than that from enraged readers who accused him of slandering Jesse James.[17]

Such dramatic incidents notwithstanding, Owen continued to write lower-octane material. To varied reading audiences he described the advent of baseball in West Texas, populated with such Runyonesque characters as Give-a-Damn Jones and One-Armed Anderson; the pampering of modern prizefighters, who no longer fought until a knockout, and the shame of fans who supported them; and the misguided sentimentality of current Western writers, who romanticized the American Indian and frontiersmen. The public devoured it: *Collier's* doubled its newsstand sales in 1926 and he was named in "Who's Who at Texas" that year. With his accustomed self-deprecation Owen pled not worthy of the honor, insisting that he acted as "a mirror that will faithfully reproduce the impressions it has received." Nevertheless, it allowed him to pontificate on his native state, which didn't "believe in doing anything like anybody else." Once again employing humor to score a point, White added, "Why shouldn't we, down in Texas, if we want to, take evolution out of the schoolbooks, equip persons with pocket pistols, house University students in barns, elect lady governors, distribute booze-bearing *bastones*, and (but not for the benefit of the K.K.K.) pass a law making bed sheets nine feet long. . . . I earnestly pray that the day will never come when [Texas] . . . will . . . behave in a normal placid manner."[18]

White's scatter-shot response presents a problem for analyzing his thought processes. Owen's natural facility with words and penchant for ironic humor first come to mind. He told a reporter that the events, taken at face value, made Texas "the most colorful, interesting and prolific news-producing state in the Union," an authentic response of a writer. He obviously disdained the Ku Klux Klan and had kiddingly criticized the appearance of the University of Texas. White had sardonically reported on the availability of weapons in the New York area. Contrarily, Owen on several occasions exhibited a fondness for Governor Amanda Ferguson. The other statements lie in the category of either revelation or rhetoric.[19]

Although Owen's sentiments distinctly favored nineteenth-century

Texas, current events in his native state kept calling him back to the present. The 1926 gubernatorial election, more specifically the Democratic primary, drew the attention of many Texans because of the attempt of Amanda Ferguson to win a second term. Owen, who had written sympathetically about her, was in that legion. Her chief opponents were Attorney General Dan Moody and, less so, Lieutenant Governor Lynch Davidson. Moody, born in Taylor, Texas, in 1893, received a law degree from the University of Texas and served in the First World War, after which he won a series of public offices as the youngest candidate in the race. As attorney general, concurrent with Governor Ferguson, he also opposed the Ku Klux Klan, prosecuting a number of its members for criminal activities. James Ferguson's clammy hold on his wife's administration produced scandals related to highway contracts and made Moody a logical challenger in 1926. Davidson, a Louisianan who prospered in the Texas lumber industry, won legislative offices before his election as lieutenant governor in 1920. He supported rural education and good roads, as had James Ferguson during his governorship. Thus both of Amanda's leading opponents took reform issues from the Fergusons, while making Jim the focal point of their campaigns. Moody ran a progressive campaign, endorsing women's suffrage, to Mrs. Ferguson's silence, and also criticized the removal of evolution from textbooks. White offered that Jim's critics generally liked Amanda. No matter: the voters apparently disliked Jim, too. Moody took 49 percent of the vote in the first primary and defeated Mrs. Ferguson in the runoff by 495,723 to 270,595 votes.[20]

Owen presented a rawer view of Texas in, appropriately enough, the free-thinking Mencken's *American Mercury*. In an issue also featuring literary heavyweights Marquis Childs, Sherwood Anderson, Edgar Lee Masters, Nunnally Johnson, and Duncan Aikman, Owen wrote "Reminiscences of Texas Divines." White conceded that

> the State leads the Union in many ways. But religion, unfortunately, isn't one of them. We haven't been able to do anything with our corn-fed clergy. They are the same, yesterday, today and forever.... [From his youth] children were taught to *fear* God and *hate* the Devil.... Christ, in fact, is merely the Devil's policeman ... who catches them in the commission of a sin ... and

slaps them down on the red-hot griddle. . . . The Texas Fundamentalists are so thoroughly wedded to the thought of a bellicose Jehovah that it would be very bad business . . . to talk about a more kindly God. . . . [It]might mean the damming up of the stream of shekels which is now flowing with undisturbed serenity into the coffers of the evangelical churches. . . . The Episcopalians, when sober, are not very comical. Moreover, they are far too intelligent to cut much ice in Texas.[21]

Writing for the eccentric Mencken, shortly to become a partner in correspondence, White doubtless felt secure in stating in print normally unwelcomed opinions. His writing's editorial and public acceptance additionally facilitated an approaching series on the foibles of prohibition. He remained cagy in stating a religious preference, offhandedly complimenting the family religion after a teasing preface.

Owen's writing interests again involved him with the neighboring nation that had influenced much of his early life in El Paso. In a letter to a hometown friend in March 1927, White apologized for the delay in his correspondence: "I have been too busy recovering from my Mexico trip and then writing about it to attend to anything else." The statement failed to reveal the full weight of the journey and its aftermath. *Collier's*, recognizing White's knowledge of Mexico, sent him south to interview President Elias Calles for his view on the still-turbulent revolutionary nation. Owen, as an astute reporter, got more than he or his editors had expected. The revolution had not ended with the death of virtually all the leaders of the anti-Díaz movement. The Constitution of 1917, the main legacy of President Carranza, continued to cause consternation on both sides of the border. American conservatives particularly joined hands with their Mexican counterparts on the issues of land and religion. Articles 3 and 130 radically separated church and state, placing severe restrictions on the Catholic Church and clergy and secularizing education. The Vatican prohibited parishioners from pledging loyalty to the constitution, and armed fighting broke out between the faithful and supporters of the document. American Catholics, inspired by the Knights of Columbus and other lay associations, unabashedly called for U.S. intervention.[22]

Article 27 aroused strong sentiments among American and other landholders and corporations. The provision made the Mexican nation the owner of mineral rights, along with other restrictions on private property, which alarmed oil companies in particular. The dictator Porfirio Díaz had granted oil companies full use of the subsoil rights while turning Mexico into a major oil-producing country. Early revolutionary regimes had largely continued Díaz's policy with verbal agreements of noninterference. American and British corporations, in particular, lobbied for a written statement to that effect, and the acrimony intensified when Obregón demanded affirmative action on petroleum still in the ground in exchange for a fifty-year leasehold. The recent inauguration of Calles, an avowed atheist and socialist former schoolteacher, pushed the religious and corporate factions into a state of panic.[23]

Owen came away with a series of articles entitled "Mexico's New Dictator—the Dollar," which included information about the tentative center of a governmental investigation of alleged briberies by oil companies in Mexico. Naturally critical of both government and companies, White reported that unnamed American interests had paid $10 million to the Mexican government and that "one of the largest financial institutions in the country" was aware of a proposed revolution. The People's Reconstruction League asked President Calvin Coolidge to investigate. The league secretary, Benjamin C. Marsh, was a naturalized Bulgarian, lifelong reformer, and Georgian single- taxer. The *Times*, a venue friendly to White, editorialized support for an investigation and quoted Owen:

> Certain American interests (and my informants named them and I will not) merely paid to the Mexican Government some time ago the sum of $10,000,000 and took a receipt for it in the nature of advanced royalties on production. One of these [candidates], strange as it may seem, is Alvaro Obregon. Frequently, while in Mexico, I heard rumors to the effect that he would lead a revolt against Calles, and on the very day that I arrived in New York I had the same story told to me in the office of one of the largest financial institutions in the world. By what authority do American oil interests seek to bribe the Mexican Government, which interests are these, and how do American financiers know the details of proposed Mexican revolutions and why?[24]

Nothing materialized about the investigation or the revolution. President Coolidge dispatched Wall Street magnate Dwight Morrow to Mexico City, and he quickly befriended Calles. Morrow, coincidentally the father-in-law of aviation hero Charles Lindbergh, convinced the worried bankers and oilmen of the Mexican president's credibility. Indeed, a year later the man supposedly at the center of the plot, Obregón, lay dead at the hand of an assassin. In fact, the close cooperation between Calles and Obregón likely prompted the act by a known religious zealot. Acting on a recent constitutional amendment that allowed nonconsecutive presidential reelections, Obregón had won a second term in 1928 after having sat out the previous four years. Amid rumors of a conspiracy between the two presidents to rotate in office, the culprit struck, forever ending the likelihood of a Mexican president serving a second term. The shocking event produced uproar in the already unsteady Mexican political scene. The American journalist and historian Carleton Beals sent a special item to the *Times*, seconded by a companion article from White, saying that Calles would have to resume power. Owen, considering his skepticism about Mexican politics, wrote of the two leaders in a surprisingly constructive manner. "Obregon [was] the one outstanding leader created by eighteen years of Mexican revolution. . . . Calles is hardheaded, stubborn and dictatorial. Obregon, on the contrary, was suave, diplomatic . . . tolerant, wise and, like Porfirio Diaz, a staunch believer in the doctrine that, where his country's interests were involved, the end justifies the means. . . . [Their] differences . . . were probably honest differences. The men had divergent views on vital subjects and yet they were close friends. . . . An answer must come soon. Mexico is a country which brooks little delay."[25]

White's clean prose demonstrated how well he had mastered the journalistic style that had concerned *Times* editor Markel only a few years earlier. To the continued regret of American students of Mexican history, Owen did not pursue the subject consistently thereafter. His next entry, a piece for *Collier's* a year later, reported a Mexican ring counterfeiting U.S. dollars. As with his reportage on the Mexican Revolution, White's sporadic coverage of this crucial period in that nation's history creates a sadness in the interested reader that he did not devote more of his skilled analysis to it. Calles indeed returned to power by naming three presidents to fill Obregón's term, increasingly controlling their administrations and establishing the party system that would rule the nation for the next seven decades. Owen returned to the period in his autobiography almost twenty years after the events; he identified the offending company as owned by the Teapot Dome instigator Edward Doheny. Through interviews with trusted sources outside the government White had pieced together a sequence of events that verified an agreement between Calles and Obregón and that included Morrow quietly giving the green light for more payments to restore decorum. Owen heartily approved of the latter maneuver, to the point of having expressed his opinion in advance of the transactions. With the repetition of Owen's dismissal of a Communist threat, his autobiography recalled the outlines of the reported situation, minus the original indignation at the audacity of the oil company. He now referred to the People's Reconstruction League, which had demanded an investigation, as a nuisance.[26]

White explained the brevity of his series as stemming from the desire of his editors to concentrate on audience building back home. Owen certainly had a demanding agenda awaiting him. To bolster *Collier's* intensified circulation campaign, Owen reverted to writing about Old West gunmen, although he feared the magazine might forfeit its quality for the larger readership. The articles remained widely popular and served the magazine and White well financially, even as the subject of the week blurred in Owen's mind. An article on modern Chicago racketeers must have seemed only a slight deviation. There was, nevertheless, opportunity for more serious material: after the Mississippi River flooded in 1927, White inveighed against the Mississippi River Commission as unworthy of further funding pending reforms in its complete control over the great river. White had acquired intimate familiarity with water projects over the years, from playfully bemoaning the banning of swimming in El Paso's irrigation ditch, to criticizing his hometown's irrigation project that created a land boom and bust, to speaking publicly for the construction of the Elephant Butte Dam in southern New Mexico.[27]

The commission dated to 1879, the pet project of Mississippi senator L. Q. C. Lamar and Louisiana representative Randall L. Gibson, in collaboration with navigation and flood-control interests. The passage of the bill to centralize authority over the area followed decades of jurisdictional, constitutional, and engineering disputes, but controversies over levee construction and river improvements continued. In the most destructive river flood in the history of the United States, the Cumberland River at Nashville topped levees of more than fifty-six feet in height on January 1, 1927, after pounding rains. Floodwaters covered an area more than fifty miles wide and one hundred miles long to a depth of thirty feet, killing 246 people in seven states and leaving seven hundred thousand people homeless in Mississippi and Louisiana. To spare New Orleans, authorities ordered the unnecessary dynamiting of levees that flooded upriver parishes. Whites' conscription of African Americans to build levees and racism exhibited in refugee camps accelerated the movement of blacks out of the South. Under the resultant Flood Control Act of 1928 the U.S. Army Corps of Engineers constructed levees to divert excessive flow from the Mississippi River, an action that became the source of heated contention after the 2005 flooding of New Orleans during Hurricane Katrina.[28]

Throughout his writing career, Owen found time to encourage fellow or aspiring writers. When El Paso printer Carl Hertzog suggested an article in *Collier's* on home furnishings, White thought the subject outside his expertise but suggested that Hertzog write it. Owen even suggested a follow-up: "If Colliers don't want it—and they probably won't if they have already published a similar article . . . then try it out on Woman's Home Companion and Good Housekeeping. Both of these magazines pay high prices and you ought to be able to get an article across. With best regards and hoping that I'll see the article with YOUR name on it in some magazine."[29]

Hertzog would see his name on a lot of publications, as printer and writer. Destined to be the "printer without peer between the Atlantic and Pacific," in the words of folklorist J. Frank Dobie, Hertzog was born in Lyon, France, in 1902. He entered the United States at two years of age when his father, a native Ohioan, took a position at the University of New Mexico. Hertzog came to El Paso in 1923 and worked with McMath, who published White's early books and poems. Hertzog had briefly left the printing business when he corresponded with Owen, but he returned to the trade in 1930 and opened his own shop in El Paso four years later. His fame soon followed.[30]

A few months later, Owen encouraged another El Pasoan, Dr. J. F. Jenness, to publish an article. In so doing, White revealed something of his trade to a friend of his and Mike's:

Personally I like the story very much. It has all the material necessary for the making of a salable yarn. Please note that damn word "saleable." It doesn't mean the same as "good." I think the story "good" as you have done it, but it isn't saleable because it lacks the trick stuff that the editors and public like. But don't let that discourage you . . . all you need is a little practice and you'll put it over. Rewriting, of course, is a mean job and we all have to do it. For instance, after all these months of writing about gunmen I have had to rewrite the last two pieces for Collier's before the editor would take 'em, so you see the fact that when an editor says "do it again" [it] indicates that he is not only interested in that particular job, but in the writer also.[31]

Subsequently, in early 1928, Owen took the manuscript and turned it in personally to his editors. "I think it is full of fact, satire, and humor," he assured the author. "That combination, in my opinion, always makes readable stuff and I'll be disappointed if they disagree with me." Following a particularly demanding year, Owen took noticeable pleasure in stating that he would work in a brief period of leisure among his travels: "I'll not be here to get the verdict on it as I am leaving tomorrow for Denver, El Paso, San Antonio, Austin and Houston. I'll be in El Paso for only two days, though, so will not have time to see much of anybody as I plan to spend practically all of my time down on the ranch with my sister."[32]

The Houston visit doubtless involved the Democratic Party national convention, scheduled for the Magnolia City in the summer of 1928. The first major presidential convention held in the South since before the Civil War owed its presence to the political and financial prowess of Jesse H. Jones. A native of Robertson County, Tennessee, Jones followed his father into the tobacco business and managed his uncle's lumberyard as a teenager. Moving to Houston in 1898 at age twenty-four, Jones established a lumber business on his own and branched out into other profitable pursuits. Already gaining recognition as "Mister Houston" by the time of the election year, Jones had bought an interest in the *Houston Chronicle*, constructed the largest hotel in the city, and was a leading banker. He envisioned placing the political spotlight on his adopted city, raised the finances to acquire the convention, and promised the party a ready-made site. The resultant Sam Houston Hall, a temporary structure with a capacity of twenty thousand, witnessed the nomination of New York governor Alfred E. Smith after a nominating speech by Franklin Delano Roosevelt, former unsuccessful vice presidential candidate and future chief executive of the United States. The lynching of Robert Powell, a twenty-four-year-old African American man, by a group including an ambulance driver incensed over the shooting death of a policeman, earned a companion piece in the national news. A perplexed Jones decried the killing as "a stigma and a blot on the good name of Texas."[33]

Like White, a Houstonian recalled the Democratic convention years after the event, with a major similarity. After noting the sight of men in white suits and Panama hats enjoying the new refrigerated watercoolers, young Rollin H. Baker and friends sighted other means the delegates used to slack their thirst. "We peeked into garbage can after garbage can just to note empty bottles. Some in standard long necked quart bottles and others in Mason jars, indicating that both the Galveston-based rum-runners and the East Texas moonshiners in the case of the latter were profiting on this rather wide-open political occasion."[34]

Owen concurred in his rumination on the convention as a means of publicizing the city and also the ship channel, opened in 1914, that connected Houston with the Gulf of Mexico, fifty miles distant. "A million [dollars] was chicken feed," he pronounced, "and what better way was there to demonstrate the true value of the ship canal than by bringing up it a few boatloads of that distilled inspiration without whose aid democratic reasoning and oratory have never yet been able to function constructively." White partied with the rest, kept both ears open, decided that the farm issue backed by both parties was inauthentic, and concluded, elsewhere, that Smith had no chance.[35]

In a not-unaccustomed manner, White arrived at decisions about the presidential race independently of the staged celebrations in Houston and Kansas City regarding the candidates. The continued sale of farm machinery and increased purchases at country stores dismissed the complaints of agriculturalists in White's mind. Owen retained this modest bit of information and continued to view agricultural issues skeptically even as the economy deteriorated. Visits to Protestant churches in the South persuaded him that the Bible Belt, in the words of H. L. Mencken, would not warm to the "wet," Roman Catholic son of immigrants. When a fundamentalist preacher shouted that he would swallow a greased n—before voting for Smith, Owen knew the political game was up. The racial and religious bigotry enthusiastically proclaimed by elements of the southern clergy unsettled even the hard-shelled reporter. Owen wrote sympathetically of Smith, despite the man's Tammany Hall connections and advocacy of reform by governmental initiative. Smith's stand, though modulated, against the Volker Act doubtless helped his candidacy with White, and the attacks by preachers and Klansmen surely carried influence with the Texan. Smith's later criticisms of Roosevelt obviously pleased Owen. The electoral results, by which Herbert Hoover carried forty of the forty-eight states, failed to surprise White, but he expressed admiration for New Mexico publisher Bronson Cutting, whom he credited with delivering the state to the Republican candidate after having done the same for the Democrats in a senatorial election four years previously.[36]

The November election carried over into the next year as far as Owen was concerned, embroiling him in a bitter political dispute that threatened his physical as well as professional welfare and placed his employer in jeopardy. In mid-1929 Collier's ran an article by White entitled "High Handed and Hell Bent," in which he referred to Yancy Baker as the "perpetual sheriff" of Hidalgo County, South Texas, who remained in office on the basis of Mexican citizens' votes and collusion with "their loyal Republican friend, Hon. R.B. Creager." For good measure, Owen dubbed the pair the "Texas Tammany boys." He promptly found himself knee-deep in the Hidalgo County Rebellion.[37]

White had personally witnessed an aspect of boss rule in his early life, when both political parties rounded up legal and illegal voters, plied them with liquor, confined them overnight, and had them vote "early and often," in the parlance of Texas politics. Yet the notorious examples of the phenomenon resided in the rural counties of South Texas. Business or political leaders, often Anglo, moved into positions of power in the late decades of the nineteenth century by appealing to both influential and marginalized populations. The former group, consisting of ranchers, developers, bankers, and merchants, received favorable legislative and judicial decisions, taxes, and assessments and armed authority to protect their advantages. Like their northern urban counterparts, the political bosses extended welfare to the immigrant poor in return for their votes. Perhaps the most notorious of ringleaders, Archer Parr and James B. Wells established fiefdoms in Duval and Cameron Counties, respectively. Attacks from Progressives and other advocates of honest, businesslike public administration, aided by urbanization and out-of-state immigration, had placed the traditional bosses on the defensive by the 1920s, but certain machines showed their resiliency well into the twentieth century.[38]

The first subject of Owen's scorn, Anderson Yancy Baker, was born in 1874 in Uvalde, Texas, the son of a Spanish-American War veteran. Baker moved to the Rio Grande Valley as a young man after enlisting with the Texas Rangers, where he escaped prosecution for the murder of two men. He soon after retired, took a position as a mounted customs inspector, gained a fortune in agriculture and real estate, and eventually became political boss of the region. Baker's source of power lay with Mexican Americans, toward whom he dispensed charity and support of education. With only a slight alteration from White's terminology, Baker's critics dubbed him the multimillionaire sheriff of Hidalgo County, who, with his wife, lived in a palatial mansion. At the time of Owen's article, Baker was president of the Edinburg State Bank, a position he held until his death.[39]

Rentfro Banton Creager, born in Waco in 1877, held two college degrees, including a doctorate of law from the University of Texas. He undertook a lucrative practice in Brownsville, serving as customs collector under Theodore Roosevelt and William Howard Taft. Creager testified in favor of the prosecution in the investigation of the Brownsville Affray of 1906, in which black troops of the Twenty-Fifth Infantry purportedly shot up the town. Creager was the unsuccessful gubernatorial Republican candidate against James Ferguson in 1916 and seconded Warren Harding's presidential nomination in 1920. Later President Harding visited Creager and his wife at Brownsville and offered him the ambassadorship to Mexico, which he declined. Creager subsequently refused the same invitation from Calvin Coolidge. Indeed, the *New York Times* reported a rumor in 1921 that Creager had been appointed as a special agent to negotiate with Obregón, who considered him the next ambassador. More recently, Creager had become the first national committeeman to support the presidential nomination of Herbert Hoover. The Creagers bought the splendid Celaya House in the 1920s, ultimately designated a Historical Landmark in Brownsville.[40]

The object of controversy and litigation, "High Handed and Hell Bent" developed from an interest by *Collier's* editor William Chenery in the rapid growth of Hidalgo County. In the space of twenty years irrigation had transformed the formerly underdeveloped, mesquite-covered flatland into a prosperous fruit basket. Dispatched by Chenery to write an article on the transformation, Owen captured various sources of amazement, including the political scene. White summarized the success as "GRAFT and GRAPEFRUIT." He stated his amazement at Creager's apparent endorsement of the defeat of his Republican Party at the hands of Baker's Democratic candidates and hit his stride, verbally. "The Texas Tammany boys not only tell the taxpayers to go to hell, but, out of the goodness of their hearts, provide them with a handy route in the shape of a heavily bonded high-way and a costly toll bridge which lands them right at the very door of the place. A committee of Congressmen went to Hidalgo County and studied the technique of Baker, Creager & Co, when they were ready to remark: 'Well, this is all too fancy for us, Philadelphia at its best was never like this.'"[41]

Meticulous detail accompanied the verbosity of White's conclusions. He cited the "Nickel Plated Highway to Hell" that connected McAllen and Hidalgo, fewer than eight miles apart over flat terrain, at a cost to taxpayers of a million dollars and ended at a toll bridge owned mainly by Sheriff Baker. First, the bridge led to a saloon and dance hall, the property of a Hidalgo County public official. Second, road costs were padded with bonds sold to friends of county officials at attractive rates and deposited in friendly banks chosen by county officials. Third, a school for Mexican children, built at an inflated price, languished with uncrated equipment years after its construction. Finally, a series of elections that many voters did not know about because of obscure posting, accumulated a school bond indebtedness of millions of dollars, prompting an administrator to resign in protest. B. D. Kimbrough, a local lawyer, told a group of congressmen who were visiting McAllen to investigate allegations of election fraud that reformers found the Democratic primaries closed to them. The skeleton Republican Party demonstrated its unconcern by declining to send a slate of candidates to the state convention.[42]

Only a week before White's article appeared, fellow *Collier's* writer William G. Shepherd included Creager in an article entitled "A Job for Jack." Like White, Shepherd had reported critically on crime, prohibition, and the Ku Klux Klan and carried journalistic authority. Shepherd gained national attention as a reporter for the *Milwaukee Journal* in 1911 when he phoned in an eyewitness account of the Triangle Shirtwaist Factory fire to United Press. The muckraker likewise spared no sympathy on Creager: "Many citizens of Texas who are lucky enough to have been named by Republican Washington for Federal jobs . . . have gone through the very realistic ceremony of actually signing notes carrying Mr. Creager's name. . . . Collecting Republican money in Texas is high-pressure business; Creager has a $10,000-a-year assistant." Shepherd reported the Baker-Creager alliance with material drawn from a bipartisan U.S. Senate investigation, concluding that Creager did not wish to share patronage power with elected Republican officeholders.[43]

The cited investigation, which corroborated what many South Texans believed, was chaired by Senator Smith W. Brookhart, an "insurgent," or Progressive, Republican from Iowa. A true maverick, Brookhart's experience combined service in two wars, the presidency of the National Rifle Association, support of liberal causes, and endorsement of Democrats against his own party members. He lost favor with Republicans by favoring the presidential candidacy of Robert M. La Follette in 1924, was once evicted from his seat by his colleagues, and eventually lost his Senate seat to party rivals. While he served in the Senate, Brookhart remained an implacable foe of political corruption.[44]

The political and legal battle that followed publication of White's article resulted from a chain of events that began when a Republican good government group in Hidalgo County sent two thousand telegrams petitioning President Coolidge for federal supervision of the 1928 elections. An assistant U.S. attorney responded that the citizens should take their appeal to H. M. Holden, the federal district attorney in Houston.

Mayor F. B. Freeland of McAllen, a member of the reform group, explained to the official that "election irregularities without parallel . . . have been in custom here for several years. . . . We must have federal relief." The mayor of neighboring Weslaco signed the missive. Holden responded to a question from the *McAllen Daily Press* that he had requested that the FBI make a "preliminary investigation" to establish the necessity of a formal inquiry. Discouraging to the reformers, the district attorney admitted "no reason for any rush." Pressed by the supplicants, Holden stated the impossibility of undertaking an investigation prior to the elections. Governor Dan Moody, for his part, ordered Texas Rangers to Edinburg to preserve peace but withdrew them when he learned that Sheriff Baker, ironically, had deputies guarding the precincts. Inasmuch as the Baker machine counted the votes, ballot theft was not the issue; at length the announced results maintained the Democrats in control. A disputed Weslaco box, tossed because the envelope was unsealed, would have given the election to a Republican county judge.[45]

Fearing a physical clash between the factions and frustrated by an electoral outcome that repudiated the actual winners, Mayor Freeland addressed a plea to Representative Frederick R. Lehlback (R-New Jersey), the chairman of the House Committee on Campaign Expenditures and a former prosecuting attorney. Freeland sought a delay of the proposed hearing until the reformers had an opportunity to supply the committee with "certified evidence." Lehlback announced the inquiry for the morning of November 26 at Edinburg and told Freeland to present witnesses and statements. The remainder of the committee consisted of John E. Nelson (R-Maine), Carl R. Chinblom (R-Illinois), and Loring M. Black (D-New York). The citizens' representatives placed three allegations before the committee: (1) county officials rejected returns and would not count votes in Weslaco; (2) several thousand non-English-speaking voters, citizens and noncitizens, voted in the elections; and (3) votes from legal voters were thrown out without justification. The county's team of lawyers countered that the committee had no jurisdiction over a state election, recommended a court as the proper setting, and denied the veracity of the accusations. After hearing a parade of witnesses testify about absent people voting, padding of the voting lists, disqualification of legitimate ballots as mutilated, and the discarding of the box of Weslaco ballots without justification, the committee opined that "the Hidalgo County election . . . was tainted with wholesale fraud in various forms" and recommended a searching investigation by the U.S. attorney general.[46]

Energized by the findings of the congressional committee, Hidalgo reformers tried to block the validation of the Baker candidates. A caravan of five hundred protesters drove 350 miles to Austin, imploring the Texas Legislature not to certify the victory of W. R. Montgomery, who also sought the House speakership, in advance of an investigation. The eight-page petition failed to muster the two-thirds vote necessary for consideration, alongside a motion to investigate the election, but the Good Government group drew some solace from the defeat of Montgomery's bid for Speaker of the House. Their attempt to seat a candidate for county judge began auspiciously when a district court issued an injunction against the Democratic nominee and subsequently accepted the disqualified ballots from Weslaco, making the reform candidate the winner. Barely had the celebrations subsided, however, before the state supreme court overruled the decision, clinching the Baker machine's victory.[47]

Repercussions followed in the wake of the decisions. A litigant sued Mayor Freeland for swindling the city of McAllen; strong support for the official from the chamber of commerce resulted in the suit being dropped. A county deputy tax collector and reform member suffered prompt dismissal for disloyalty to his superior; dozens of disloyal teachers met the same fate, and others resigned under pressure. A night intruder attacked a reform participant with a blunt weapon, leaving the victim in a pool of blood. Although the man initially recovered, he never regained speech and died three months later. In a lengthy court case two men received life sentences for murder and conspiracy to murder, although apparent collusion with county officials could not be proven. The official Democratic candidates continued to win in Hidalgo County until the ringleader's death from a stroke in November 1930.[48]

In light of disclosures prior to and after the 1928 elections, White's disdainful remarks appear almost understated. Yet he would join the parade of victims of retaliation. Creager claimed that Owen and *Collier's* had libeled him by implying that he sold federal offices for personal profit, switched votes, escaped jail through control of the courts, and connived with the Democratic Party to defeat Republican contenders. He filed suits against the journal for $1 million in the friendly Brownsville court's December session. A history of violence, even death, that hung over the venue was by no means unrecognized by Owen. By late 1929 Owen White was lodged at the El Jardin Hotel in Brownsville, edgily eyeing the court calendar. Despite the seriousness of the matter, an editor felt obliged to remind White of his assignment deadlines and to joke that a friend expected "that you will all see jail. If so, I hope you will meet . . . Creager there. If you must choose jails, Matamoros has a nice clean one. That's where they took me."[49]

The tension in the city obviated any kind of relief other than gallows humor. Over a decade later White still remembered that the populace fully expected him to fall victim to foul play during the course of the trial, which was delayed until early May. Indeed, the man victimized by a night intruder, the son-in-law of a prominent banker, had permitted Owen to peruse records damaging to the political ring only hours before the assault. A group of locals visited White in the night, clearly to intimidate him, but left without incident. Even Governor Dan Moody, who had stood against the Ku Klux Klan, appeared to Owen to be reluctant to involve himself in the South Texas controversy. White maintained his fearless persona throughout the ordeal, while the litigant, Creager, deteriorated. Described as "tanned and grizzled," by a reporter, the writer spent the first day in court explaining, sentence by sentence, the substance of his article, while his wife, Mike, sketched likenesses of the participants. White denied that he intended to charge Creager with anything other than failing to support Republican candidates against incumbent Democrats. In a moment approaching levity, Charles Kelly and the *Collier's* defense team asked federal judge W. Lee Estes to subpoena from Washington, D.C., Senator Brookhart and five House representatives, including Representative Harry Wurzbach of Texas, to testify on corruption. Creager's chief counsel, George Hill Jr., denounced the move as a "grand stand play," leaving the magistrate doubting that he possessed such authority and declining to rule on the motion.[50]

On the day scheduled for Creager to testify, the public interest necessitated moving the trial to a larger location. With Baker and others of his friends in attendance, Creager, dressed to the nines, replied to his attorneys with supreme confidence. He had promised the townspeople that he would contribute his award to creating parks and other physical improvements. The decision of the magazine's lawyers not to interrogate, in order to close off debate, stalled the litigant's momentum, while the selection of distant jurors offset his expected advantage. The jury's decision of not guilty came as no surprise to Owen but apparently surprised the *Brownsville Herald.* The newspaper missed its usual publication delivery by hours as the staff hurriedly rewrote the morning edition that had headlined Creager's victory. Deflated, Creager withdrew his suit against Shepherd and *Collier's,* ending the magazine's and White's association with Hidalgo County. The Baker ring approaching collapse, Creager remained paramount in Republican politics. He was an early backer of Kansas governor Alfred Landon's quest for the 1936 presidential nomination and floor leader for Ohio senator Robert A. Taft at the 1948 party convention. Creager, president of an oil company, died two years later at Brownsville. Owen always considered *Collier's* role in bringing down the county ring to be its greatest achievement during his association with the magazine.[51]

CHAPTER 5

"Like a terrier in a barnful of rats"

The year 1929, in the words of Owen White, was the last before "the big hang over." His prose described not only his reportorial activities on the failings of prohibition but the binge of the economy. Since 1920 the U.S. population had grown by twenty-five million and the nation had added 70 percent to the gross national product, more than trebled the index of common stocks, and almost quintupled the volume of stock sales. A less bright side, however, also showed itself. The number of bank suspensions had accelerated before the Wall Street crash, average weekly earnings for production workers had fallen slightly, and wholesale commodity prices had dropped sharply. The clearest indicator, agriculture, showed a substantial loss in farm products generally and wheat specifically, defying Owen's optimism. The Texan doubtless took pleasure from the court verdict that found Albert B. Fall, former secretary of interior, guilty of accepting illegal loans from oilmen and receiving a year in prison as the Teapot Dome scandal finally wound down. White's career prospered as *Collier's* published a three-part series titled "A Frontier Mother" in October, followed by a hardback book version, both of which pleased readers and critics. An editor recognized the manuscript's appeal, even before publication. "Will you return the corrected set [of proofs] with the copy as soon as you conveniently can?"

one asked. "They look pretty good to me." Owen's fame was spreading across the Atlantic: an English publisher asked permission to reprint the series. The irascible H. L. Mencken repeatedly told Owen not to forget his journal as a market for his writings.[1]

The praise increasingly included personal touches. White's old friend William S. McMath wrote, "I am at a loss for words to tell you what I think of 'A Frontier Mother.' It is a little gem that comes agitating close to being masterly . . . slyly humorous . . . a little classic of the pioneer west. . . . I prize the book for itself and for the inscription on the fly-leaf." A reader who knew Owen's mother recalled, "Mrs. White was a lady of the highest character and intellect and as I look back over my early years in El Paso it seems a great privilege to have known and had such a person for a friend." Another reader wondered if White's father might have treated the wounds of his own father at Fort Garland.[2]

The *Collier's* issue following the serialization of "A Frontier Mother" contained Owen's article "Setting Them Up in Ohio," illustrating another successful series by the Texan. Although White had written on the fallacy of enforcing prohibition for the past several years, the editorial staff decided to throw its full support behind the repeal of the Eighteenth Amendment, as a result of either soul searching or head counting. As one who had despised hypocrites since the time in his youth when he would regularly recognize the town fathers in compromising situations in south side bars and brothels, Owen eagerly accepted the assignment of seeking out politicians, preachers, and bootleggers whose candidness he admired in a nationwide trek. He found all of those types and more for his opening articles on New Mexico and Ohio towns, New Orleans, and Dallas. While the ambience and types of spirits varied, the spigots flowed in every location. White and his employer narrowly escaped a second lawsuit that year when the mayor of Dallas, in a five-hundred-word telegram, threatened legal action over Owen's revelations. The suit fizzled but Owen rankled his own hometown by stating that young girls "just beyond spanking age" served whisky "in luxurious flats" in Oklahoma and Texas, including El Paso. Accordingly, a criticism from a reader who said, "I strongly suspect that your observations . . . of Ohio must of a necessity have been obtained from the rear platform of an observation car" seemed faint praise. *American Mercury* editor H. L. Mencken's encouraging words were, "I hope the Washington bootleggers don't poison you." Threats not-withstanding, White continued debunking temperance morality, bolstered by his employer's knowledge of the popularity of the series. The theme even inspired Owen to write several pieces of fiction with a bar-room setting.[3]

White's fourth-estate exploits carried over into the Depression-ridden 1930s. With all economic indicators plummeting, Owen's world endured better than most. His name recognition and reputation at an all-time high, the Texan's long suit of scofflaws and Old West gunmen appealed mightily to seekers of escapist literature. White witnessed the publication of two books, *Lead and Likker* (1932) and *My Texas Tis of Thee* (1936), to brisk sales before the decade barely hit midpoint. *Collier's* remained abreast of the weekly journals with a stable that included Ernest Hemingway, Martha Gellhorn, and Winston Churchill. Owen's correspondence attested to his stature. A grandson of Texas Ranger John Coffee Hays expressed gratitude for the virtually exclusive treatment of his ancestor, extending a lunch invitation and adding that "practically nothing heretofore has been written about his career and experiences." A nephew and namesake of Hays echoed the opinion, adding, "I knew [Hays] from my earliest days up until the time of his death." The cynical Mencken always maintained a cordial attitude toward White, even when occasionally turning down submissions. The editor apologized for returning a story from a writer recommended by Owen, exhorting him, "I surely hope you don't forget the *American Mercury* in the course of your peregrinations."[4]

Eclipsing his success and influence was the deepest personal loss White had suffered since the death of his mother. In June 1931 White sadly witnessed the death of his older brother, Alward, who had turned to the practice of medicine in the Big Bend mining town of Shafter. The tragedy followed an undisclosed but apparently serious illness Owen had experienced several months earlier. Editorial comments showed that even those concerned over his health still desired his productivity. In late April Tom Cathcart, an editor at the *Country Home*, a companion publication to *Collier's*, wrote him, "We missed you around here, and on inquiring found that you were doing a little recuperating out in Santa Fe." While expressing sympathy, Cathcart expressed hope "that the good old

sunshine has fixed you up in good stead ... [to] dig up something for us."
Andrew S. Wing, a fellow editor, added, "You certainly picked an ideal
spot to rejuvenate yourself." Disavowing any intention to encourage
Owen to overexert himself, Wing offered, "This thing we had in mind is
an article which you probably could do without a great deal of running
around or research." Two weeks later, William Chenery entered the competition for the recuperating White's talents: "The most important thing
is to get thoroughly well [but] ... I think there might be a good personality article in Senator Cutting."[5]

The *El Paso Times* stated on June 20, 1931,

> Dr. Alward H. White, 55, of Shafter, Texas, died at an El Paso
> hospital yesterday morning following a brief illness. He was
> rushed here Thursday night after being stricken with a hemor-
> rhage of the spinal cord, and died 18 hours later. He was a mem-
> ber of a pioneer El Paso family, and a brother of Owen P. White,
> New York author. He came here from Colorado with his parents,
> Dr. and Mrs. Alward White, while a small child. He was reared
> and educated in El Paso, and opened his practice here immedi-
> ately after receiving his medical degree from the University of
> Maryland.

Funeral services pended the arrival of Owen, who, along with his sister,
Leigh, now Mrs. O. S. Osborn, were Alward's only surviving immediate
family members.[6]

The article might have said much more. While in medical school, from
which he graduated about 1905, Alward lost an eye in an accident and
developed a tremor in his lips. To compensate for the alterations in his
appearance, White wore a glass eye and grew a beard. After returning to
El Paso he obtained the position of company doctor for the American
Smelting and Refining Company. In a bizarre instance of infatuation, the
wife of the smelter superintendent began to press him for an intimate
relationship. To escape her attentions, Alward requested transfers, first to
Chihuahua and then to Shafter, only to have her pursue him to each location. When the doctor rejected her advances another time, she took a
pistol out of her purse and killed herself with a shot in the head. The

shocked Alward arranged a formal burial and constructed a shrine in the form of a satin-lined small stone-block house. Alward enjoyed several years of happiness after he married a traveling companion of the deceased woman, adopting her two small children. Unfortunately, his wife died not long afterward, prompting Alward to construct a second chapel over her grave. Several years later, Dr. White married the adopted granddaughter of the prominent landholder and rancher Milton Favor, a native Virginian and personal hero of Owen's. Afterward Alward contented himself with raising figs and comanaging a service station and tire store, as the number of personnel employed by the silver-mining company declined. The owners closed the silver mines in early 1930 due to flooding. Dr. White considered leaving the dying town in the concluding months of his life but could not abandon the remaining settlers.[7]

Owen described in a letter to his sister, Leigh, his and Mike's journey to Shafter, the selected site of the burial. White dreaded witnessing the mourning but was pleasantly surprised by the strength of the grievers. He was touched by the affection the small community and residents of nearby Marfa and Presidio had for his brother. A Catholic priest agreed to the people's wish that Alward receive burial in the church cemetery, notwithstanding the doctor's Protestant faith. A kindred soul to Owen, the priest reiterated the kindnesses and charities Alward had bestowed on the poor: "It doesn't make any difference to me that Dr. White was not a Catholic. . . . [He had] the spirit of God, and my church will never be closed to a man who has that in him." The writer counted perhaps fifty bareheaded men walking behind the hearse as it slowly moved to the cemetery. Owen, obviously tired from travel, bereaved, and only recently recovered from his own illness, told Leigh, "If when I die, such a tribute is ever paid to me . . . I will be happy." He then threw himself into arranging his brother's papers and estate.[8]

The Great Depression, which White and many others attributed to stock market inflation and speculation, brought governmental growth as well as economic reverse. Herbert Clark Hoover, born in 1874 at West Branch, Iowa, was both cause and effect of the growth phenomenon. The embodiment of a rugged individualist, Hoover worked as a mining engineer in the United States, Australia, China, Africa, South America, and Russia before assuming leadership of the American Relief Commission,

U.S. Food Administration, and American Relief Administration under President Woodrow Wilson in the First World War. Widely popular, he served as secretary of commerce under President Warren Harding and easily won the Republican presidential nomination in 1928. The severity of the Depression converted him from a laissez-faire advocate to a limited interventionist. Shortly after the market crash of October 1929, Hoover called leading industrialists to Washington and extracted promises that they would rehabilitate and modernize their equipment and plants in order to restore employment. White and his editors approved of the plan, but the employers failed to enact it, pushing the economy farther downward. Hoover's subsequent programs, requiring federal structures, aroused Owen's skepticism.[9]

Presidential attempts to rescue agriculture offended White, who thought them unnecessary, and much of the public because of their ineffectiveness. Hoover promised farmers relief during his presidential campaign and acted to raise tariffs on agricultural imports after taking office. He asked Congress to reduce tariffs on manufactured goods to balance his request for higher farm duties, but the chambers responded with the Smoot-Hawley Tariff, or the Tariff Act of 1930. The bill raised tariffs on more than twenty thousand imported goods to record levels, facing possible veto from Hoover. In the end the president signed the bill despite vocal opposition from various quarters and a disapproving petition from a thousand economists. An international trade war followed, as other nations retaliated against the United States by raising their tariffs. The teetering national economy collapsed, prompting some economists and historians to blame the act as the actual cause of the Great Depression.[10]

Hoover's support of agricultural protection was only one component of a larger plan to aid farmers. The Agricultural Marketing Act, passed before the market crash, established the Federal Farm Board with a revolving fund of half a billion dollars. The legislation sought to buy, sell, and store agricultural surpluses by loaning money to farm organizations. The board would stabilize prices by holding surplus grain and cotton. Congress created the Cotton Stabilization Corporation and the Grain Stabilization Corporation in 1930 to centralize marketing. The entities complemented the preexisting Federal Farm Loan Board, which dated to 1916 and organized and administered land banks. As with Hoover's other interventionist programs, limited funding and narrowness of scope thwarted his intentions so that they failed to reverse the downward spiral.[11]

White's increasing unease with Hoover stemmed from policy, rather than personality. Owen felt no animosity toward the president, though he credited his election to the religious intolerance of voters rather than to organization or appeal. The writer perceived the Farm Board as wholly dedicated to one segment of the society, with no interest in the others. In one piece White suggested that the federal government team up with the boll weevil to limit cotton production, "as the bug does it better than the Farm Board." Several other critical articles made his editors squirm, while they led to a radio debate between Owen and the Farm Board chairman. The Texan acquitted himself well, convincing an NBC official to suggest a radio program: "I was distinctly impressed with the quality of your voice and your mannerisms. . . . I believe you would make a distinctive hit . . . [with] the sharp incisive somewhat sarcastic inflections which you have." However, linking the president to critical assessments even gave pause to the fearless Mencken. "This is amusing stuff," the Baltimore lion wrote, "[but] the hook-up with Hoover is rather strained and that, set forth in cold type . . . would seem gratuitous." Mencken posited a safer article on Bill Hickock, to which Owen quickly assented.[12]

Well before the 1932 presidential conventions, Owen had lost interest in the outcome. Obviously, the Republicans would renominate the frustrated Hoover, while New York governor Franklin Delano Roosevelt seemingly had pocketed the Democratic nomination. A cousin of Theodore Roosevelt, the subject of an early White poem, the Hyde Park Roosevelt had served the Wilson administration as assistant secretary of navy—while Owen chafed at military regulations at a field hospital in France—before running unsuccessfully for vice president in 1920 and suffering an attack of poliomyelitis the following year. Owen preferred fellow Texan John Nance Garner, despite the man's early connections to political machines in South Texas. Garner's propensity for "striking a blow for liberty" through defiance of prohibition doubtlessly endeared him to Owen, though White gave him scant chance of winning. Born in a log cabin in Detroit, Texas, in 1868, Garner held a succession of offices in his adopted Uvalde, Texas, before becoming Speaker of the House of

Representatives in 1931. Disillusioned with the incumbent, White would come to disapprove of the next chief executive even more but was circumspect in his assessments of the man. Jaded from his experiences with politicians, Owen penned a curiously optimistic essay for the occasion, "In the Nature of Prophecy." Circumstances would transform the campaign winner into "a great man," he claimed. "Driven to it by the necessities of the case, we will ignore the politicians, recapture control of our business affairs from the Federal Government, reassert our right to attend to our own morals, declare for a doctrine of decent treatment to be accorded to people less fortunate than we are, tear down our tariff wall, forgive Europe its debts, and shake hands with the world."[13]

With the inquisitive mind of the newsman, White arranged a meeting with the rising star of the Democrats in early 1931. The Texan asked for an interview with Governor Roosevelt on the rumored state investigation of New York City political corruption. His staff responded with an invitation to lunch. In Owen's lasting memory of the convivial occasion, the future president came across as the epitome of ambition and expediency. Whether by preconceived notion or observation, White would sympathize with the irascible Mencken's unguarded assessment of Roosevelt as "a cheap and trashy fellow." Mencken's view and White's developing opinion notwithstanding, Roosevelt defeated Hoover, as expected, by 472 to 59 electoral votes, accompanied by Democratic majorities in both houses. The ensuing repeal of prohibition in 1933 removed Owen's favorite target only partially, as two-thirds of the states, predominantly southern ones, continued some form of local option and dry counties.[14]

White's reference to according "decent treatment . . . to people less fortunate than we are" in his essay "In the Nature of Prophecy" formed an integral part of his world view. While opposing government agricultural programs, he lamented the fact that farmers were not allowed to produce their way out of their plight, leaving the market to other nations. Irrigation projects by the Reclamation Bureau, he believed, raised land prices, encouraged speculation, and drove farmers into debt, rather than benefiting them. As, typically, Owen's strongest views developed from personal experience, he recounted the irrigation of El Paso's valley in the past century that attracted naïve individuals to plant pears and cotton, ventures in which "they lost everything." Genuinely alarmed by the toll of soil erosion on farmland, caused by rainwater running down hillsides, White endorsed the recommendation by the Soil Erosion Service of terracing and contour farming to cure the condition.[15]

The Plains Indians, who literally threatened his and his family's existence in his youth, now drew his respect. In an article entitled "Scalping the Indian," Owen declared that "the entire United States army never really did defeat the redskins," whom the government tricked with "scraps of paper . . . ironically called 'treaties' and . . . plenty of bad whisky." Their current plight provided White another example of the evil of government interference, notably the Bureau of Indian Affairs squandering tribal funds and legislation requiring the placement of minor or incompetent Native Americans under court-selected guardians. White returned to the plight of the Indians several years later when New Mexico federal senators blocked a bill by the late Senator Cutting that provided for the addition of "No Man's Land" to the Navajo reservation. Owen blamed "a dozen big-hatted, high-booted stockmen, whose pockets are deep and whose political influence stretches from Santa Fe to Washington." He predicted the death of four thousand square miles of land and nine thousand human beings. In other acts of graciousness, White continued, with mixed success, to introduce untried authors to publishers.[16]

Whether acceding to demands of his editors or, more likely, following his own individualistic inclinations, Owen White presented in print an orthodox Progressive side. Unlike many avowed conservatives, White never subscribed to the Red Scare, which sounded alarms against Communist encroachments on or near U.S. soil. Fellow Texan Martin Dies would open House of Representatives investigations of Communist infiltration after 1937, anticipating Senator Joseph R. McCarthy by a decade. White increasingly flayed the Roosevelt administration, particularly Harold Ickes and Hugh "Iron Pants" Johnson, but he never accused the White House of Moscow connections. White believed that Mexican president Lázaro Cárdenas used Communist tactics in taking over foreign oil companies, following a favorable Supreme Court decision, although the administration paid off the companies in Mexican bonds. As a reporter, Owen observed a street demonstration of the American Communist Party, noting the ease with which they moved about and the innocence of their convictions, but felt no threat from their presence.[17]

In several instances White wrote favorable articles about Progressive individuals and programs. His selection of the National Recovery Administration, one of the most visible of the early New Deal agencies, was surprising only in his evaluation, which he later repudiated. The agency authorized businesses to draw up "fair labor codes," avoid antitrust prosecution, and stimulate hiring. Although the agency eventually became unpopular and was found to be negligent in its regulation of labor contracts and declared unconstitutional, Owen viewed its popularity up close. White toured the nation in late 1933, the first year of the New Deal, and compared the mood of the public to that in the previous year. He noted a complete change, from pessimism to optimism, in their view that government now favored them, not only the rich. Everyone spoke favorably of the National Recovery Administration to him, even businessmen and politicians, who knew it was popular. Some people expressed fear that vested interests would try to defeat the agency. Owen could not persuade a mechanic to work on his car until he could show that it was an emergency in order not to violate hours limits. To the challenge to the National Recovery Administration, White boasted, in clear contrast to his later expressed opinion: "Well let 'em try. If Wall Street wants to lock horns with Main Street over the issue of the Blue Eagle, then I'm betting on Main Street. I'll give odds too."[18]

White portrayed Senator Robert F. Wagner sympathetically in a mid-1934 article, "When the Public Needs a Friend." To many the conscience of the New Deal, Wagner was an immigrant, born in Prussia in 1877. He entered the United States at age eight, with his family, settling in New York City. Wagner attended local schools and was admitted to the bar in 1900. After serving in both houses of the New York legislature, he was continually elected to the U.S. Senate through 1944, establishing himself as a defender of public housing, unions, and legal protection of workers while crafting, among other bills, the National Labor Relations Act (aka the Wagner Act). The legislation created the National Labor Relations Board, which mediated between unions and corporations, finally allowing collective bargaining for union workers. Wagner participated in writing the Social Security Act and tried unsuccessfully to pass a federal anti-lynching bill and, later, successfully admitted twenty thousand Jewish youths from Nazi Germany to the United States.[19]

White not only noted the highlights of Wagner's career to date but praised him for building "a brilliant political career upon the steady refusal to subordinate that ideal to political expediency. . . . [H]e is still in the forefront of the fight, battling for the public good." A fighter for safety conditions after the 1911 Triangle Shirtwaist fire that claimed 146 young women's lives, Wagner helped pass landmark protections in the Empire State. Several aspects of Wagner's political life apparently impressed the libertarian Texan. Owen credited him with shaking loose his early connections with Tammany Hall and for concocting an industrial philosophy that placed "as much interest in men as in machinery." In the manner that industrialists set aside reserves to replace obsolete equipment, they should do the same for employees, which would benefit them during periods of unemployment. This "social insurance," which White lauded in other venues, "would travel up instead of down"—in other words, from the workplace rather than the federal government. In the spirit of his previous article on the National Recovery Administration, Owen named "the big employees" as strongly aligned against the plan.[20]

White commended New Mexico U.S. senator Bronson Murray Cutting as an independent-minded Progressive Republican only seven months before the wealthy newspaperman's death in 1935. Cutting, a native New Yorker who traveled west because of frail health, had impressed Owen a decade earlier during his intercession in electoral politics. The Texan credited Cutting with influencing consecutive elections for both major parties. In "Cutting Free," White noted the base of Cutting's strength in the "Spanish-American" vote, minus the corrupted machine that White attributed to Y. A. Baker in South Texas. Doubtless, the senator's opposition to a federal censorship bill, in which he compared the condemned literature to certain stories in the Bible, met with White's full approval. Perhaps this stance ameliorated Cutting's early support of New Deal positions favoring federal labor exchanges, unemployment insurance, anti-injunction laws, and "huge building programs." Owen always took pride in dissuading Cutting from accepting Roosevelt's offer of the position of secretary of interior.[21]

White's ingrained instincts for protecting natural resources curiously placed him on the side of New Deal regulations against extractive industries. Years later, Owen recalled that he had supported Secretary of

Interior Harold Ickes on most issues, despite considering the man a light-weight. White, in a 1935 article, coined a proverb for lumbermen: "Waste makes wealth." He bemoaned the abandon cutting of trees "ever since we took the country away from the Indians" while the industry claimed to be conservationist. Owen reserved praise for an Arkansas lumber mill he viewed in his travels that actually cut only what the growth accommodated. White also credited the Roosevelt administration with attempting to enforce the federal lumber code. The proper remedy, he insisted, "should be compulsory and not merely suggestive." Elsewhere, Owen compared the fate of American farmland to the destruction of the ancient Tigris and Euphrates Valleys through soil erosion. He cited dust storms, depleted forests, polluted waterways, abandoned oil fields, exhausted gas wells, and stripped coal mines as contributing to "a coming American desert." Blaming greed and ignorance, Owen lashed out at politicians who, over time, gave away the public domain in land grants to states, sales to land speculators, and passage of a homestead act that created dust bowls by encouraging the plowing up of grasslands on the Great Plains. Uncharacteristically, White scored "rugged individuals who could do what they pleased with their lands and with all that those lands produced." Theodore Roosevelt, a man he admired, erred by thinking that people would correct the course when informed of our dwindling resources. Still, White held hope that Americans could reclaim their treasure for themselves and their grandchildren by "working hard and paying the bills."[22]

Owen White's writings by no means turned to somberness during the early Depression. He managed potboiler articles on Belle Starr, "queen of the highwaymen," and Hendry Brown, "the two-gun reformer," among his more serious essays. His baiting of Texas Christians even went past Mencken's toleration point on one occasion. "I can imagine nothing more unpleasant than losing a chance to print you," the Baltimore mogul confessed. "But ... I suggest playing down the Holy Ghost a bit. You probably work Him a bit too hard." Although usually quite receptive, Mencken shortly afterward declined another submission with "I wish I could take this very amusing piece, but at the moment I have a number of other tales and articles dealing with ladies of joy in type." Two days later the editor hastened to urge White to call on him when in the city and supplied his office schedule. As a sign of the hard times, however, a reader asked if Owen was writing a book on the unemployed. "I wish to secure a copy of such a book written by you."[23]

White's outspoken nature kicked up sand in his home state on more than one occasion but rarely so much as when he tied the oil industry to corruption. Lieutenant Governor Elect Walter Woodful fired off a telegram to the *Collier's* managing editor complaining that an article published that very day in early 1935 constituted "malicious fraud on the senate of Texas." Owen had quoted an unidentified East Texas oil operator saying that he "lined up 16 state senators at $500 apiece to kill [a] house bill" that would create a court in that area to prosecute producers of hot oil. The term referred to the production of petroleum in excess of standards imposed by federal or state law, which drove down the price of oil. The result of the East Texas oil boom of the early 1930s, overproduction at that time caused the Oklahoma and Texas governors to declare martial law to stem the flow. Despite such efforts, the excess increased. The Laredo-born Woodful, former Texas assistant attorney general and counsel for major railroads, vehemently denied the statement, touting the success of the Texas Railroad Commission in suppressing the illegal production. Stopping short of threatening legal action, Woodful advised the editor to make "more use of the editorial pencil in articles written by this bird White" and added with a flourish, "So far as I am concerned his name is marked out and entirely obliterated as a Texan."[24]

Assuming the official meant to silence Owen, the attempt failed. A week later White served another hard-hitting article describing the East Texas oilfields, "the most lucrative in history," as being worked in defiance of unenforceable federal law. The Texas "allowable," a production limit set by the state railroad commission, lacked control, according to the writer, because an oilman could circumvent it by paying a fine of a thousand dollars a day, far less than the amount of profit. Owen again praised Secretary Ickes for pursuing federal legislation that would permit states to limit well production, over the opposition of producers. He slammed the Texas Legislature, governor, and judges for supporting hot oil "in utter disregard of the fact that oil is an irreplaceable resource, necessary for national defense and that today we are consuming more than we are discovering." White, a man philosophically in favor of states' rights, charged his home state of hiding behind that rubric "to carry on with the most reckless program of waste, coupled with political chicanery and law evasion, that this country, or any other perhaps, has ever seen." Special Texas Rangers, he wrote, physically attacked oil inspectors or bribed them. Such actions on the part of Texas affected the entire nation in that the state extracted more oil and gas, wasting much of the latter, than virtually the rest of the country. Neither Senator Tom Connally nor House Speaker Sam Rayburn would introduce restrictive federal legislation, while "someone" deleted a paragraph from the National Industrial Recovery Act that would have empowered the federal government to control oil. Consequently, Owen affirmed, administrator Hugh Johnson remained unaware of his authority.[25]

White's final statement stemmed from Title 1, Section 9, of the National Industrial Recovery Act, which prohibited the transport of petroleum that exceeded state quotas. The controversy widened when C. B. Ames, chairman of the Texas Corporation, denied allegations that he was refusing to submit operating and cost data. Harry F. Sinclair, convicted for contempt of court in the Teapot Dome bribery scandal that imprisoned Albert Fall, publicly urged full government regulation, also denying refusal to provide data. The U.S. Supreme Court intervened in May 1935, unanimously declaring the National Industrial Recovery Act unconstitutional for excessive delegation of congressional powers and regulation of intrastate commerce. The Connally Hot Oil Act of 1935 passed Congress to fill the void created by the *Schechter v. United States* decision, prohibiting the shipment of hot oil in interstate commerce and authorizing the president to prescribe regulations and require certificates of clearance. The law survived a court challenge and remained in effect past the designated ending date of 1937, with responsibilities transferring to the Federal Petroleum Board of the Department of Interior.[26]

White doubtless reddened more Texan faces with a report on the gas industry published a few months after his critique of East Texas hot oil. Under the uncharitable title "Texas Cuts Off Her Nose," Owen scathed the industry on the enormous amounts of natural gas wasted in the stripping process and the Texas Railroad Commission for neglecting existing laws of conservation. The commission held the authority to cap gas wells until they could provide light, heat, or power. White noted the strong demand for natural gas outside the state at the current low cost of production and the simplicity of restraining the emission of gas into the air. Sardonically, the Texan added, "Such an action would also . . . convince many skeptics that Texas is still a part of the Union."[27]

Owen seldom shied away from an opportunity to criticize aspects of the state he loved when he saw the necessity. Arriving in Austin to review recently uncovered documents on the King Ranch, White encountered a covey of reporters. The celebrated writer lampooned "professional Texans" for creating the public impression of a booted and two-gunned population. "You know what I mean by 'professional Texans,'" he told the press. "I mean those people who wear boots and ten-gallon hats when they go out of the State. That may be the romantic side of Texas; but there's also another side." Owen quoted a New Yorker who told his son, "They [Texans] eat hay son. They're only partly civilized, you know." White promised future books on the Texas Rangers, cattle trails, and schools. The resulting article told of the purchase of the Santa Gertrudis grant in South Texas by Richard King, a New Yorker, and his business partner Gideon K. Lewis, an Ohioan, in 1853. After a later partnership dissolved, Mifflin Kenedy, a Pennsylvanian, secluded his adjacent ranch behind a fence that still existed in 1935, with no roads entering the property. Owen marveled that the present Kenedy County thrived without bonds, a jail, or unemployment.[28]

Notwithstanding the recurring threat of lawsuits, an officer of the Crowell Publishing Company, which owned *Collier's*, congratulated the salty writer for his part in "a hard-hitting, fast moving organization." Thomas H. Beck referred to statistics that showed the magazine carrying more advertising than any other five-cent weekly at the end of 1935. Perhaps to skirt controversy, Owen also wrote his share of more mundane articles, including ones on Texas drinking history in the wake of prohibition repeal, a Chilean blacksmith, and the dour consequences of civilization arriving in the Big Bend area, while collaborating on a book about the Texas Rangers.[29]

Huey Long, the Louisiana "Kingfish," probably generated more consternation and, eventually, fulfillment in Owen White than any politician of his time. Huey Pierce Long Jr., the subject of fictionalized and historical books and several movies, was born August 30, 1893, in Winnfield,

Louisiana. Raised in a farm-owning middle-class community, Long could trace his ancestry to the Revolutionary War. While excelling as a student with virtually a photographic memory, Long was expelled for vocally opposing a newly added twelfth grade. Unable to afford college textbooks, he became a traveling salesman and an auctioneer. Long married, tried his hand at seminary training and law, each time abandoning his studies, and passed the bar exam after self-study in 1915. As a practicing attorney in Shreveport, he bragged that he never took a case against a poor man. A successful suit against Standard Oil brought Long fame and catapulted him into a rapidly rising political career. An elected member of the Louisiana Railroad Commission, Long continued to win awards against corporations, once arguing before the U.S. Supreme Court and greatly impressing Chief Justice William Howard Taft.[30]

Long gained national recognition as governor (1928–1932) and U.S. senator (1932–1935) from Louisiana. In 1928, making his second run for governor, the candidate conducted a populist campaign, even borrowing the slogan "Every man a king, but no one wears a crown" from William Jennings Bryan. To the surprise of cynics, the victorious Long fulfilled his promises to the poor, providing free textbooks, adult literacy programs, and a torrent of much-needed public works programs, constructing roads, bridges, hospitals, and schools. The improvements came at a price: political kickbacks and slush funds, followed by a tax on the production of refined oil, led to impeachment efforts, but they failed. After suffering reverses in party support in the 1930 legislative elections, Long announced his bid for a federal Senate seat. The Louisianan's term as senator coincided with the full brunt of the Great Depression. At first a supporter of President Roosevelt, the Democrat became a rival in his own right, utilizing radio and loyal newspapers to publicize his "Share Our Wealth" program. In concert with other radical New Deal challengers, such as Father Charles E. Coughlin and Dr. Francis E. Townsend, Long's redistribution plan would cap incomes in order to grant every American family a living income supplemented by old-age pensions, college scholarships, aid to farmers, and public works. None of Long's bills passed, Roosevelt ordered an investigation of his income tax payments, and the senator's political future seemed questionable at the time of his death. His shocking assassination on September 8, 1935, from pistol shots fired in the state capitol by Dr. Carl Weiss, son-in-law of a political opponent, removed Long from the political scene. Nevertheless, his family and organization continued to govern Louisiana for decades.[31]

Owen White never had personal contact with Long, but he had studied the phenom and learned to detest him. While shaking his head at the corrupt and inefficient ruling establishments, as he gauged them, in many states, White reacted against the scale of the Long machine, the perceived threat to the public order, and the appeal to populism in its rawest form. With the covert cooperation of government staffers, Owen assembled sufficient information on Long's practices and tax returns to attest that he could bring down the powerful leader at the apex of his career. The aforementioned Dr. Weiss and Long's enemies prevented the exposure, but White took delight in hearing and perpetuating the story of an embarrassing incident for the self-ascribed Kingfish. Although the perpetrator of the deed remained anonymous, the various versions of the story told of an angered man who punched Long in the eye at a Long Island bathhouse in the summer of 1933. The site of the publicized punch, Sands Point, Long Island, was a curious location for the famed leveler to be in that its scenic five square miles gracing Long Island Sound enclosed estates of some of the nation's richest families. Reportedly, author F. Scott Fitzgerald modeled the fictionalized East Egg in *The Great Gatsby* on the lucrative community. Supposedly attending a charity event at the Sands Point Bath Club, Long, according to observers, entered the men's room and left shortly afterward, sporting a black eye. Rumors spread that Long urinated on the man at the adjacent urinal or perhaps burst into the facility, angering the occupant. Newspapers as distant as the *Times* of London brandished raucous variations of the story.[32]

Owen appreciated a good story and resolved to make it better. With the assistance of his friend George De Zayas, a *Collier's* artist, White designed a medal struck to the "Unknown Hero who had hit Huey." White's plan extended a conflict between Long and *Collier's*, as one of the magazine's writers had criticized the Kingfish in an article, prompting a Long diatribe against the publication and its Wall Street parent corporation. Owen made an apt choice in De Zayas: born in Mexico City in 1895, he was listed in *Who's Who in American Art* three times and in *Who Was Who in American Art* after his death in 1967. A New York newspaper displayed a two-column photograph of White watching De Zayas at work with a picture of Huey Long and a can of sardines on the desk "to provide greater inspiration." The product, which depicted a fist striking a pained, open-mouthed fish with a star above its head, set in motion two national campaigns instigated or supported by Owen—a search for the puncher and a fund drive to defeat Long and his Senate colleague John H. Overton. The sought man never emerged to claim his prize and the anti-Long Women's Committee of Louisiana failed to prevent Overton's re-election after Long's death, but the medal gained notoriety. It found a home in the collection of the American Numismatic Society and sold numerous times at auction into the twenty-first century. A plaster model in the shape of a toilet seat was mounted in the public men's room of the Medallic Art's Danbury plant in 1972, surviving all of the participants in the incident.[33]

Historians have treated the bathhouse incident in various ways. In the same year that Long died, Carleton Beals, the noted biographer of Porfirio Díaz, told the story cryptically within a longer recounting of Long's downward spiral: "Every turn of publicity seemed to be unfavorable, and he couldn't keep out of the news." Beals stated only that "Huey got into some sort of a jam and was punched in the eye." Long claimed that he was beaten by a gang in the pay of the House of Morgan, the parent corporation of *Collier's* that Long had attacked verbally on the Senate floor, though eyewitnesses faulted his story. A "national magazine" collected funds and newspapers published lists of people who denied hitting him. Arthur M. Schlesinger Jr., celebrated for his biographies of Andrew Jackson and Franklin Roosevelt, briefly mentioned the "comic episode" in 1960. Songwriter Gene Buck invited the Kingfish to spend an evening at the Sands Point Club on Long Island. According to one account, Long was drunk and may have tried to urinate between the legs of an unidentified man in front of him in the restroom. Long responded to the jubilation by writing an open letter to the imprisoned crime lord Al Capone suggesting that Wall Street would arrange a pardon for him if he would confess to having planned the attack.[34]

T. Harry Williams devoted more space to the incident in his monumental biography of Long in 1969. By various accounts, some wildly imaginative, Long had drunk considerably before going to the restroom.

He emerged a half hour later with a cut over his eye and left immediately for New York. Wags most often conjectured that pilot Al Williams, standing at the next urinal, landed the punch, an action he denied. Later drawn out by reporters, Long stated that he was besieged by three or four men, one lunging at him with a knife that only grazed his head. Will Rogers commented on the rumor that Long tried to urinate between a man's legs: "Huey didn't recognize him in the disguise. Dress suits are only used in Louisiana to encase dead politicians."[35]

A spate of books on Long appeared in the 1990s carrying vignettes of the incident. William Ivey Hair, in 1991, described Long as drunk and obnoxious, insulting a piano player with racial slurs. One of the few accounts to mention *Collier's* as a publicizing factor, Hair's failed to identify White as the person who commissioned the medal. Hair quoted persons close to Long who said that he had urinated on people deliberately on several occasions. Although Long had entrapped himself in more serious difficulties in the past, the burlesquing of "Huey Pee Long" almost wrecked his career, according to the writer. Five years later Richard C. Cortner became the first historian to recognize White as the instigator of the medal. The author claimed that Owen initially intended the award as a joke and then adopted a serious stance, though in his autobiography White described his response as an instant of mental aberration. Garry Boulard in 1998 mentioned the incident only briefly and without reference to White or his magazine. Richard D. White Jr. in 2006 added a story that one of Long's bodyguards blackjacked an Associated Press photographer and smashed his camera at a subsequent public appearance by the Kingfish, but he neglected White, *Collier's*, and the medal.[36]

The year that Huey Long died, 1935, marked the time that Owen's editors asked him to examine and explain New Deal policies to their readers. The exercise had the effect of turning the Texan's attention away from his home state to Washington D.C. The Silver Purchase Act of 1934 authorized the president to increase the treasury's silver holdings until they reached one-fourth of the monetary reserve. Reminiscent of the "free silver" proposal of the Populists and Democratic candidate William Jennings Bryan in the nineteenth century, which would have essentially increased the money supply to fight the Panic of 1893, the bill received backing from inflationists and the silver bloc. The act, which nationalized the silver holdings of most Americans and required the sale of silver to the government for fifty cents an ounce, exhibited the sort of coercion and potential for mischief that rankled White. Although Owen had defended some New Deal programs in previous articles, in "The Silver Mirage" he quoted critical experts and reported that the ensuing rise in the cost of silver had strained the supply of nations such as Mexico and China that used the silver standard. Owen told his readers, "Just settle . . . down for a good long spell of watchful waiting, because we won't be through with the job for some years yet." Disruptions in the market and the recovery of the economy led to the repeal of the legislation in the 1960s.[37]

Anyone who had read Owen White's critiques of President Hoover's farm policies could anticipate his evaluation of the Agricultural Adjustment Act. The legislation created the Agricultural Adjustment Administration, which sought to restore the purchasing power of farmers to the prosperous 1909–1914 level through a complicated combination of crop reduction and subsidies. It included refinancing of farm mortgages through federal land banks, which Owen had rebuffed when it was proposed by the previous administration, and inflation of the money through coining silver, earlier scorned by White. As they did for his assessment of the National Industrial Recovery Act, the Texan and Mike embarked on an extensive tour to interview farmers on the issues in preparation for the article. Contrary to his finding of favorable attitudes among workers regarding the National Recovery Administration, Owen registered misgivings of farmers about the Agricultural Adjustment Act equal to his own. The U.S. Supreme Court, famously anti–New Deal, concurred. The following year the high tribunal, in a 6–3 decision, ruled the processing tax that financed the measure and federal regulation of agriculture unconstitutional. White combined assignments on his driving tour, refusing a story on the Memphis murder rate and writing admiringly about the ability of North Carolina to escape federal taxes on its bootlegging industry. For his praise, antitax Tar heels burned his likeness in effigy.[38]

"Rattlesnake Pete," as Owen described himself jokingly and critics called him seriously, needed his thick skin as his fame and sardonicism mated. A new book, *My Texas 'Tis of Thee*, appeared on the shelves in early 1936, the centennial of the independence of Texas, for his fans to celebrate and his critics to dissect. The Texan's renown insured manifestations of each. Historian Wayne Gard, in the *Dallas News*, recommended the collection of essays as "excellent entertainment not only for outsiders but also for Texans who have not become unduly touchy about the heroic age in which their grandfathers lived." The reviewer referenced local chambers of commerce as likely antagonists, but he could have included the preachers that Owen lampooned in "The Holy Ghost Takes Texas," an article and title suggested by Mencken. The *New York Times* reviewer took umbrage at the book generally, below the headline "Tall Tales of Texas." R. L. Martin doubted the existence or actions of some of the protagonists and pronounced "the line between fact and fiction" as "never strictly defined." Martin took the author to task for perceived unfair conclusions about Texas's pro–New Deal governor James Allred, a clear difference of political opinion, as Owen also castigated his personal hero, Sam Houston. C. A. Benson denounced White as "careful of neither feelings nor facts," accused him of betraying Texas for the amusement of "strangers and foreigners," and compared his conclusions to those of "spokesmen for the Republican National Committee and the American Liberty League." A *Houston Post* reviewer, under the headline "Owen White Pans Texans," took White's exaggerations and sarcasm more lightly. John W. Yeats, after crediting the Texan for his "meteoric" success, pronounced them part of "Owen P. White's style, the manner of a man who swings the ax with gusto, let the chips fall where they may." F. G. Forti, in the *El Paso Times*, liked the book but joined the collective opinion with his own: "It seems . . . that there is very little difference, to him, between what he might have seen for himself, and the things he may have 'heard tell of.'"[39]

My Texas 'Tis of Thee, White's sixth book in a period of slightly more than a dozen years, offered a microcosm of his convictions: regret for the passing of the West, a theme later taken up by other writers; a humorous, larger-than-life description of people and events; a sarcastic denunciation of hypocrisy and wrongheadedness; and an ability to credit the actions of persons with whom he otherwise disagreed. Readers quickly grasped his propensity to employ language for effect, most acquiescing to the greater truth. Others failed to see his prose as poetry and his audience as generalists, interpreting his writings too literally. In common with many writers of the period, Owen attracted more justified criticism from his emphasis on Anglo-Saxon contributions to borderland history, to the exclusion of Spanish and Mexican contributions. He devoted less than 10 percent of *Out of the Desert* to El Paso's Hispanic origins and included unflattering stereotypes in "Conchita," a story in *My Texas 'Tis of Thee*.[40]

Cleofas Calleros, destined to become a major El Paso historian, rebuked White in a letter to the editor of the *Herald-Post*. A native of Chihuahua state, Calleros arrived with his parents at the Pass of the North at age six. Like White, Calleros saw duty in the First World War, receiving a Purple Heart. Unlike Owen, Calleros personally experienced racial prejudice in education and employment at the Pass. In the postwar period he entered social service, becoming a specialist on immigration affairs for the National Catholic Welfare Conference, and gathered historical material for the Texas Centennial. In a scathing attack, Calleros deemed White's historical books "more or less incorrect," his writing style more suited to "modern red ink cheap magazines": "Mr. White, like other western life writers, would have us believe that our fair city, prior to their arrival, was a hot bed of Mexican bandits, snakes and prostitutes. El Paso owes Mr. White nothing. He has been repaid . . . in the sale of this and other books . . . [for] publish[ing] . . . junk under the name of truthful history and mak[ing] the public believe things that never existed or were not done."[41]

Calleros closed his letter by stating that White's account of the Salt War was 99 percent "fictitious and libelous." Ironically, little more than a year later the city of San Antonio, Texas, actually filed a libel suit against White and *Collier's* for an exposé of a municipal scandal. A September 1937 issue of the magazine charged the health department with extorting prostitutes, gamblers, and liquor dealers for protection money. While denying the allegation, the administration focused much of its attention on Owen's description of the relationship between a black political leader, Charles Bellinger, and the mayor's office. Born in 1875 in Caldwell County, Bellinger learned to play cards and progressed so successfully that he soon was made a dealer in a gambling hall and made his employer wealthy. With his profits he moved to San Antonio and bought a home and a string of businesses. He brought together African American pastors to organize black voters, which gave him domination over the city's electoral process, landed improvements for the black neighborhoods, and increased his own wealth, accelerating the movement of his enemies for a white primary. By the time White took up the story, Bellinger had been convicted of tax evasion, gained a parole from President Roosevelt due to illness, and died in June 1937. Although the district attorney charged White and the magazine with criminally libeling the city department of health, Owen believed his implication of the superiority of a black political leader over whites raised the ire of his prosecutors.[42]

When the story broke, Mayor Charles Kennon Quin failed to appear at his office the next morning, to the chagrin of the local press. Quin's reputation could not have pleased White. A native of Louisiana, Quin moved with his family at an early age to Columbus, Texas, where he eventually practiced law. He later arrived at San Antonio, where he served as city attorney, won election to the mayoralty, and refashioned the existing political machine. With the aid of Bellinger and other political allies, his black- and Hispanic-based organization beat back reform candidates until he was temporarily unseated by Fontaine Maury Maverick, a former liberal congressman and member of a prominent local family. Quin managed to return to office during the following election and then won a state district judgeship that he held until his death in 1960.[43]

The suit bore the markings of the Creager case of eight years prior—a corrupt political machine, albeit sans the customary violence—but it played out minus the drama of shadowy hotel rooms or courtroom theatrics. In March 1938 the Bexar County district attorney moved for dismissal of the libel charges on the grounds that the state could not compel a nonresident to appear in court on a misdemeanor offense. White believed that his appeal to Vice President John Nance Garner had provoked the decision. Their shared appreciation of good whisky and dislike of the New Deal certainly provided some commonality. While neither vouchsafed the opinion, the two met on occasion and exchanged correspondence. A Garner missive of the previous year thanked Owen for a letter, expressing, "I appreciate what you say. . . . Wishing you long life, health and happiness." Unexpectedly, the county grand jury indicted Quin and two other city officials later that same year for misapplication of funds for paying more than four hundred precinct workers in the July primary. The prosecution again withdrew the indictments, but the threat of conviction doubtless pleased White.[44]

By contrast, White won at least one admirer for his research on Reginald Aubrey Fessenden, who did pioneering work in radio. A naturalized American citizen born in Canada in 1866, Fessenden came to New York as a young man and worked with Thomas Edison and George Westinghouse. By the end of the century he had perfected a wireless communication system within the state of Pennsylvania. Fessenden apparently performed the first audio radio transmission of one mile in 1900. Listeners on ships at sea heard him play "O Holy Night" on the violin and read a passage from the Bible. Fessenden eventually held over two hundred patents, including a version of microfilm and an early form of sonar. He volunteered his expertise to Canada in the war effort. White linked Fessenden with Ernst F. W. Alexanderson, a Swedish electrical engineer who developed an alternator based on Fessenden's research, giving America its start in the field of radio communication. In "H-e-l-l-o P-a-r-i-s" Owen stated that in spite of American ownership of the wireless system, the foreign-owned undersea cables transported 80 percent of the transoceanic business. White feared a movement in the U.S. Congress to break up the domestic conglomerate. Owen returned to the subject in 1939, emphasizing after the beginning of the European war that America's link to the world could not be broken by any nation.[45]

Helen M. Fessenden, the widow of the inventor, praised White for a broadcast tribute to her husband. "Fessenden's work in radio and sound production and transmission," she wrote, "has been so consistently minimized and suppressed by 'big business' policies that it is heartwarming and a bit breathtaking suddenly to find someone aware of the real history of early radio."[46]

Owen sometimes caused lifted eyebrows over the objects of his scorn and approbation. His liking for conservative vice president Garner stood in sharp contrast to his impatience with presidential policies. The Texan's criticisms of his state's political and economic establishment flustered many, while his indulgence of the Fergusons sparked incredulity or worse. White's near-embrace of W. Lee O'Daniel, a lightning rod for diverse opinion, lengthened the string. Born in 1890 at Malta, Ohio, O'Daniel finished a two-year Kansas business college curriculum at age eighteen and entered the flour business, eventually rising to sales manager at Burris Mills in Fort Worth, Texas. Assuming responsibility for the company's radio advertising, he wrote songs, read the Bible on the air, and organized the legendary Light Crust Doughboys, featuring Bob Wills and Milton Brown. The program became one of the most popular on the Texas Quality Network, making stars of the musicians and O'Daniel. "Pappy" formed his own flour business in 1935 and at the urging of his listeners announced his candidacy for governor three years later. Campaigning on the Golden Rule and the Ten Commandments, the political novice defeated a range of candidates without a runoff in the Democratic primary. Despite, or perhaps because of, the astonishing victory, a number of critics ridiculed the result and the winner. Owen White was not among them.[47]

Enjoying a respite at El Paso en route to New York, White sat on the porch of his sister's home and entertained the local press with his impressions of the newly elected governor. Scoffing at editors who put their "foot in their mouth," Owen described a 350-mile auto trip with O'Daniel from Raymondville to Houston only a few days previously. "I spent eight hours alone with him," White expounded, "which is more than any other person has done since he began his flour and dance song campaign, and the thing he didn't talk about was politics." Owen pointed out that O'Daniel had increased his business 350 percent during the Depression and, flaunting his political skepticism, opined that "Pappy" would have to be "a master-genius at bad government" to worsen the current situation. "No matter how fast you are," White told reporters, "O'Daniel is eighteen feet ahead of you." White, who reminded the *El Paso Times* representative of the flailing the newspaper gave him for some comments in *Out of the Desert*, had just seen publication of a poem, "The Mountains," in a local journal.[48]

The year 1938, in which White and *Collier's* withstood a legal attack from San Antonio and Bexar County prosecutors, also marked the uncoupling of the formal relationship that had brought success to both for nearly fourteen years. The writer later confided that his editors had embraced the Roosevelt administration so warmly in its second term that they vetoed direct criticism of the New Deal. According to Owen, his superiors permitted him to strafe Lázaro Cárdenas's Mexican expropriation policy but not to comment on the quiet support from Washington; his interview with the increasingly critical vice president, Garner, never saw the light of day. An auto tour of the South convinced White that the lot of sharecroppers showed no improvement under the Agricultural Adjustment Act, and he blamed the agency's structure. After a friendly meeting with Chenery, the men amicably agreed to remove White's name from the magazine's masthead. Nevertheless, Owen continued to submit articles to his former employers and found time to branch out into radio, which pleased him greatly. An old friend and interviewee, Frank Mullen, remembering an article that Owen had once done in the field of television and radio, offered him a program, *Radio, the Voice of the World*, with Radio Corporation of America over a national connection.[49]

The selfsame Mullen, in a deceptively calm message of August 2, 1940, submitted a surviving reference to a brief but dangerous period in White's life. "I was delighted to get your letter of the 29th. . . . The news of your complete recovery is fine. . . . I knew you were spending your time in the country and that you'd probably be getting in touch with me. . . . I shall be glad to see you whenever you are able to get into town."[50]

Owen White later told the story in more emotional terms. Despite the onset of the European phase of World War II, he felt a certain optimism that plummeted on the morning after Thanksgiving, when he hemorrhaged from his right lung. Although the bleeding continued for four or five days, the fullness of his work schedule, perhaps enhanced by his durable persona, prompted Owen to silence. After several weeks, his weakened condition forced a confession to Mike, who rushed him to a doctor within the hour. Owen nevertheless ignored medical advice to enter a sanitarium for several more months, until he reported a lump in his neck. Even then the doctor delayed several more weeks, monitoring the growth until a biopsy indicated malignancy and the necessity of surgery. Responding as if "he had hit me on the head with a pick handle," Owen accepted the prescription, humorously deeming it the one thing in his life to serve as an example to others. The surgeon and patient proclaimed the operation a success, providing the Whites the opportunity to move from their Kew Gardens apartment to a more restful setting at Peconic Bay, previously purchased as a summer camp.[51]

Originally an art colony, the site, named for its location by the body of water touching Suffolk County, Long Island, allowed Owen a respite but not sustained relief from his writing and broadcasting. Within months an article on counterfeit detection for his old employer *Collier's* engendered more than the usual fan mail. "Camera Dick" attracted the attention of Doubleday, Doran and Company, a representative of which stated the publisher's interest in expanding the material into a book, if enough material existed and in lieu of a contract with Putnam. Owen reciprocated interest, though nothing resulted from the exchange of messages. Perhaps White's latest book occupied his time.[52]

The new entry, *The Autobiography of a Durable Sinner*, left the presses in early 1942 and captured a new audience in addition to fans of the Old West and political currents. It differed from his previous books and articles in that Owen emerged from the wrappings and wrote of himself, family, friends, enemies, celebrities, scoundrels, and his philosophy of life for the first time. Indeed, scoundrels in the form of hypocritical religionists, politicians, and community leaders abounded, and all suffered the cut of his acerbic wit. Vignettes, self-deprecation, and controversial opinions filled the pages, in White's breezy writing style, that encompassed his whole life to that date. While Owen had previously treated aspects of his early life in the serial and book *A Frontier Mother*, much was new, some conspicuously so. His earlier criticisms of certain Texas political leaders, his admiration for John Nance Garner the major exception, appeared intensified, and his disdain for Franklin Roosevelt, his "nit wit" appointees, and the New Deal was never before so deep. White's opinions challenged the electoral majority, who had recently elected Roosevelt to an unprecedented third term over challenger Wendell Willkie. Indeed, White's memory of a person or event sometimes seemed asymmetrical with his reporting or comments of the time. The jarring conclusion fanned a considerable array of comments: "The inevitable war had started. Honolulu had been attacked without provocation . . . and in the depravity and wickedness of my soul I was glad of it. . . . It woke up the American people; it cleared their minds for them; it caused them to realize for the first time in twenty years that they are the American people and that they are not a conglomerate mass of alphabetically designated organizations under all kinds of un-American leaderships."[53]

Reviewers in unison accorded White a gifted writing style, vivid portrayal of characters, and readability, although his larger-than-life portrayals earned differing tributes. C. L. Sonnichsen, whose long tenure at the Pass gained him singular distinction, largely summarized the story, teasing readers with undisclosed hints and characterizing the El Pasoan's "almost complete skepticism about lawyers, uplifters, politicians, and 'Christians.'" Sonnichsen predicted objections "concerning some of his facts and prejudices" but promised interesting reading. Edward Frank Allen, whose domain included both writing and public speaking, credited "a racy style of writing" for making the book "so interesting." An unidentified reviewer for the *Kansas City Star* extolled the "high colored brand of journalese English" as "the best thing he has written to date," adding, "He rather misses the underlying essentials on a great many of the issues of the day, but he is like a terrier in a barnful of rats—he gets action." Stanley Walker viewed the book as "lusty, gusty, salted, and crowded with adventures" but, in concert with many White watchers, thought, "It is probable that Mr. White lays too much emphasis upon his own alleged sinfulness." For all the controversial points in Owen's autobiography, Walker considered the author's disregard for Wyatt Earp the most potentially explosive. Herbert Gambrell, a Southern Methodist University history professor, reviewed the publication quite favorably: "In the drab plain of autobiographical writing," the critic stated, "this book is refreshing for its lustiness and unblushingness and for the unerring way in which the author writes himself down a harder customer than he probably is." Ira Cain judged "this one-man saga" to be "of particular interest to Texans."[54]

Owen's sister Leigh, Mrs. O. S. Osborn, insisted on the nonsinful nature of Owen White twenty years later. Donating Owen's early columns to the El Paso County Historical Society in 1961, she told a *Herald-Post* reporter that her sibling "was not as mean as he made himself out to be" in his autobiography: "I wouldn't read that book because I knew he wasn't that bad. Imagine him saying that our mother let us children run around naked!" Mrs. Osborn joined a list of White admirers who loved his writing despite exaggerations. He "was not one to let facts get in the way of a good story."[55]

The Autobiography of a Durable Sinner dominated Owen's personal correspondence for months, singularly favorable. Owen instigated one affirmation by sending a copy to his doctor, Alexander Zimany, "as a punishment for having kept me here on this earth long enough to enable me to write it. . . . I send it to you however in deep appreciation of what you did for me." Praise from William S. McMath, White's first publisher, must have particularly pleased him. "I sat down after supper," his El Paso friend wrote, "and read line by line until three a.m. last night. I finished it still hankering for more." A chaplain at the Ohio penitentiary, after an unsuccessful request to the publisher, asked Owen for a complimentary copy of the book based on requests from a number of inmates. Only a few days later the pastor thanked White profusely "for this very generous contribution." A fan of the book compared White to Mark Twain and insisted that he "write for current magazines so that you can reach some real circulation." To this naïve but genuine praise, Owen responded, "You flatter me, and of course as old Mark Twain is dead he can't resent the comparison you make. . . . I wrote exclusively for [*Collier's*] for thirteen years . . . [but] would like to hear from you again at any time." An El Pasoan remembered White's feed store from so many years ago. A reader disclosed that he had not disappeared in Mexico as White reported. A widow stated that the book was the last her husband read. On request, Owen sent an autographed copy of *The Autobiography of a Durable Sinner* to a fan in Edinburg, Texas, who had interested him in the Hidalgo County political scandal.[56]

H. L. Mencken, whose modulated enthusiasm for *Out of the Desert* launched Owen's literary career, was now emphatic: "I went down to the *Sun* office yesterday, howled and roared half an hour, and finally unearthed the book. . . . It is swell stuff . . . [but] might get you into trouble when the Japs take New York." Typically, the Baltimore sage offered an irreverent story. "Lent damn nigh wrecked me this year. My spiritual advisor put me on a diet that was really brutal. I discovered on Easter Sunday that he had done so in violation of canon law, Article XX-A of which provides that men above sixty shall have all the privileges of pregnant women. You are still a long way from that age, but nevertheless I advise you seriously against the practice of pious rigors."[57]

In contrast to his famous review of White's first book, Mencken declined extending other than personal congratulations on *The Autobiography of a Durable Sinner.* "I am under a bloody oath to avoid all book reviews for the rest of this mortal life, so there is no danger I will foment that libel suit. I sincerely hope you dispose of it without actually going to court. Such combats are a lot of fun, but they certainly cost money. . . . I only trust that the revision doesn't damage it, and that the sales break all records."[58]

Mencken referenced the threatened suit of Rentfro Banton Creager, the same man who brought an unsuccessful action against White and *Collier's* in 1929. While Owen White's expose of Hidalgo County corruption had facilitated the fall of the Baker gang, with prosecutions as late as 1941, Creager's influence had continued unabated. The owner of an oil company and one of the first to support the presidential candidacy of Kansas governor Alfred Landon in 1936, Creager remained a dominant financial and political power. A chapter in *The Autobiography of a Durable Sinner* treating the Baker-Creager relationship again brought a threat of a lawsuit against the publisher and author. Mencken's hope prevailed, with Putnam deleting the offending pages in subsequent printings, but the threat surely generated publicity for the book. Perhaps it was a silver lining to the publisher's lament that "we are having a discouraging time getting the right people in the trade to read THE AUTOBIOGRAPHY OF A DURABLE SINNER but we're doing everything we can. . . . The book itself has cheered us that end." A Santa Maria, California, reader confirmed the problem "with the discriminating reader," noting that no store in her town or the neighboring community carried the book. While unprovable, Owen's provocative statement on Pearl Harbor and his criticism of the Roosevelt administration at a time when the nation rallied around the president likely dampened the book's appeal.[59]

Another threatened litigation, also blunted, converted the book into the most potentially actionable of White's career. This challenge, more personally vexing to Owen than Creager's, emanated from the scion of one of Texas's most controversial figures, Joseph Weldon Bailey. Born in Crystal Springs, Mississippi, in 1863, "The Last Democrat," as his biographer named him, refused to testify before a U.S. Senate investigating committee in 1884 over charges that Mississippi Democrats had employed violence in the previous year's elections. Bailey moved to Gainesville, Texas, in 1885, where he practiced law and endorsed a prohibition amendment. Subsequently elected to the federal House of Representatives and Senate, he took a Populist position on free silver and anti-imperialism and opposed the resurrected Ku Klux Klan. Bailey increasingly supported corporations, however, and suffered an irreversible setback over disclosures that he legally represented the Waters-Pierce oil firm after its eviction from Texas under the antitrust law. He resigned from the Senate in 1911 and practiced law in Dallas until his death in 1929.[60]

In *The Autobiography of a Durable Sinner* White described a scene between Joseph Weldon Bailey Jr. and him in an Austin hotel dining room. Owen had infuriated the political establishment with an article in which he reported that twelve Texas legislators had defeated an oil regulation bill after having received $500 each from lobbyists. Bailey, a former congressman, exhibited public anger at White, only to whisper a social invitation. Owen praised both Baileys in the book but referred to the senior as an impeached senator. Forthwith, Putnam's received a missive from Bailey's law firm that did not mention the incident in Austin but expressed "a distinct distaste for a remark which Mr. White makes and you print concerning my Father, who is now dead. . . . At no time in my father's lifetime was he ever impeached by anybody under any circumstances." The younger Bailey insisted on a public retraction as widely circulated as the book.[61]

White initially reacted a little more testily than his diplomatic letter to Bailey revealed. He sent a copy of his message to a publishing official, referring to Bailey as "my offended friend" and citing the source of his description of the late senator. To "Dear Joe," contrarily, Owen offered a deep apology for his use of the term "impeached," stating that it was used casually in Texas at the time. "It was a satirical use with the satire directed at the Texas Legislature," he explained, and "more of a distinction than a dishonor." White expressed the highest admiration for both father and son and released the letter to his correspondent to distribute as he wished. Bailey replied in similarly friendly fashion, assuring White of his certainty "that you had no intention to reflect upon my Father and I rather felt it was the publisher's fault for not caching the statement." He found White's explanation "entirely satisfactory" and reaffirmed their friendship. In conclusion, Bailey informed Owen that he was closing his law office to enter active duty as a marine captain, a position recently secured with the aid of a former campaign opponent, Senator Tom Connally. A more relaxed Owen White responded with a description of his own aspirations.

Well that's settled, you're off to the wars, and, God man how I envy you. I've tried a dozen ways to get into the thick of it but can't seem to make it. However, I haven't entirely given up hope of killing off a German, a Jap, or a Dago. Perhaps I can even shoot one on my own door-step. At any rate half of the saboteur group that was picked up by the F.B.I. day before yesterday landed on the shore just a few miles from where I live. . . . If you'll let me know [when you return] I'll have a party for you.[62]

Sadly, the reunion of the two reconciled friends never took place. Bailey suffered fatal head injuries in a car wreck en route from his Norman, Oklahoma, base to Dallas a little more than a year later.[63]

Reflections on his life and correspondence enabled White to express to fans his personal convictions. He responded to an old friend, "I . . . hope that many El Pasoans will share our feelings about it [the book]. But a lot of them won't. They're the ones who think El Paso is a better town today than it was forty years ago. It isn't but why argue about it." Of his latest book he wrote a well-wisher,

It is an uncompromising statement of the way I feel and it is naturally gratifying to me to discover that a good many people, like yourself, agree with me. Don't be discouraged about the future of the American way of life. After all there isn't anything to it except hard work and economy, plus the privileges of enjoying the fruits thereof. All the rest, such as laws to restrict working hours for labor, and production for farmers, is just so much damn nonsense that this war will entirely destroy. If it doesn't it will destroy us which is a consummation I cannot conceive of.[64]

White replied to a friend of long-standing in a similar vein, ranging from reaction to critics to concern about the progress of the war:

Naturally, because it is courageous writing, it had made a good many people pretty mad, but what of it. You didn't give a damn, and said so, about what people thought, and neither do I. It pays to be that way. Perhaps not in cash but certainly in self respect. . . . As for the War, it's got me badly worried. Everything looks bad,

and frankly I think it's very poor psychology for the people in
Washington to tell us that eventual victory is absolutely certain.
To do that slows up the war effort.[65]

Offering a deep insight into his outwardly crusty, inwardly gentle nature, "Rattlesnake Pete" confided to a liberal judge in Texas his ability to
like a person with whom he disagreed. "I had the same feeling . . . for
Morris Shepherd. Morris and I disagreed on pretty much everything.
Nevertheless we were very good friends simply because each believed the
other to be sincere. Unfortunately, I am unable to say the same thing
about some Texans now in Washington." Perhaps the moment of seriousness made him self-conscious, for Owen felt compelled to add a story
showing his humorous, self-effacing aspect. "And may I extend my congratulations to your wife on the privilege of having you for a husband. In
one respect she is far more fortunate than Mike. When Mike and I are
in the car together . . . [I make her] do all the driving herself. I just sit
there, saying nothing, except that sometimes, after we have landed in a
borrow-ditch or climbed a telegraph pole I have been known to remark,
timidly, 'Will you please tell me, darling, how the hell we ever managed
to get here?'"[66]

White obviously enjoyed the banter with H. L. Mencken that *The
Autobiography of a Durable Sinner* enhanced. Doubtless, the Texan's de-
tailed examples of his libertarianism, his self-effacement, and his witty
skepticism appealed to similar characteristics in the Baltimorean, still pri-
vately grieving over the death of his wife seven years earlier. The most
prominent issue that separated the men, Mencken's opposition to the war,
remained off the table for discussion, while Mencken's health and jousts
at religion amused both. Yet the exchanges also concealed an awareness
of mortality in the two senior citizens. In a light response to one of many
Menckenian complaints of imminent death, Owen offered,

I will be very glad to cooperate with Dr. Boyd in his plan to erect
a monument to you, made with bricks of your own fashioning,
that you can contemplate while you are still alive. After you have
gone, of course, it won't do you any good, because as I understand
it the view from down under is not very inspiring. And how

about a stained glass window in a Baptist cathedral[?] . . . I regret your two illnesses since Christmas and am glad you are still able to take your liquor. . . . I am a bit under the weather myself.[67]

The humorous letters also included hard information. "Dr. Boyd" referred to Julian P. Boyd, a Princeton librarian who had approached Mencken with a proposal to collect and publish a volume of his letters. Mencken joked, "There is a stained glass window to me in one of the Baltimore breweries. I have left instructions that my ashes are to be deposited immediately under it. It is my hope that this window will attract many pious tourists to Baltimore in the years to come." The statements about mutual health problems were based on fact, and the collection project offered White wider exposure to Mencken's readers. At Boyd's request, Owen dispatched all the letters in his possession, apologizing that those from 1923 and 1924 were missing. He strongly endorsed Mencken's boast of having discovered Owen: "He dragged me from obscurity into columns of his magazine; gave me a very swift and dizzy correspondence course in how to write—at times he was openly insulting about it—and then when I had graduated, and had been offered a job on the New York Times, he tried his best to dissuade me from accepting and coming back East to live in the anus of the world. . . . [But] frankly, I feel flattered that Mencken mentioned my name to you."[68]

As it turned out, the project was never completed, as Boyd turned his attention to the papers of Thomas Jefferson, an enterprise that lasted from 1944 until his death in 1980. The Boyd and Mencken papers lie together in the archives of Princeton University. A later compilation of Mencken's papers somehow overlooked Owen White, whose correspondence with the Baltimore lion resides in the archives of the University of Texas at El Paso.[69]

CHAPTER 6

"Dammit Sis, I've got to finish this book"

Owen and Mike's change of address to Peconic Bay did not by any means signal the end of White's writing career, despite his numerous references to his peaceful surroundings and tributes to the Americanism of his neighbors. The hamlet Cutchogue, designated "principal place" by the Algonquin Indians, certainly had a lot to recommend it as a break from the bustle of New York City, whose editorial offices Owen had long frequented. Settled by English and American colonists in the seventeenth century, the portion of Southold, in Suffolk County, covered approximately eight square miles of fertile land that was conducive to production of merlot grapes. Albert Einstein, a sailing devotee, thought the adjoining bay "the most beautiful sailing ground I ever experienced." Indeed, a meeting of Einstein and fellow physicists in Cutchogue in 1939 laid the groundwork for the Manhattan Project, which created the first atomic bomb. From his scenic settlement, Owen planned further books and articles and carried some to fruition.[1]

The war, whose outcome deeply concerned White and millions of Americans, almost imperceptibly had begun to turn away from the dictatorships. Within days of the bombing of Pearl Harbor, Honolulu, the Philippines, Wake Island, Guam, and Midway, the Japanese captured Guam, Wake, and Hong Kong. They followed with occupations of Malaya,

Singapore, most of the Dutch East Indies, and, eventually, Thailand and Mandalay, bombing Dutch Harbor, Alaska, and seizing two of the Aleutian Islands. The United States' chances of victory indeed appeared small when General Douglas MacArthur retreated to the Bataan Peninsula and evacuated to Australia in March 1942, and General Jonathan Wainwright surrendered Corregidor in May. Yet in April Lieutenant Colonel James H. Doolittle bombed Tokyo and in May and June the U.S. Navy scored smashing victories in the Coral Sea and at Midway. Within two months the Americans had Japan on the defensive in the Pacific.[2]

The European theater followed a similar pattern. After Germany's attack on Poland in September 1939 launched the western phase of the world war, the Third Reich, in collusion with Italy, quickly overran most of the continent, strafed England, and pushed back the British in North Africa. Germany's invasion of its former ally Russia in June 1941 created a powerful enemy to its east, however. With the American entry into the war, on December 8 Britain and the United States undertook sustained bombing attacks and won the Battle of the Atlantic against German submarines. The Allies combined forces for decisive victories in North Africa, while the Russians defeated the Germans at Stalingrad and drove toward Poland by the end of 1941. The Anglo-American Sicilian campaign, the precursor of Allied victory, was underway in mid-1943.[3]

Closer to Owen White, the War Department established fortifications along the eastern tip of Long Island at Montauk and Camp Hero, across Peconic Bay from Southold. The navy tested torpedoes and docked ships and dirigibles within the vicinity. In Operation Pastorius, in June 1942 a German submarine landed the four German agents that White referenced in a letter to Bailey. A Coast Guardsman apprehended the men but lost them as he sought out his supervisor. Guard reinforcements discovered German cigarettes and hidden boxes of high explosives on the beach. The German agents escaped to New York City but were captured, along with a band that came ashore at Jacksonville, Florida. After thwarting one of the most daring espionage attempts on American soil, the government executed six of the agents. In a more mundane manner, Cutchogue shared with the nation blackouts, alerts, and rationing.[4]

The war was heating up the economy, fueled by the production of military weapons and equipment under profitable government contracts, high wages paid to scarce workers, and the direction of a large portion of working-age men into the armed forces. At the beginning of the European war in 1939 the United States had climbed out of the recession of 1937; subsequent cutbacks in spending had then set the economy back three years. American participation in the war lifted the economy well above the 1929 standard and virtually eliminated unemployment. There was no relief for Owen White from New Deal bureaucracy, however, as wartime regulations instituted such agencies as the War Production Board, the Board of Economic Warfare, the National War Labor Board, the Office for Civilian Defense, and the Office of Price Administration.[5]

Several potentially attractive offers reached White amid the correspondence generated from *The Autobiography of a Durable Sinner*. In one of the most promising, an officer from Twentieth Century-Fox Film Corporation wrote, "We have had an excellent outline made of your book, which we received from Putnam's. This is a delightfully written autobiography. To me, the most interesting part is the early days in the great Southwest." The writer, from the New York Story Department, frankly thought the remainder "not quite as glamorous" but promised to advise White "should there be any definite reaction." Silence from the source indicated that the Hollywood moguls were unconvinced or that the manuscript was overpowered by events of the war. Apparently there was some interest in selecting White as a government representative to Mexico in mid-1942. Given Owen's familiarity with the neighboring nation, its people, and its language, the idea contained merit. An assistant to Vice President Henry Wallace dampened the idea to Frank Mullen of NBC, stating, "Frankly, I believe that what White would like more than anything else is an assignment to write some articles about what is going on. . . . He is too much of an individual, it seems to me, to fit into a job, no matter how important the job is." Owen never commented on the matter, but in the closest reference said of a government official, "I envy . . . his trip to Mexico. It's an interesting country at any time but right now must be exceptionally so. . . . Tell him that if I ever get down to Washington again I will certainly call on him." Chenery, of *Collier's*, thought the military would veto on security grounds Owen's proposal of an article on prisms. While encountering reluctance to accept some of his proposals, Owen intervened with his publisher on behalf of a promising writer.[6]

Interestingly, the U.S. government extended an offer that White could accept. Throughout his printed criticisms of the administration, Owen had retained friends in official places. Reacting to the publication of *The Autobiography of a Durable Sinner*, the assistant chief of the Soil Conservation Service had invited him to visit and lauded "your fine conservation article in Collier's of a few years back." As noted, someone in good standing with the White House had suggested Owen for a position in Mexico. White had become impatient with his lack of a military role: "Besides buying a dimes worth of stamps now and then I want to help win it. I don't know how exactly but did have a letter from Washington this morning suggesting a way. I may adopt it." Perhaps it was the one Owen in fact signed onto. The Treasury Department concocted a plan for authors to combine patriotism with publicity for their publications. The department asked for a paragraph or two, consisting of one hundred to two hundred words, promoting the sale of U.S. savings bonds and stamps. Resembling somewhat the reciprocity in the National Industrial Recovery Act, the government would encourage the publisher to carry the statement on the author's book while it would circulate the endorsement throughout the media, "always with full credit to you and the title of your latest book."[7]

As one of the most widely read writers in the nation, Owen obviously acted on patriotism, rather than a desire for publicity. Responding to the request, he prefaced his essay with a comment that it was "pretty concise and convincing. At any rate it is an exact expression of my sentiments. . . . Would be very glad to see this on the jacket of Durable Sinner:"

BUY UNITED STATES WAR BONDS.
Save America and you save everything! You
save civilization, sanity, yourself and your freedom.
Your dimes and your dollars will do that!
Your future is the future of America. America's
future is the future of the world.
Save America and you save everything!
BUY UNITED STATES WAR BONDS.[8]

Owen White performed the tasks of a civic leader, supporting national defense and the sale of Christmas seals to fund the treatment of tubercu-losis since his age and health barred him from participating in a second world war. The sheriff of Suffolk County appointed him to the position of county special deputy sheriff, assisting the sheriff in the maintenance of peace and order. The Suffolk County War Council issued Owen "a Certificate of Merit as a Minute Man in recognition of Patriotic Voluntary Service as a member of the Civilian Protection Corps during the emer-gency period of World War II" and another for emergency medical ser-vice. The second award indicated that White put his medical training and experience from the First World War to good use in World War II. Perhaps the awards consoled White, who chafed at not participating di-rectly in the war and noted friends, and even his doctor, entering military service. In recognition of his service to the War Finance Program, the U.S. Treasury struck a medal for White and only twenty-nine others in Suffolk County. The National Arts Club celebrated his literary achievements on Author's Night at the Commodore Club in New York City, declaring White "an authority on the great Southwest because he is a part of it." The announcement repeated the fiction, constantly corrected by Owen, that he was the first white child born in El Paso.[9]

A new entry into the book market at the end of the war no doubt cheered Owen after the disappointing sales of his autobiography. A Putnam's representative lamented that it should have sold widely but en-joyed "only a fair sale.... At any rate for the millions who know, love, and live in the Lone Star State, there's a treat in store ... undoubtedly the best book that anyone has ever written on or about Texas. With publication date a month off, we have reprinted twice and our fourth printing is now in the press." Then the representative printed a double error, designating Owen the first white El Pasoan and compounding it with the fallacy that White had "broadcast and capitalized upon" that "fact." Owen alluded to his new book, *Texas: An Informal Biography*, in a letter to his publisher, confessing, "I'm ... having a hell of a time settling down to it" because of the war. He half-joked to correspondents that his planned criticism of Texan politicians and religionists would make a return to his home state impossible. A panoramic sweep of Texas, the book ranged from the Spanish involvement with the region to the present. In his usual unfalter-ing style, Owen refused to spare anyone from deserved criticism, calling

Sam Houston and other legendary figures to task along with recent Texas officials. Contrary to allegations that Texans lacked patriotism, White stated that the common folk, not supposed leaders, brought Texas from the wilderness. "This was a tremendous achievement. They had conquered an area approximately four times the size of the combined areas of the thirteen colonies, and yet the activities of the men who actually accomplished it have been studiously neglected by history in favor of the politicians who have more often succeeded in making Texas appear ridiculous than in making it appear great."[10]

Owen White's last book drew the usual spectrum of commentary. Some viewed it as sentimental, neglectful of other than the Anglo contributions, mindless of the role of state and national government in the development of Texas, and tending to tell a good story at the expense of detail. The larger reading public enjoyed its wit, unprecedented sweep, and compass for Texas's destiny. Aside from the size of the canvas, little had changed in White's portrayal of history in the twenty-plus years that separated *Out of the Desert* from *Texas: An Informal Biography*, indicating to a portion of the public a narrow-visioned stubbornness and to others stalwart conviction.

A number of reviewers took a middle path, admiring Owen's skills while throwing up a cautionary flag. *El Paso Times* reviewer Marian Howe Broaddus reported that Joske's department store in San Antonio had ordered twenty-five hundred copies, "the largest initial order ever placed by any book store in the state for any book" and opined, "His version of history makes tasty reading, provided the reader applies salt to some of his findings." Horace Reynolds, whose reviews and essays considered the writings of James Joyce, William Faulkner, Henry David Thoreau, and Woody Guthrie, took a similar tack: "One suspects that Mr. White allows preconception to tyrannize over fact . . . [but] he is never dull." Herbert Pulsifer, who wrote the book cover notes, agreed, calling the book "a piece of tongue-in-cheek history, to be taken with a full salt-shaker, but with plenty of truth in it." Wayne Gard, a veteran at reviewing White's books, offered it "as a healthful antidote to the stuffed-shirt type of historian, of which Texas has had is full share. . . . Readers . . . run some risk in regard to instruction, but none in regard to entertainment."[11]

There was no lack of positive comments from reviewers and readers.

A writer for the *Pasadena Star-News* harbored no reservations in endorsing *Texas: An Informal Biography*, stating, "It is a gay charming book, yet a rugged one, written with gusto." Stanley Vestal, author of more than two dozen histories of the American West, pronounced White's book "a subject made to his hand," adding, "and he takes full advantage of his opportunity." A Long Island reviewer praised it as "not the usual debunking type, which has been so common of late, still it handles those who occupied the seats of the mighty with bare hands." A review from *American Mercury*, the public podium of H. L. Mencken until his retirement, judged Owen's "informal roundup of Texas history . . . pretty much a model of its kind—learned, outspoken, and lively." Mencken liked the book before and after reading it. "The book came in safely this morning, and I hope to tackle it within the next few days," wrote the sage of Baltimore. "You are precisely the man to do a history of Texas and I am looking forward to the reading of it with the pleasantest anticipations." Mencken could not allow the moment to lapse without his customary note of irreverent levity: "I only hope that you make it clear that the Texans are diligent students of the Holy Scriptures and unfailing supporters of Christian democracy."[12]

Readers' mail almost universally acclaimed *Texas: An Informal Biography*, many asking for autographs, telling of past meetings with White, and encouraging him toward a further venture. "*Why* isn't your 'Texas, An Informal Biography' brought more forcibly to the attention of the reading public," one avid but irate fan demanded. A soldier complimented the book on the basis of a review that he read in the *Kansas City Star*; a marine requested an autographed copy of the book. A sympathetic Chicago Universalist pastor, apparently a friend, rendered to Owen his personal critique: "It gave me many a chuckle and a picture of Texas and her people that was new and different—How the Catholic church must love you!—second only to the Orthodox church—Holy sinners! I like your racy, free and easy style, though there are times when I think you need a stiff right to the jaw. . . . That adds pleasure to anyone's reading to feel that an author is doing something he gets a kick from. My best to Mrs. White and the season's greetings to you both."[13]

Various aspects of the book displeased some. Stanley Walker, who favorably reviewed *Them Was the Days* and *The Autobiography of a Durable*

Sinner, held scant patience for *Texas: An Informal Biography*: "He has merely put together some nostalgic, swashbuckling essays and called it history. . . . It is hardly history, and not of very high rank as straight reporting." William H. Burges, head of one of El Paso's most prestigious law firms, delivered probably the harshest cut. "You haven't done yourself justice," he admonished Owen, "and what I feel as a native Texan [is that] you haven't done the State justice. The latter is impossible in the tone that you wrote and in the light of the State's own history. . . . You have . . . drawn your picture giving too much prominence to the men who have made lawless Texas, instead of the Texas that now at any rate reasonably well enforces its laws." Burges, born in Seguin, Texas, in 1867, migrated to the Pass of the North for his health in 1889 and quickly established himself as a leading citizen, progressive reformer, and cofounder of the Toltec Club, later having a street and school bear his name. At the base of his differences with White lay the age-old argument of whether El Paso had improved or deteriorated since its hell-for-leather frontier days.[14]

The Autobiography of a Durable Sinner produced an extra virtue of reacquiring air time for White. The publicity director of G. P. Putnam's Sons helped schedule Owen for a popular radio interview show over a New York station. The host, Bessie Beatty, a native Californian, had established herself in journalism, movie scripting, and book writing well before attracting the largest audience for women's programming on WOR for the past three years. Whether Beatty's support of labor unions and liberal causes caused hesitation in Owen is not recorded, but their mutual promotion of war bonds doubtless appealed to him. The publicist presented the appearance in plainly drab terms. Citing a format of product promotion, Maureen McManus predicted that the routine "will probably be pretty dull for you, however, the rest of the time is given over to interviewing you and this sort of thing really does sell books." Clearly the interview satisfied the publisher and listeners. McManus judged Owen's performance "grand" and promised other interviews "if you like this kind of thing." A fan sent "congratulations on your very interesting and well done interview. . . . I'm certainly glad they could shoot straight in Texas and miss you."[15]

Owen and Mike last visited El Paso in February 1946, their first return since 1938, spending several days with his sister, Leigh. Much publicized in the local press, the respite allowed Owen to ready himself for writing another book for Putnam's. He hoped to renew old friendships but, sadly, noted that many had passed on. "Often I have been embarrassed by asking a man how his wife was or vice versa and finding she or he had died, without my knowing it," White lamented. Even so, Owen found some humor in the situation: on one occasion a man responded, "Oh, my wife's fine. . . . But she's not the one you're thinking of. I divorced that one." One old friend, Carl Hertzog, introduced him to a local, "very influential in the book business." His arrival incited some disagreement among prominent locals over Owen's criticisms of modern El Paso. Burges Johnson, a faculty member at the College of Mines (now the University of Texas at El Paso), responded that Owen's criticisms were "a strange thing for anyone to say," citing bilingualism, contrast of lifestyles, and beneficent climate as characteristic of the area's virtues. Johnson's colleague C. L. Sonnichsen, the chairman of the English Department, submitted, "El Paso hasn't changed as much as Mr. White says it has. . . . That's partly because it never was as tough as he pictures it and because it isn't as 'honest' now as he seems to think it is."[16]

The news reports of Owen's vacation at the Pass prompted fans to contact him with various desires. An Arizonan asked where he could obtain copies of *Out of the Desert* and *Them Was the Days*. A citizen of Ohio took the liberty to compare parallels in their lives, including parents and residency in El Paso and Mexico: "My mother too was not disagreeably religious. . . . Like your father, mine knew and loved Shakespeare." By June 1946 Owen was back at Cutchogue, intensely working on his projected book on western exploration, "Western Trails." Pressured by declining health, White still found time to encourage a prospective writer, suggesting regional publishers less interested in profit than the major nationals. Apologizing for the delay in response, due to his being so "busy writing that I've neglected everything else," he opined, "Publishers . . . are peculiarly human in that they are more interested in the salability of a book than in its *true* value."[17]

Describing his project as "perhaps very ambitious" but requiring for its success "only a hell of a lot of hard work," Owen planned to treat the westward movement "from the Mississippi to the Pacific." As with the settlement of Texas, he saw the people, not the publicized leaders, as the true heroes.

The spirit for none of this great movement to the west originated with statesmen (?) or politicians. It all stemmed from the initiative of the American people, they won the western country for themselves, and as I read it in their records simply team with colorful incidents, thrilling adventures, humorous happenings and finally magnificent achievement.

Obviously the book will be a long one, but as there should not be a dull page in it that should not be a drawback.[18]

The promised manuscript, in second draft, covered a wide expanse of history, meeting controversial issues and interpretations head-on. White endorsed Álvar Núñez Cabeza de Vaca as the first European to enter the Southwest in advance of settled opinion and surmised from the "very dim and erratic trail" of the explorer's narrative that the Spaniard crossed the Pass in his wanderings. The *gran entrada* of Francisco Vásquez de Coronado White judged as "the most ridiculous wild-goose-chase in American history" short of the Pershing expedition. General James Wilkinson, Owen asserted, sent Philip Nolan, the mysterious mustang catcher, to Texas in order to steal it from Spain, while "all the intelligent people in Mexico" turned against independence leader Father Miguel Hidalgo for inciting a class war.[19]

White also treated the divergence in opinions among Americans in the nineteenth century on the eventual acquisition of Texas, New Mexico, and Oregon. Most believed the first two areas would gravitate to the United States, with the third debatable. Some intellectuals thought the region between the Rocky Mountains and the Pacific of no value. With his patented sardonic style, White pitched the rivalry between the United States and Britain over control of the continent as a question of the right of the human race or of fur-bearing animals (referring to the English Hudson's Bay Company monopoly) to occupy it. American missionaries Dr. Marcus A. Whitman and Reverend H. J. Spaulding brought Christianity across the Rockies in 1836 after centuries of neglect by the Catholic Church. In the final words of the unfinished manuscript, and arguably the last he ever wrote, White playfully imagined the missionaries' wives at the summit of South Pass on July 4, 1836: "[They] probably amused themselves as tourists do to this day by carrying water from one side of the Divide to the other and pouring it into some spring or brook thus robbing each ocean of something that rightfully belonged to it."[20]

Owen White's last, half-finished writing effort bore the customary strengths and minor weaknesses of his literary career. Solidly researched from the author's extensive reading and photographic memory, the manuscript couched an array of facts and observations in a facile writing style. Tellingly, it also contained disputable judgments about the efficacy and effort of Catholic missionaries and assumed the natural leadership role of Anglo-Americans. Racial and national generalizations, while supportable, reached the level of stereotyping. Had the book reached publication, one might have expected the critical reaction to approximate that of *Out of the Desert*. Prophetically, White penned an undated poem, framed within the pages that forecast the immediate future.

A Soul's Soliloquy,
Today the journey is ended,
    I have worked out the mandates of fate,
Naked, alone, undefended, I knock at the Uttermost Gate—
    Lo, the gate swings open at my knocking;
        Across endless reaches I see lost friends, with laughter,
            come flocking
        To give a glad welcome to me.
        Farewell, the maze has been threaded,
        This is the ending of strife;
Say not that death should be ended,
Tis but the beginning of life.[21]

In September 1946 Owen White wrote to Earle H. Balch, vice president of G. P. Putnam's Sons, forthrightly stating the condition of his health, which he viewed as declining precipitously. Owen disclosed a history of illness that included erysipelas and cancer and concern for the completion of his ninth book. In typically scrupulous fashion, White requested the withholding of further advances from the publisher pending the outcome of his illness. Balch, a friend as well as a business associate, attempted encouragement through his shock and sadness.

I am more sorry than I can express that you have this new anxiety about your health. . . . You have thumbed your nose at more bad diseases and laughed your way out of them than any other two men. I have strong faith that this is another instance where you will do exactly the same thing. . . . As you get better and the end of the book is a little nearer, you will be developing other plans for more books to come, or I don't know Owen White. . . . I hope when you come to town in the next couple of weeks you will be completely reassured.[22]

Both men's forced optimism came to naught. There would be no more books from Owen White. As late as December 1946 his fans could read an earlier article on the history of Mobile, Alabama, in which Owen seemed his old self, mocking modernism and glibly characterizing his subjects. "Although this writer hasn't been there since before World War II, he knows that Mobile owes its charm, its wealth, and its bewildering beauty and its glorious self-respect to the disdainful manner in which it has repulsed promoters who would turn it into a modern, typical American city. . . . Unlike the Spaniards, who believed [in] Christianizing the Indians with Bibles, bullets and bullwhips, the French, who cared no more for the souls of the savages than they did their own, believed in fraternizing with them."[23]

White's letter to Balch in September forecast his immediate future. Pressed by his perception that his time was short, Owen sent an outline and eight chapters to an undisclosed New York publisher, likely Putnam's, who asked to see the rest of the book. He told his sister, Leigh, "Dammit Sis, I've got to finish this book!" Five weeks before his death, White entered the veterans' hospital in the Bronx after sustaining a nervous breakdown at his home. As Owen's condition deteriorated, Leigh hurried from El Paso to comfort him. At two o'clock, Eastern time, White succumbed to "chronic illness" on December 7, 1946, exactly six years after the Japanese attack on Pearl Harbor that shaped the last part of his life. Funeral services at the Universalist Church at Southold three days later preceded his burial at the Cutchogue Cemetery on Long Island. Creedless Universalism, a historic American religion emphasizing salvation for all, must have appealed to a religious man such as Owen White, who harbored misgivings about aspects of orthodoxy.[24]

Obituaries in newspapers and magazines extolled White's popularity as a historian, journalist, and author, some repeating the fiction of that we was the firstborn white in El Paso. The *New York Times* emphasized Owen's contributions to that newspaper in the 1920s and marveled at the diversity of his life and career. "He knew all kinds of people," stated the writer, "—Indians, outlaws, peace officers, Texas Rangers, Mexicans, cattle kings. At different times he was a lawyer, newspaper man and rancher. Thus when he came to New York about twenty-five years ago, he could draw upon a large fund of information on the Old and the New in Texas." The *Frontier Times* reprinted a death notice from the *San Angelo Standard* describing the deceased as Texas's "most colorful and beloved narrator," stating "The history of Texas, and the literature of the world, have been made richer because he lived." The managing editor of the *American Mercury*, the magazine that launched White's writing success, appropriately responded painfully to Mike White.

> I want to tell you how sorry I was to hear about your husband's death. We in THE MERCURY were particularly saddened . . . for . . . the relationship between him and us was quite close throughout the years. He was a gentleman and a very able writer, and there are not many like him left in the world. We recall that some time ago he submitted to us an article on the Strange Doings of the Huey Long Machine. For one reason or another we did not take it at the time, but if you have it around, we would be delighted to see it once more.[25]

Hazel (Mike) White focused her energies on having "Western Trails" published. Encouraged by El Paso's premier printer, Carl Hertzog, she envisioned the volumes crafted by Hertzog and engraved by El Paso's renowned artist Tom Lea. She immediately undertook a frustrating search of their home for an outline of the uncompleted chapters. When nothing turned up, Mrs. White contacted Putnam's, who professed to have only the original memorandum, which they retained. Hesitating, the publisher eventually released a sketchy outline, apparently the product of Owen's reliance on his retentive memory at the expense of written form. A review of the completed portion convinced Mrs. White that "a writer with interest in the subject should be able to take it from where Owen left it." She collected the marginal notes, corrections on the original manuscript, and a map and, unable to control her enthusiasm, approached Hertzog: "It is hard for me to tell you how much your idea for the book appeals to me. I think of Owen having written his first book in El Paso and that it was printed there, that you came to El Paso about that time . . . and that Owen's last manuscript comes back to the place where he started and into your hands. I hope so much it can be done this way. What a kick Owen would have gotten from it."[26]

Hertzog responded favorably on April 10, 1947, asking to see the offered materials but not promising a hasty resolution. "I hope to clear the decks by summer so we can do something with the 'Trails.' I'm anxious to see what Tom Lea says of the project. He hasn't seen the manuscript—perhaps it would be better to wait until I can show him the original." Lea, a nationally recognized artist and author, was a fine choice as a prospective illustrator but his consistently busy schedule virtually guaranteed delay. Mrs. White reacted promptly, dispatching by express mail the manuscript and appendices a few days later. "I hope Tom Lea will think well of the project," she wrote Hertzog from Cutchogue. "It sounds good that by summer something can be done about it."[27]

Mike's enthusiasm melded into anxiety with the passage of time. On July 28 she wrote Hertzog, "When you wrote me on April 10th you thought you would be ready to begin work on Owen's 'Trails' by summer. Naturally I think about it and am interested if you are doing something about it. At that time you had not talked with Tom Lea but hoped he liked the idea, all of which seemed perfect and pleased me very much." Hertzog's response arrived almost a full month later, collapsing prospects for immediate publication. The printer confided that he had sold the business earlier that month at the instigation of a partner who owned two-thirds of the partnership. "I was so tired of the commercial business that I didn't protest. . . . This means that I have no way of producing a book on the basis we discussed. . . . I hope to produce books only in the near future but equipment is so high priced and scarce that I will have to design books on a fee basis and sub-contract the production. Perhaps these crazy conditions will level off before long, and then we can do something."[28]

Inexplicably, the manuscript never reached publication, despite the interest of at least one publisher before Owen died. Perhaps no competent writer capable of finishing the work stepped forward and Mike lacked the resources to see the El Paso venture through. Why Putnam's or another publisher failed to print the last work of a best-selling author remains unrecorded. Correspondence between Mike and Hertzog ceased after August 1946. Hertzog briefly turned to designing rare book collections, joined the faculty of Texas Western College (now the University of Texas at El Paso), and launched Texas Western Press. He died at El Paso, still practicing his craft, in 1984.[29]

Owen White's name dimmed in the public mind in the ensuing decades, but his legacy remained strong among his fellow El Pasoans and academicians. In 1961 his sister Leigh, Mrs. O. S. Osborn, donated "Mesquite Smoke" columns that White had written for the *El Paso Herald* in the 1920s to the El Paso County Historical Society. The donation of Mencken's correspondence with White to Texas Western College the following year produced, in the words of a reporter, "almost stylistic twins." A few years later, Texas Western College librarian Baxter Polk accepted White's literary effects, including the "Western Trails" manuscript and correspondence from Mike White. Leigh presented the materials due to Mike's inability to travel from her Cutchogue home. The donation emerged from a chance meeting between Leigh and assistant librarian Frances Clayton at a local grocery store. Leigh asked if the college would like a copy of *Out of the Desert*, and the favorable reply prompted Mike to ask if the library wanted the rest of White's "junk." Mike expressed doubt that she would ever return to El Paso and considered the Texas Western library an excellent choice for the material. Leigh agreed: "Owen's papers are where he would want them to be." Appropriately, the El Paso County Historical Society inducted White into its Hall of Fame in 1986 and its Hall of Honor in the year 2000, as the first El Paso writer to achieve national and international fame. The management of the El Paso International Airport framed poems from White's 1921 publication *Southwestern Milestones* as captions for paintings by local artists placed in the main concourse.[30]

Owen Payne White was a singular personality conditioned by a singular lifespan that incorporated frontier and modern times. He experienced and participated in that most alluring time in American history, the passing of the Old West. Only with difficulty can one envision White in a different era. He literally lived the history that subsequent authors and historians approached only secondarily. Born in 1879 in an isolated village hundreds of miles from the nearest railroad and less than a mile from a foreign nation, young Owen witnessed marauding Indians and outlaws in the regular course of events. The famous Battle of Little Big Horn, in which General George Custer's death demonstrated that the West was far from "won," had occurred only three years before White's birth. However, the time held a contradiction. The same year as the battle the Centennial International Exhibition in Philadelphia heralded American advances in metallurgy, manufacturing, mining, education, and science, and by the following year the victorious Sioux were in flight. The Southern Pacific and other railroad lines introduced a fascinating blend of transients to the Pass of the North for the admiration of White, but permanent residents also arrived, and families, and churchmen, and people who dreamed of the scattered huts along the Rio Grande blossoming into a modern, respectable city. Periodically throughout the twentieth century the nation flirted with a return to a perceived simpler time.

Owen never discarded the comfort of that childhood, in which parents and law officers protected him from the dangerous elements of society, while he could accompany his father, in the course of the elder's medical practice, into the mysterious byways of the town. At first hand Owen witnessed virtue, vice, and hypocrisy, instantly categorizing each. Yet Owen's father imported the most modern medical advances known to him, and both parents acted as civilizing agents on the children by teaching them the arts and classics. White railed against the changing of the societal guard that ended swimming and bathing in the town canal, constructed brick structures in place of the adobe, and attempted, with less than complete success, to eradicate the traditional sin and violence. However, Owen profited from the public school system, graduating at the head of his class and toasting Julius Caesar in his valedictory. As a young man he frequented the posh Toltec Club and worked in virtually every field of economic endeavor offered by a modern, growing city. Ironically, when El Paso became too modern for him, by the 1920s, White moved to New York City, the epitome of urban growth and culture, and never lived again in the place of his birth. A constant critic of government, Owen spent his last weeks in the care of the Veterans' Administration.

A Jeffersonian by instinct, White developed his libertarian philosophy from his frontier experiences, particularly as recorded through a post-frontier filter. His sharp perception of right and wrong, his inquisitive and retentive mind, and his talent for the written and spoken word made him a natural muckraker. Behind his gruff "Rattlesnake Pete" exterior lay an idealist who rankled at hypocrisy, exploitation of power, and pretension. Malefactors with great wealth, in the words of Theodore Roosevelt, whom he honored with a poem, repelled him as much as any New Deal "pin head." Indeed, White's respect for Harold Ickes and Morris Shepherd demonstrated his ability to appreciate the sincerity in a person despite philosophical differences. His constant support for fledgling writers and attentiveness to mail from his readers identified a caring individual.

Owen White's writing career, actually dating from midlife, profited from the era and place of his birth. While he was plainly not the first white man born in El Paso, a myth he refuted throughout his career, as a man in his forties with firsthand knowledge of the Old West, White had an advantage over most of the field of western writers. Although only a generation into the past, the days of John Wesley Hardin, John Selman, and Bat Masterson seemed a world away to many readers. White referred to Hollywood Westerns as publicity agents for "dude ranches" and communities commercially propagandizing their Old West origins. Nevertheless, the romanticizing of the West in film and pulp fiction benefited Owen's historical accounts. Consciously or otherwise, Owen's fast-paced and tongue-in-cheek writing style attracted many fiction adherents, despite his criticism of the fantasy mills. Critics accused White of romanticizing Old El Paso in his own right, and Leigh commented that he was not one to let facts get in the way of a good story. He clearly painted his words with broad strokes, at times suggesting metaphor. In any case, he acknowledged falling back to his favorite subject to impress editors. Yet White's serious investigative reporting also had its roots in the muckraking period of the early twentieth century, when he reached his maturity. His factual accounts of political corruption in Hidalgo and Bexar Counties and collusion of civic leaders and bootleggers and his exposés of corporate influence in Mexico and

Texas earned him high marks as a true journalist, including lawsuits, threats of bodily harm, and censorship.

Owen White passed his entire life in the years before major civil rights successes. His was a world of racial segregation in his home state, national disrespect for minorities, and outspoken racism and gentlemen's agreements in so-called polite society. He overtly opposed the Ku Klux Klan and other nativistic groups as well as prohibition, which sought to impose the will of the cultural majority, while distancing himself from the Red Scares that followed both world wars. However, White spoke and wrote in the currency of his time, sometimes employing words that clatter on our ears today. His companionship with the Mexican people from his early youth notwithstanding, White considered them unready for self-government and deprecated their political movements. Perhaps this limitation explains his absence from major reportage on the Mexican Revolution, which he apparently regarded as a minor power play. Contemporary readers and later researchers of the most important event in Mexican history would have profited greatly from his insights. Although White denied objective reporting, his talent for journalism may have contributed to the allegation that his strongest opinions lacked historical perspective. Conversely, history has denied him his due by neglecting his role as a muckraker and instigator of the campaign to memorialize the famous punch that, by all accounts, torpedoed the political career of Huey Long.

Yet White's successful career relating stories of the Old West and corruption in modern America obscured his literary talents in other fields. Owen's first love was poetry, some of it whimsical and satirical but much of it compassionate and descriptive. His local columns on everyday life in El Paso anticipated widely read writings on the social scene in New York City. He interspersed serious reporting in national magazines with humorous short stories, while his early writings on pre-Hispanic Mexico, the epic *Out of the Desert*, and his last, unpublished manuscript, "Western Trails," bore the imprint of a solid historian. White applied the same high standards in his approach to journalism, history, fiction, and poetry, carefully selecting his words to convey precise shadings to larger meanings. No critic dismissed his writings as banal, thoughtless, or lacking integrity. White's written record sustains his credibility in the individual fields and in the collective. Curiously, White, conspicuously outspoken on controversial issues and individuals, refrained from commenting on contemporary writers in his published works, including his autobiography, interviews, and private correspondence. He withheld opinion on his editors, positive in the case of the *New York Times* and negative toward *Collier's*, until *The Autobiography of a Durable Sinner*, published years after he severed both connections.

White lived out the contradictions of his time. An exponent of frontier life, he chose to spend his writing career within the shadows of Manhattan skyscrapers. An avowed libertarian, he embraced some individuals and programs of Progressivism and the New Deal. A religious skeptic, he wrote deeply religious poetry. A self-identified realist, he arguably romanticized the frontier past. A bilingual and authority on ancient Native Americans, he undervalued attempts by Mexican nationalists to create a twentieth-century democracy. Ardently supportive of the Anglo Protestant westward movement, he opposed its most visible manifestation, prohibition.

Straddling two worlds, Owen Payne White acted as a conduit between them. While the popularity of the Western genre in fiction and history continues unabated, the frontier and its most ardent advocate have passed from the scene.

Notes

CHAPTER 1

1. The best sources on Owen Payne White are Christian, "Always in His Heart"; White Papers, C. L. Sonnichsen Special Collections Department, University of Texas at El Paso (cited hereafter as White Papers, SSC); El Paso County Historical Society; vertical files at the El Paso Public Library and the Dolph Briscoe Center for American History, University of Texas at Austin; Farah, "White, Owen Payne"; and White's books, particularly *The Autobiography of a Durable Sinner.*

2. Roosevelt, "Man with the Muckrake"; Gambrell, "Rattlesnake Pete," 31; Christian, "Always in His Heart"; Knight, "Owen Payne White."

3. Donkin, *Blood, Sweat and Tears*, 129; Kobre, *Development of American Journalism*, 349–51.

4. Fite and Reese, *Economic History of the United States*, 299, 395, 397, 401, 404–5, 503; Filler, *Muckrakers*, 20–23.

5. Connery, *Journalism and Realism*, 13, 15, 166; Filler, *Muckrakers*, 25, 41, 60, 80, 121, 134.

6. Filler, *Muckrakers*, 45–48, 63, 381; Fite and Reese, *Economic History of the United States*, 123, 503; Billington, *Frontier Thesis*, 1–8.

7. Filler, *Muckrakers*, 25–26; D. Malone, *Dictionary*, 6:331–32.

8. Connery, *Journalism and Realism*, 246; Kobre, *Development of American Journalism*, 718–19; Filler, *Muckrakers*, 250; Malone, *Dictionary*, supplement, 3:674–78.

9. Malone, *Dictionary*, supplement, 4:516–19; Connery, *Journalism and Realism*, 246; Kobre, *Development of American Journalism*, 513, 528, 529, 718.

10. Kobre, *Development of American Journalism*, 337, 528, 721; Connery,

Journalism and Realism, 72–75, 79, 84, 101–3, 119, 123, 154, 162, 187, 198; "Atlantic Monthly," Things-and-Other-Stuff.com.

11. Filler, *Muckrakers*, 57, 85, 133–34, 140, 151–56, 164–67, 187, 194, 197, 211, 214, 231, 232, 289, 310, 316–17, 320, 329–36, 338–39, 345–47, 352, 354, 357, 360, 362, 363, 378. "Collier's Weekly," Spartacus Educational, www.spartacus-educational. com/USAcolliers.htm.

12. Kobre, *Development of American Journalism*, 337, 339, 528, 530, 531, 721; Connery, *Journalism and Realism*, 105–7, 111–18, 127, 145, 151, 152, 160, 170–71, 187, 198, 234, 245; "About Harper's Magazine," *Harper's Magazine*, harpers. org/harpers/about; "Scientific American," *New World Encyclopedia*, www. newworldencyclopedia.org/entry/Scientific_American.

13. Malone, *Dictionary*, 3:477–78; Filler, *Muckrakers*, 9, 39–42, 197, 211, 241, 279, 299, 341–42, 361, 365; Connery, *Journalism and Realism*, 163–64, 240.

14. Fite and Reese, *Economic History of the United States*, 338, 496, 506, 507; Lorant, *Life and Times of Roosevelt*, 370, 472, 473.

15. "The Press: Comeback," *Time*, March 30, 1931.

16. Darity, *International Encyclopedia*, 437–39; Sapon and Robino, "Right and Left Wings"; Otteson, *Adam Smith*, 7; Murray, *Alexander Hamilton*, 2–3.

17. Mayer, *Constitutional Thought of Jefferson*, 185–86; Kelly and Harbison, *American Constitution*, 179–80, 207–9, 306–11, 936; Fite and Reese, *Economic History of the United States*, 443, 447, 452.

18. Stettner, *Shaping Modern Liberalism*, 38–45, 72–73.

19. Malone, *Dictionary*, 4:211–15; Fite and Reese, *Economic History of the United States*, 304.

20. Malone, *Dictionary*, 4:211–15.

21. M. Mason Gaffney, "Henry George 100 Years Later, The Great Reconciliator," Association for Georgist Studies, www.georgiststudies.org/ george100years.html.

22. Frederick Jackson Turner, "The Significance of the Frontier in American History," in Billington, *Frontier Thesis*, 13.

23. W. Timmons, *El Paso*, 4–24.

24. Ibid., 71, 74, 100, 116, 132.

25. Strickland, *Six Who Came to El Paso*, 26–37, 39; Hamilton, *Ben Dowell*, 5, 7, 11, 29, 47; White, *Out of the Desert*, 179. 184, 191; W. Timmons, *El Paso*, 146–51.

26. W. Timmons, *El Paso*, 166–68; *El Paso Times*, April 30, 2011; White, *Out of the Desert*, 128–30.

27. White, *Texas*, 189, 199, 201; "Stoudenmire, Dallas," in Metz, *Encyclopedia of Lawmen*, 234–37.

28. White, *Them Was the Days*, 80–91, 94, 104–11. "Selman, John Henry," in Metz, *Encyclopedia of Lawmen*, 216–18.

29. White, *Lead and Likker*, 3–11; "Hardin, John Wesley," in Metz, *Encyclopedia of Lawmen*, 108–10.

CHAPTER 2

1. White, *Autobiography*, 7.

2. Walker and Bufkin, *Historical Atlas of Arizona*, 10, 13, 17, 23, 25, 26, 38, 48, 60; Population Schedules of the Ninth Census of the United States, 1870, Arizona, www.archive.org/details/populationschedu0046unit.

3. Mrs. Rebecca C. Shatto to Garna Christian, Houston, November 20, 2009, document in possession of author.

4. Ibid.; Metz, *John Wesley Hardin*, 99.

5. White, "A Frontier Mother," *Collier's*, October 12, 1929, 18, 21, 83, Box 2, Folder 3, White Papers, SSC.

6. Ibid., 18.

7. Ibid., 25, 55.

8. White, *Autobiography*, 14–16.

9. "Arizona, History," *Collier's*, October 26, 1929, 52.

10. White, *Autobiography*, 22–25.

11. Ibid., 28; "Arizona, History," *Collier's*, October 26, 1929, 54; Osborn, "Scenes of My Childhood," 187.

12. White, *Autobiography*, 29–32; White, *Southwestern Milestones*.

13. White, *Autobiography*, 45–46; *El Paso Herald*, May 9, 1902; January 7, 1906; *El Paso Herald-Post*, May 28, 1936; Knight, " Owen Payne White," 54; Population Schedules of the Twelfth Census of the United States, 1900.

14. *El Paso Herald*, December 20, 1882; January 20, 1893; February 1, 1893 (quote); December 31, 1898; November 20, 1899; *El Paso Herald-Post*, December 31, 1934; May 17, 1940; June 1, 1940; June 11, 1940; June 14, 1940; August 10, 1940.

15. Sonnichsen, *Pass*, 254, 258–60, 262, 269, 270–71; W. Timmons, *El Paso*, 194; Osborn, "Scenes of My Childhood."

16. Sonnichsen, *Pass*, 274–75, 358–62; White, *Autobiography*, 60–62.

17. White, *Autobiography*, 44–45, 48–50.

18. Ibid., 50–51.

19. Ibid., 57–58, 102; White, *Lead and Likker*, 16–25.

20. White, *Autobiography*, 60, 63–70.

21. *El Paso Times*, March 11, 1898.

22. Hailman, *Thomas Jefferson on Wine*, xi, 7, 8, 13; McCullough, *John Adams*, 36; Mayer, "Woman Wagoners"; "Prostitution," in Kutler, *Dictionary of American History*, 513–14.

23. Sonnichsen, *Pass*, 277; Rose, *Storyville, New Orleans*, 1, 82.

24. Smith, *Daltons!*, 3, 19.

25. *Greensboro News Record*, May 24, 1998; McComb, *Houston*, 105–7; Humphrey, "Prostitution and Public Policy"; W. Timmons, *El Paso*, 173, 192–93; Humphrey, "Prostitution in Texas," 27–43.

26. McComb, *Houston*, 46; Sonnichsen, *Roy Bean*, 112; Campbell, *Gone to Texas*, 318, 341–44; Frantz, *Texas*, 146–47.

27. W. Timmons, *El Paso*, 172; Newman, "Newman, Simeon Harrison."

28. Ibid; Sonnichsen, *Pass*, 353–57; W. Timmons, *El Paso*, 192–93.

29. Sonnichsen, *Pass*, 362–70.

30. White, *Autobiography*, 75; *El Paso Herald*, August 7, 1903; *El Paso Times*, August 7, 1903.

31. White, *Out of the Desert*, 398–401.

32. White, *Autobiography*, 75–76, 90–91; *El Paso Herald*, May 9, 1902; January 7, 1906; *El Paso Times*, January 11, 1905 (quote); *El Paso Times*, undated 1911.

33. White, *Autobiography*, 92–100.

34. Ibid., 100–102; The Editors, *Collier's: The National Weekly*, to Owen Payne White, New York City, February 25, 1909, Box 1, Folder 13, White Papers, SSC; "Toltec Club," City of El Paso, Texas, yearbookdigital.com/historical/Toltec_club.htm.

35. "Toltec Club," City of El Paso, Texas, yearbookdigital.com/historical/Toltec_club.htm; White, *Autobiography*, 100–102; "Elephant Butte Dam," Absolute Astronomy, www.absoluteastronomy.com/topics/Elephant_Butte_Dam; *Los Angeles Times*, October 20, 1916.

36. White, *Autobiography*, 106, 109–11; Garner, *Porfirio Díaz*, 98–133; Meyer, Sherman, and Deeds, *Course of Mexican History*, 435–39; Bazant, *Concise History of Mexico*, 122–24.

37. Harris and Sadler, *Secret War*, 1–13, 24, 87–93; Meyer, Sherman, and Deeds, *Course of Mexican History*, 539–40; W. Timmons, *El Paso*, 198–200.

38. Harris and Sadler, *Secret War*, 29–30, 37–38, 42, 51, 53.

39. Bazant, *Concise History of Mexico*, 125–38; White, *Autobiography*, 109–110; *El Paso Times*, May 12, 1911.

40. Harris and Sadler, *Secret War*, 63, 162, 175, 203, 247; Bazant, *Concise History of Mexico*, 151; W. Timmons, *El Paso*, 214.

41. Meyer, Sherman, and Deeds, *Course of Mexican History*, 518–20, 547, 556; W. Timmons, *El Paso*, 219–21.

42. W. Timmons, *El Paso*, 221–22; Sonnichsen, *Pass*, 404–5; Meyer, Sherman, and Deeds, *Course of Mexican History*, 556–57.

43. Christian, "Sword and Plowshare," 243–51; W. Timmons, *El Paso*, 245.

44. White, *Autobiography*, 118–28; Leigh W. Osborn Photographs, PH026, White Papers, SSC.

45. White, *Autobiography*, 129–43; White, *Them Was the Day*, 11–32; Smith, "Shafter, Tx"; *Houston Chronicle*, December 2, 2007. For the life of William R. Shafter, see *Boston Daily Globe*, November 13, 1906.

46. *El Paso Herald*, January 28, 1915.

47. White, *Autobiography*, 146; Manzo, "Alfred Henry Lewis."

48. White, *Autobiography*, 146–49.

49. Esler, *Human Venture*, 561–68; Bass, *America's Entry*, 1–7.

50. W. Timmons, *El Paso*, 223; Meyer, Sherman, and Deeds, *Course of Mexican History*, 525.

51. W. Timmons, *El Paso*, 223–24.

52. Ibid., 224–25; Christian, *Black Soldiers*, 128, 132, 145.

53. White, *Autobiography*, 150–53; *El Paso Herald*, February 1, 1918; *Washington Post*, November 9, 1932.

54. White, *Autobiography*, 150–53; John D. Rockefeller Jr. to Owen Payne White, New York City, December 8, 1917; Rockefeller to White, December 15, 1917; Military Attache, Regia Ambasciata D'Italia to White, Washington, July 13, 1918, all in Box 1, Folder 13, White Papers, SSC; Owen Payne White, "To the Papago," *The Indian Sentinel: Official Organ of the Catholic Indian Missions* 1, no. 5 (July 1917), Box 1, Folder 21, White Papers, SSC (quote).

55. White, *Autobiography*, 154–55; Owen P. White, "I'm a-Going to Join the Army," undated, Box 1, Folder 13, White Papers, SSC.

56. White, *Autobiography*, 154–63.

57. White to Leigh White Osborn, n.p., July 1918; White to Osborn, Toul, December 22, 1918, both in Box 1, Folder 13, White Papers, SSC.

58. Grayzel, *First World War*, 128–29; "First World War Casualties," History Learning Site, www.historylearningsite.co.uk/FWWcasualties.htm.

59. White, *Autobiography*, 159–62.

CHAPTER 3

1. White, *Autobiography*, 164; *USA Today*, March 27, 2007; Dillingham, *Federal Aid to Veterans*, 13–15, 42, 145–156, 163–65; *Cleveland Call and Post*, June 16, 1956.

2. Degler, De Santis, and Ver Steeg, *Introduction to American History*, 211; W. Timmons, *El Paso*, 226–31, 235.

3. W. Timmons, *El Paso*, 231–35; Campbell, *Gone to Texas*, 364–66.

4. White, *Autobiography*, 164–65; *El Paso Times*, October 12, 1919; Garner, *Porfirio Díaz*, 1–2. While still representing a minority opinion, Garner joined an increasing number of historians who would agree with White that Díaz was unfairly maligned.

5. White, "Mesquite Smoke," Box 1, File 21, White Papers, SSC.

6. Ibid.; *El Paso Herald*, February 23, 1923.

7. White, "Southwestern Ballads," 1–15, White Papers, SSC (quote); White, *Southwestern Milestones.*

8. White, *Autobiography*, 165; *El Paso Herald*, January 23, 1920.

9. White, *Autobiography*, 165–67.

10. Ibid., 167; *El Paso Herald*, February 23, 1923 (first quote); February 24, 1923 (second quote); Bode, *Mencken*, 100; Rodgers, *Mencken*, 1.

11. W. S. McMath, "Looking Backward," Box 1, Folder 15, White Papers, SSC.

12. T. E. Sharp, "Cabbages," Box 1, Folder 15, White Papers, SSC.

13. W. Timmons, *El Paso*, 125, 144–58; Metz, "Mills, William Wallace."

14. Mills, *Forty Years at El Paso*, vii, xii.

15. Ibid., 9, 12–13, 23, 91, 175–92.

16. White, *Out of the Desert*, 1, 9, 76, 174, 203, 288.

17. Ibid., 130, 149, 174, 203, 305.

18. Ibid., 150, 171, 196, 296.

19. Meyer, Sherman, and Deeds, *Course of Mexican History*, 351; Vargas, *Crucible of Struggle*, 146–47; W. Timmons, *El Paso*, 162; Fite and Reese, *Economic History of the United States*, 501–2; Berg, *Latino Image in Film*, 38–40, 68, 71. Nearly ninety years after the first, racist-laden edition of the textbook was published, the Texas State Historical Association acquired the rights and published a sanitized version of the book by Jack Jackson. See Jackson, *New Texas History Movies.*

20. White, *Out of the Desert*, 95–96.

21. Ibid., 3, 96, 100, 113 (quote), 115, 123, 128, 249, 252, 263.

22. Ibid., 269, 275, 284, 321.

23. White, *Autobiography*, 168–69; *New York Morning Telegram*, December 1, 1923 (first quote); *El Paso Herald*, April 8, 1923 (second quote); *El Paso Post*, October 27, 1923.

24. *El Paso Herald*, March 8–9, 1924; March 25, 1924; Project, Box 67, Carl Hertzog Papers, SSC; Box 1, Folder 16, White Papers, SSC (quote).

25. W. S. McMath, "Looking Backwards," Box 1, Folder 15, White Papers, SSC; Bode, *Mencken*, 9–26; Stenerson, *H. L. Mencken*, 3–33.

26. H. L. Mencken, *American Mercury*, April 1924, Box 1, Folder 15, White Papers, SSC.

27. White, *Autobiography*, 169 (first quote); White, "El Paso," 444 (second quote).

28. White, *Autobiography*, 170–73; "Adventure (Magazine)," contextualization by Jon Cotton, in Newsstand: 1925, directed by David Earle, University of West Florida, http://uwf.edu/dearle/enewsstand/enewsstand_files/Page2834.htm; "History of the Adventurers' Club," Adventurers' Club of Los Angeles, www.adventurersclub.org/information_about_the_club.php.

29. "Markel, Lester," in Berenbaum and Skolnik, *Encyclopedia Judaica*, 13:549; Markel to White, New York City, November 22, 1924, Box 1, Folder 9, White Papers, SSC (first quote); Markel to White, December 6, 1924, Box 1, Folder 9, White Papers, SSC; "Cattle Kings Pass with the Vivid West," *New York Times Sunday Magazine*, December 7, 1924 (second quote); White, *Autobiography*, 174.

30. White, *Autobiography*, 174–76; Fernlund, "Senator Holm O. Bursum"; "Sam Gilbert Bratton," *Judgepedia*, last modified October 25, 2011, http://judgepedia.org/index.php/Sam_Gilbert_Bratton.

31. White, *Autobiography*, 177 (quote); Brown, *Hood, Bonnet, and Little Brown Jug*, 95–97; Gould, *Progressives and Prohibitionists*, 130–31.

32. Brown, *Hood, Bonnet, and Little Brown Jug*, 218–39; Gould, *Progressives and Prohibitionists*, 281; Buenger, *Path to a Modern South*, 214–17.

33. Brown, *Hood, Bonnet, and Little Brown Jug*, 246–51.

34. Markel to White, NYC, December 5, 1924, (first quote); December 15, 1924 (second and third quotes); December 26, 1924 (fifth and sixth quotes); January 6, 1925 (seventh quote), all in Box 1, Folder 9, White Papers, SSC; White, *Autobiography*, 177 (fourth quote).

35. White to Markel, January 9, 1925, n.p. (first quote) Box 1, Folder 9, White Papers, SSC; White, *Autobiography*, 177–78; *New York Times Sunday Magazine*, February 1, 1925 (second quote). Brown cites the article with White's name appearing in the footnote in *Hood, Bonnet, and Little Brown Jug*, 253.

36. *New York Times Sunday Magazine*, April 5, 1925.

37. White, *Autobiography*, 177–78; *New York Times*, February 1, 1925; *Dallas Morning News*, January 11, 1925 (first quote); *New York Times Book Review*, February 1, 1925; *Denton Herald*, November 27, 1925; Markel to White, NYC, February 13, 1925, Box 1, Folder 9, White Papers, SSC (second quote).

CHAPTER 4

1. Lester Markel to Owen White, New York City, March 4, 1925 (first quote); White to Markel, n.p., May 9, 1925 (second and third quotes), both in Box 1, Folder 9, White Papers, SSC.
2. *New York Times Sunday Magazine*, March 1, 1925.
3. "A Picture History of Kew Gardens, NY," kewgardenshistory.com; Biographical-Articles Acc. 11, Box 1, Folder 2, White Papers, SSC; *El Paso Times*, December 8, 1946; *New York Times Book Review*, September 13, 1925 (quote). The 1930 federal census listed White and his wife at 115 Metropolitan, with his place of birth stated erroneously as Virginia. See Department of Commerce, Bureau of the Census, Fifteenth Census of the United States: 1930 Population Schedule for Queens, New York City, New York City Public Library. Celebrities Charlie Chaplin, Billy Rose, and Dorothy Parker lived in Kew Gardens at different times, while Burt Bacharach and Rodney Dangerfield were born there. *New York Times*, February 4, 1990.
4. *Dallas News*, September 13, 1925 (first and second quotes); *St. Louis Post-Dispatch*, September 19, 1925 (third quote); *New York Sun*, October 1, 1925 (fourth quote); *Saturday Review of Literature*, December 5, 1925 (fifth quote).
5. White to Dear Grant, NYC, April 29, 1925, Box 51, Folder 7, General Correspondence, White Papers, SSC.
6. White, *Autobiography*, 179; *New York Times Sunday Magazine*, April 19, 1925 (quote).
7. *New York Times Sunday Magazine*, April 19, 1925.
8. *New York Times Sunday Magazine*, May 12, 1925.
9. White, *Autobiography*, 180–81, quote on p. 180; *New York Times*, August 19, 1917; January 12, 1936.
10. *New York Times Sunday Magazine*, May 3, 1925; Pringle, "Oil and the Permanent University Fund," 277–82; Battle, "University of Texas at Austin."
11. *New York Times Sunday Magazine*, May 3, 1925.
12. White, *Autobiography*, 181–82.
13. Ibid., 182–83, quote on 182.

14. Chenery, *Industry and Human Welfare*, x.

15. White, *Autobiography*, 183.

16. Ibid., 184–91.

17. Ibid., 191–92, 196–200. The *New York Times*, March 7, 1915, describes a raid on the Bradley brothers' Palm Beach casino.

18. *New York Times Sunday Magazine*, April 26, 1925; *New York Herald Tribune*, March 14, 1926; White, "Diatribe upon a Manly Theme," 75; *New York Times*, October 26, 1926; *Alcalde* 15, no. 2 (December 1926): 95–96 (quotes).

19. *Alcalde* 15, no. 2 (December 1926): 96.

20. July 24 Democratic Primary, Box 3, Folder 12, White Papers, SSC; Brown, *Hood, Bonnet, and Little Brown Jug*, 220, 298–99, 302–5, 326, 331–32.

21. White, "Reminiscences of Texas Divines."

22. White to Carl Hertzog, NYC, March 7, 1927 (quote), Box 51, Folder 7, Hertzog Papers, SSC; Meyer, Sherman, and Deeds, *Course of Mexican History*, 521–23, 565.

23. Meyer, Sherman, and Deeds, *Course of Mexican History*, 555–56.

24. *El Paso Herald*, March 26, 1927.

25. Bazant, *Concise History of Mexico*, 170; *New York Times*, July 17, 1928 (quote).

26. Box 5, Folder 2, White Papers, SSC; White, *Autobiography*, 202–4; Bazant, *Concise History of Mexico*, 172–75.

27. White, *Autobiography*, 204–8; Box 5, Folder 1, White Papers, SSC.

28. "Mississippi River Commission," www.mvd.usace.army.mil/About/ MississippiRiverCommision.

29. White to Hertzog, March 7, 1927, Box 51, Folder 7, Carl Hertzog Papers, MS295 J, SSC.

30. Gibbs, "Carl Hertzog, Printer," 1 (quote); Lowman, *Remembering Carl Hertzog*, 5–7.

31. White to B. F. Jenness, October 29, 1927, Box 2, Jenness Papers, SSC.

32. White to Jenness, February 6, 1928, Box 2, Jenness Papers, SSC.

33. Fenberg, *Unprecedented Power*, 8, 14–20, 35–44, 137. After serving in the Franklin Roosevelt administrations as secretary of commerce and Reconstruction Finance Corporation director, Jones grew increasingly conservative and anti-Communist, as demonstrated in his *Houston Chronicle* editorials, while remaining less strident than his other wealthy colleagues. See Burrough, *Big Rich*; Fenberg, *Unprecedented Power*, 565–67; "Sam Houston Hall and 1928 Democratic Convention," http://houstorian. wordpress.com/2007/02/14/sam-houston-hall-1928-democratic-national-convention (quote). Two men were arrested for the murder of Powell and released, though they had confessed.

34. Baker, "Boy's Life in Houston," 37–38.
35. White, *Autobiography*, 211.
36. Ibid., 176, 213–17.
37. White, "High Handed and Hell Bent," Box 5, Folder 4, White Papers, SSC.
38. Anders, *Boss Rule in South Texas*, vii, ix–x, 280, 283.
39. Ibid., 37, 134, 239; Spence, "Nickel Plated," 94.
40. Olien, *From Token to Triumph*, 6–7; Casdorph, *History of the Republican Party*, 115; "Celaya Creager House, Brownsville Texas," www.waymarking.com.
41. Olien, *From Token to Triumph*, 54–55; "The Press: Scooper Scooped," *Time*, September 16, 1929, http://content.time.com/time/magazine/article/0,9171,737888–2,00.html.
42. Spence, "Nickel Plated," 37–40; White, "High Handed and Hell Bent," Box 5, Folder 4, White Papers, SSC.
43. White, "High Handed and Hell Bent," Box 5, Folder 4, White Papers, SSC; William G. Shepherd, "Eyewitness at the Triangle," March 27, 1911, in Schaller et al., *Reading American Horizons*, 2:221–22, also available at http://www.ilr.cornell.edu/trianglefire/primary/testimonials/ootss_WilliamShepherd.html; "The Press: Scooper Scooped," *Time*, September 16, 1929.
44. "Brookhart, Smith William (1869–1944)," in U.S. Congress, *Biographical Directory*.
45. Spence, "Nickel Plated," 35, 47–51.
46. Ibid., 55–70.
47. Ibid., 72–76.
48. Ibid., 77–82, 99.
49. "The Press: Scooper Scooped," *Time*, September 16, 1929; Sam T. Williamson to White, NYC, December 3, 1929, Box 1, Folder 9, White Papers, SSC.
50. White, *Autobiography*, 219–23; *El Paso Times*, May 10, 1930 (quotes).
51. White, *Autobiography*, 239–44; Olien, *From Token to Triumph*, 55–56, 110; Casdorph, *History of the Republican Party*, 137–38, 146–47, 151.

CHAPTER 5

1. White, *Autobiography*, 235 (first quote); Cole, *Handbook of American History*, 211. Fall served nine months of a one-year prison sentence and

died in El Paso in 1944. Stratton, *Tempest over Teapot Dome*, 336–38, 342; White, "A Frontier Mother," *Collier's*, October 12, 1929, Box 2, Folder 3, White Papers, SSC; Earle Balch to Owen White, Box 1, Folder 10, White Papers, SSC (second quote); Paul R. Reynolds, Jr. to White, NYC, October 18, 1929, Box 1, Folder 10, White Papers, SSC; H. L. Mencken to White, Baltimore, March 22, 1930, Box 1, Folder 6, White Papers, SSC.

2. William S. McMath to White, El Paso, October 8, n.d., Box 1, Folder 7, White Papers, SSC (first quote); H. A. Carpenter to White, River Edge, October 20, 1929, Box 1, Folder 10, White Papers, SSC (second quote); C. F. O'Hara to White, Great Falls, October 15, 1929, Box 1, Folder 10, White Papers, SSC.

3. White, *Autobiography*, 225, 228, 237–38; *El Paso Herald-Post*, August 5, 1940 (first quote); Walter A. Gorrell to White, Cleveland, n.d., Box 1, Folder 10, White Papers, SSC (second quote); Mencken to White, Baltimore, April 24, 1929, Box 1, Folder 6, White Papers, SSC (third quote); White, "Soakem O'Riley," *Collier's*, August 24, 1929, Box 5, Folder 7, White Papers, SSC; White, "Conchita," *Collier's*, October 5, 1929, Box 5, Folder 8, White Papers, SSC.

4. White, *Lead and Likker*; White, *My Texas 'Tis of Thee*; John Coffee Hays to White, NYC, April 29, 1930, Box 1, Folder 13, White Papers, SSC (first quote); John Hays Hammond to White, Washington, November 22, 1930, Box 1, Folder 13, White Papers, SSC (second quote); Mencken to White, Baltimore, March 22, 1930, Box 1, Folder 6, White Papers, SSC (third quote).

5. Tom Cathcart to White, NYC, April 21, 1931 (first quote); Andrew S. Wing to White, NYC, April 21, 1931 (second quote); William L. Chenery to White, NYC, May 4, 1931 (third quote), all in Box 1, Folder 13, White Papers, SSC.

6. *El Paso Times*, June 20, 1931.

7. "The Beloved Physician of Shafter—Dr. Alward Hamilton White," unsigned and undated manuscript in possession of author.

8. White to Leigh White Osborn, NYC, June 30, 1931, in "A Letter from the Past from Owen P. White," *Password* 46 (2001): 18–21.

9. Hinshaw, *Herbert Hoover*, 3, 59, 88, 106, 121, 145, 193–94; White, *Autobiography*, 235–37.

10. Burner, *Herbert Hoover*, 297–99.

11. Ibid., 236–44.

12. White, "Cotton Poor," *Collier's*, June 6, 1931, Box 6, Folder 1, White Papers,

SSC (first quote); Frank E. Mullen to White, Chicago, December 27, 1931, Box 1, Folder 13, White Papers, SSC (second quote); Mencken to White, Baltimore, January 9, 1931, Box 1, Folder 6, White Papers, SSC (third quote).

13. White, *Autobiography*, 250 (first quote), 256; Burns, *Roosevelt*, 6–7, 50, 105; B. Timmons, *Garner of Texas*, 3, 15–31, 134; James, *Mr. Garner of Texas*, 14, 23–34, 114; Anders, *Boss Rule in South Texas*, ix; "In the Nature of Prophecy," Box 1, Folder 2, White Papers, SSC (second quote).

14. Guernsey T. Cross to White, Albany, January 9, 1931, Box 1, Folder 13, White Papers, SSC; White, *Autobiography*, 247–49; Mencken to White, Baltimore, April 12, 1932, Box 1, Folder 6, White Papers, SSC (quote); Leuchtenburg, *Franklin Delano Roosevelt and the New Deal*, 17. Texans voted for local option while continuing to ban open saloons in 1935. *New York Times*, September 1, 1935.

15. White, "In the Nature of Prophecy," Box 1, Folder 2, White Papers, SSC (quote); White, "Wheat's Here to Stay," *Collier's*, January 2, 1932, Box 6, Folder 4, White Papers, SSC; White, "Spare That Desert," *Collier's*, June 16, 1934, Box 6, Folder 13, White Papers, SSC; White, "All Washed Up," *Collier's*, September 29, 1934, Box 2, Folder 4, White Papers, SSC; White, *Out of the Desert*, 296.

16. White, "Scalping the Indian," *Collier's*, March 3, 1934, Box 6, Folder 11, White Papers, SSC (first quote); White, "Low, the Poor Indian," *Collier's*, February 6, 1937, Box 2, Folder 7, White Papers, SSC (second quote).

17. Dies created the controversial House Committee on Un-American Activities. For his correspondence with FBI chief J. Edgar Hoover, see Federal Bureau of Investigation, "Martin Dies." See also White, *Autobiography*, 298–99; Meyer, Sherman, and Deeds, *Course of Mexican History*, 581–82; White, "The Red Racket," *Collier's*, November 8, 1930, Box 3, Folder 12 White Papers, SSC; Mencken to White, Baltimore, June 30, 1933, Box 1, Folder 3, White Papers, SSC.

18. White, "The Blue Eagle at Home," *Collier's*, October 28, 1933, Box 6, Folder 9, White Papers, SSC.

19. White, "When the Public Needs a Friend," *Collier's*, June 2, 1934, Box 6, Folder 12, White Papers, SSC.; "Wagner, Robert Ferdinand," in D. Malone, *Dictionary of American Biography, Supplement Five*, 717–19.

20. White, "When the Public Needs a Friend," *Collier's*, June 2, 1934, Box 6, Folder 12, White Papers, SSC.

21. White, "Cutting Free," *Collier's*, October 27, 1934, Box 6, Folder 16, White Papers, SSC (quotes); "Cutting, Bronson Murray," in Betz and Carnes, *American National Biography*.

22. White, *Autobiography*, 293; White, "Timber for the Future," *Collier's*, June 22, 1935, Box 7, Folder 5, White Papers, SSC (first, second, and third quotes); White, "Land of the Pilgrims' Pride," *Collier's*, July 27, 1935, Box 7, Folder 7, White Papers, SSC (remaining quotes).

23. White, "Belle Starr, Bandit," *Collier's*, February 6, 1932, Box 6, Folder 5, White Papers, SSC; White, "Bullet-Proof Brown," *Collier's*, February 27, 1932, Box 6, Folder 6, White Papers, SSC; Mencken to White, Baltimore, April 12, 1932, Box 1, Folder 6, White Papers, SSC (first quote); Mencken to White, Baltimore, June 7, 1933, Box 1, Folder 6, White Papers, SSC (second quote); Mencken to White, Baltimore, June 9, 1933, Box 1, Folder 6, White Papers, SSC; Martha Kaufmann to White, NYC, May 9, 1932, Box 1, Folder 13, White Papers, SSC (third quote).

24. *El Paso Times*, January 4, 1935 (quotes); "Texas Politics—Lieutenant Governors: Walter F. Woodful," www.laits.utexas.edu/typ_media/html/leg/ltgovernors/20.html.

25. White, "Piping Hot," *Collier's*, Box 7, Folder 1, White Papers, SSC.

26. "National Industrial Recovery Act (1933)," *Our Documents*, U.S. National Archives, www.ourdocuments.gov/doc.php?flash=true&doc=66; *New York Times*, September 8, 1935; *Washington Post*, February 4, 1965; Richardson, "Judge Charles Bismark Ames."

27. White, "Texas Cuts Off Her Nose," *Collier's*, April 6, 1935, Box 7, Folder 3, White Papers, SSC.

28. *Texan*, November 2, 1934 (quotes); White, "Walled Kingdom," *Collier's*, May 11, 1935, Box 7, Folder 4, White Papers, SSC.

29. Thomas H. Beck to White, NYC, December 16, 1935, Box 1, Folder 13, White Papers, SSC (quote); White, "A Man Called Smith," *Collier's*, January 6, 1934, Box 6, Folder 10, White Papers, SSC; White, "Big Bend—Broken," *Collier's*, August 4, 1934, Box 6, Folder 15, White Papers, SSC; *El Paso Times*, December 9, 1934; White, "Texas Thirst," *Today*, January 26, 1935, Box 2, Folder 5, White Papers, SSC.

30. Williams, *Huey Long*, 20, 36, 39–40, 48, 67, 77–78, 91–105, 125–27; Long Legacy Project, Huey Long website, www.hueylong.com.

31. Williams, *Huey Long*, 7, 251–78, 303–7, 347–55, 461, 692, 793, 862; Long Legacy Project, Huey Long website, www.hueylong.com.

32. White, *Autobiography*, 270–71, 278; Long Island Exchange, "Long Island: Sands Point" http://www.longislandexchange.com/towns/sands-point.html.

33. White, *Autobiography*, 270 (first quote); Wayne Homren, "Washroom Warrior Medal Info Sources," *E-Sylum* (newsletter) 4, no. 33 (August 12,

2001), Numismatic Bibliomania Society, http://www.coinbooks.org/esylum_v04n33a09.html; caption to photograph from International News Photograph Service, n.d., White vertical files, Briscoe Center, University of Texas at Austin (second quote). Hilda Phelps Hammonds and prominent New Orleans ladies fought unsuccessfully to have Senators Long and Overton removed from office. See *Washington Post*, May 5, 1934; July 26, 1937.

34. Beals, *Story of Huey Long*, 264 (first and second quotes), 265 (third quote); Arthur M. Schlesinger Jr., "The Messiah of the Rednecks," in Graham, *Huey Long*, 153 (fourth quote).

35. Williams, *Huey Long*, 648–53.

36. Hair, *Kingfish and His Realm*, 257–59 (quote); Cortner, *Kingfish and the Constitution*, 61; Boulard, *Huey Long Invades New Orleans*, 77; R. White, *Kingfish*, 185–87.

37. White, *Autobiography*, 280; *Congressional Record* 78 (January 15, 1934): 614–15; Fite and Reese, *Economic History of the United States*, 299; White, "The Silver Mirage," *Collier's*, July 6, 1935, Box 7, Folder 6, White Papers, SSC (quote).

38. "Burns, *Roosevelt*, 193; "Agricultural Adjustment Act," www.u-s-history.com/pages/h1639.html; White, *Autobiography*, 281–92.

39. *Dallas News*, April 5, 1936 (first quote); *New York Times Book Review*, May 3, 1936 (second quote); "A Texas 'Renegade' Entertains," n.p., n.d., White vertical files, Briscoe Center, University of Texas at Austin (third quote); *Houston Post*, April 28, 1936 (fourth quote); *El Paso Times*, April 12, 1936 (fifth quote).

40. White, *My Texas 'Tis of Thee*, 17–22.

41. *El Paso Herald-Post*, April 20, 1936 (quotes); Garcia, *Desert Immigrants*, 37, 66, 125, 143, 214, 249–50n5; Lugo, "El Paso's Own Señor."

42. *El Paso Herald-Post*, April 20, 1936 (quote); *San Antonio Light*, April 10, 1937; Barr, *Black Texans*, 124; Brown, *Hood, Bonnet, and Little Brown Jug*, 150; White, *Autobiography*, 303–6.

43. *San Antonio Light*, September 10, 1937; Barnhart, "Quin, Charles Kennon."

44. *El Paso Times*, March 25, 1938; John Nance Garner to White, Washington, July 26, 1937, Box 1, Folder 13, White Papers, SSC (quote); White, *Autobiography*, 306–7; Barnhart, "Quin, Charles Kennon."

45. Charles Susskind, "Fessenden, Reginald Aubrey," in Koertge, *Complete Dictionary of Scientific Biography*, 4:601; Fry, "First Voice of Radio"; Owen P. White, "H-e-l-l-o P-a-r-i-s," *Collier's*, February 15, 1936, Box 2, Folder 6,

White Papers, SSC; White, "America Calling," *Collier's*, November, 1939, Box 2, Folder 8, White Papers, SSC.

46. Helen M. Fessenden to White, Bermuda, March 10, 1940, Box 1, Folder 13, White Papers, SSC.

47. B. Malone, *Country Music U.S.A.*, 167; Barkley, *Handbook of Texas Music*, 233–34.

48. *El Paso Times*, July 26, 1938 (quotes); White, "The Mountains," *Sirocco*, May 1938, Box 1, Folder 15, White Papers, SSC.

49. White, *Autobiography*, 299, 308–14, 315–16, 320–21, 324–26.

50. Frank Mullen to White, NYC, August 2, 1940, Box 1, Folder 13, White Papers, SSC.

51. White, *Autobiography*, 326–29.

52. "Long Island: Peconic" Long Island Exchange, www.longislandexchange. com/towns/peconic.html; Ken McCormick to White, NYC, June 25, 1941; McCormick to White, NYC, July 7, 1941, both in Box 1, Folder 13, White Papers, SSC.

53. White, *Autobiography*, 335–36.

54. *El Paso Herald-Post*, February 16, 1942 (first and second quotes); "An Ornery Texan's Story," n.p., n.d., White File, Dolph Briscoe Center for American History, University of Texas at Austin (third quote); *Kansas City Star*, May 9, 1942 (fourth quote); *New York Herald Tribune*, May 24, 1942 (fifth quote); *Dallas News*, May 17, 1942 (sixth quote); *Fort Worth Star Telegraph*, May 10, 1942 (seventh quote).

55. *El Paso Herald-Post*, July 7, 1961.

56. White to Doctor Alexander Zimany, NYC, April 13, 1942, Box 1, Folder 14, White Papers, SSC (first quote); William McMath to White, Hollywood, New Mexico, n.d., Box 1, Folder 7, White Papers, SSC (second quote); Rev. K. E. Wall to White, Columbus, May 15, 1942, Box 1, Folder 11, White Papers, SSC; Wall to White, June 1, 1942, Box 1, Folder 11, White Papers, SSC (third quote); Julius W. Lorentzen to White, El Paso, June 5, 1942, Box 1, Folder 13, White Papers, SSC; William Guild to White, Newtonville, June 10, 1942, Box 1, Folder 11, White Papers, SSC (fourth quote); White to Guild, n.p., June 15, 1942, Box 1, Folder 14, White Papers, SSC (fifth quote); G. C. Gaither to White, Reidsville, August 30, 1942, Box 1, Folder 11, White Papers, SSC; [Undecipherable] to White, Putnam, June 18, 1942, Box 1, Folder 7, White Papers, SSC.

57. Mencken to White, Baltimore, April 14, 1942 (first quote); Mencken to White, Baltimore, April 9, 1942 (second quote), both in Box 1, Folder 6,

White Papers, SSC. Actually, White, almost sixty-three at the time, was Mencken's senior.

58. Mencken to White, Baltimore, April 27, 1942, Box 1, Folder 6, White Papers, SSC.

59. Knight, "Owen Payne White," 55; Casdorph, "Creager, Renfro Banton"; Quentin Bossi to White, NYC, April 15, 1942, Box 1, Folder 7, White Papers, SSC (first quote); Allie to White, Santa Maria, November 29, 1942, Box 1, Folder 13, White Papers, SSC (second quote).

60. Acheson, *Joe Bailey*, 1, 25, 28–29, 41–42, 114, 139–40, 151, 263, 317–22, 390, 404.

61. White, *Autobiography*, 265–66; Joseph W. Bailey Jr. to G. P. Putnam's Sons, Dallas, June 11, 1942 (quote); Earle Balch to White, NYC, June 15, 1942, both in Box 1, Folder 8, White Papers, SSC.

62. White to Balch, n.p., June 17, 1942 (first quote); White to Bailey, Cutchogue, June 17, 1942 (second quote); Bailey to White, Dallas, June 22, 1942 (third and fourth quotes); White to Bailey, n.p., June 29, 1942 (block quote), all in Box 1, Folder 8, White Papers, SSC.

63. Melusin, "Bailey, Joseph Weldon, Jr."

64. White to Dr. Asa Brunson, n.p., June 15 [1942?] (first quote); White to Mr. Holliday, n.p., July 6, 1942 (block quote), both in Box 1, Folder 14, White Papers, SSC.

65. White to Mrs. Rowley, n.p., July 9, 1942, Box 1, Folder 14, White Papers, SSC.

66. White to Judge Daniel Walker, n.p., August 12, 1942, Box 1, Folder 14, White Papers, SSC.

67. White to Mencken, n.p., June 22, 1942, Box 1, Folder 6, White Papers, SSC.

68. Mencken to White, Baltimore, July 23, 1942 (first quote); White to Julian P. Boyd, n.p., July 25, 1942 (second quote), both in Box 1, Folder 6, White Papers, SSC.

69. Julian P. Boyd, "Fundamental Laws and Constitutions of New Jersey," finding aid, Princeton University Library, findingaids.princeton.edu/getEad?eadid=C0654&kw.

CHAPTER 6

1. *New York Times*, July 21, 2007.

2. Cole, *Handbook of American History*, 226, 228, 229, 230.

3. Ibid., 223, 224, 226, 227, 228.

4. "The Coast Artillery at Camp Hero," *Skylighters*, www.skylighters.org/

camphero; Kennedy Hickman, "World War II: Operation Pastorius," militaryhistory.about.com/od/socialeffectsofwar/p/pastorius.htm.

5. Cole, *Handbook of American History*, 211, 231.

6. Dorothy Purdell to White, NYC, April 15, 1942, Box 1, Folder 14, White Papers, SSC (first and second quotes); Harold Young to Frank E. Mullen, NYC, June 3, 1942, Box 1, Folder 14, White Papers, SSC (third quote); William Chenery to White, NYC, June 10, 1942, Box 1, Folder 14, White Papers, SSC; White to J.C. Dykes, n.p., July 6, 1942, Box 1, Folder 14, White Papers, SSC (fourth quote); White to Murray Ballinger, n.p., July 9, 1942, Box 1, Folder 13, White Papers, SSC.

7. Dykes to White, Arlington, June 8, 1942, Box 1, Folder 11, White Papers, SSC (first quote); White to G.P. Putnam, n.p., June 15 [1942?], Box 1, Folder 7, White Papers, SSC (second quote); "Writers Please Note," n.p., n.d., Box 1, Folder 13, White Papers, SSC (third quote).

8. White to Mr. Boutell, n.p., June 15 [1942?], Box 1, Folder 14, White Papers, SSC.

9. "Awards 1940s," Box 1, Folder 4, White Papers, SSC (quotes); Raymond M. Dinsmore to White, Riverhead, February 18, 1946, Box 1, Folder 13, White Papers, SSC.

10. Melville Minton, "Comments on Forthcoming Books," n.d., Box 1, Folder 20, White Papers, SSC (first quote); White to Putnam, n.p., June 15 [1942?], Box 1, Folder 7, White Papers, SSC (second quote); White to Mrs. Rowley, n.p., July 9, 1943, Box 1, Folder 14, White Papers, SSC; White to Judge Walker, n.p., December 3, 1942, Box 1, Folder 14, White Papers, SSC; White, *Texas*, 140, 141 (third quote).

11. *El Paso Times*, n.d., Box 1, Folder 20, White Papers, SSC (first quote); "The Bookshelf," n.p., n.d., Box 1, Folder 20, White Papers, SSC (second quote); "Reynolds, Horace Mason, 1896–1965. Papers: Guide," updated April 24, 2012, Houghton Library, Harvard College Library, oasis.lib.harvard.edu/oasis/deliver/~hou00899; Balch to White, NYC, August 27, 1945, Box 1, Folder 5, White Papers, SSC (third quote); *Dallas Morning News*, September 30, 1945 (fourth quote).

12. *Pasadena Star-News*, November 4, 1945 (first quote); *Chicago Sunday Tribune*, December 16, 1945 (second quote); *Long Island Traveler*, September 20, 1945 (third quote); *American Mercury*, December 1945, Box 1, Folder 20, White Papers, SSC (fourth quote); Mencken to White, Baltimore, July 24, 1945, Box 1, Folder 20, White Papers, SSC (fifth, sixth, and seventh quotes).

13. Adela Shekter to White, Jamaica, October 30, 1945, Box 1, Folder 13, White Papers, SSC; Frank M. Flack to White, Fort Leavenworth, October 31, 1945, Box 1, Folder 12, White Papers, SSC; Blanche Berman to White, Jamaica, January 9, 1946, Box 1, Folder 12, White Papers, SSC (first quote); Donald K. Evans, Chicago, December 16, 1945, Box 1, Folder 11, White Papers, SSC (second quote).

14. *New York Herald Tribune Weekly Book Review*, September 30, 1945, Box 1, Folder 12, White Papers, SSC (first quote); William H. Burges to White, n.p., September 15, 1945, Box 1, Folder 12, White Papers, SSC (second quote); Hulse, "Burges, William Henry"; W. Timmons, *El Paso*, 192, 232.

15. Maureen McManus to White, NYC, October 4, 1945, Box 1, Folder 13, White Papers, SSC (first quote); McManus to White, NYC, October 12, 1945, Box 1, Folder 7, White Papers, SSC (second quote); Wilson [?] to White, NYC, October 13, 1945, Box 1, Folder 13, White Papers, SSC (third quote); "Bessie Beatty," Spartacus Educational, www.spartacus-educational. com/RUSbeatty.htm. Beatty once sold $300,000 in war bonds in a few days on her radio show. See *New York Times*, April 7, 1947.

16. *El Paso Times*, February 25, 1946 (first and second quotes); March 4, 1946 (fourth and fifth quotes); White to Carl Hertzog, Cutchogue, April 5, 1946, Box 51, Folder 7, Hertzog Papers, SSC (third quote).

17. Hans Eckel to White, Naco, March 25, 1946, Box 1, Folder 11, White Papers, SSC; Robert N. Mullin to White, Toledo, April 3, 1946, Box 1, Folder 11, White Papers, SSC (first quote); White to Frank Wells Brown, Cutchogue, June 3, 1946, Box 1, Folder 3, White Papers, SSC (second quote).

18. Undated proposal, Box 4, White Papers, SSC.

19. "Western Trails," 1, 5, 90, Box 4, White Papers, SSC.

20. Ibid., 156–62, quote on 62.

21. "A Soul's Soliloquy" is placed between the end of chapter 9 and the beginning of chapter 10 in the second draft of "Western Trails," ibid.

22. Earle H. Balch to White, NYC, September 19, 1946, Box 1, Folder 7, White Papers, SSC.

23. White, "Mobile," 697, 703.

24. *El Paso Herald-Post*, n.d., Box 2, Folder 6, White Papers, SSC (quote); *El Paso Herald-Post*, December 9, 1946; El Paso newspaper (unidentified clipping), December 8, 1946, Box 1, Folder 5, White Papers, SSC; *New York Times*, n.d., Box 1, Folder 5, White Papers, SSC; Bressler, *Universalist Movement in America*, 3–8.

25. *New York Times*, n.d., Box 1, Folder 5, White Papers, SSC (first quote);

Frontier Times, March, 1947, 363 (second quote); Charles Angoff to Mrs. Owen P. White, Baltimore, December 12, 1946, Box 1, Folder 5, White Papers, SSC (block quote).

26. Mike White to Carl Hertzog, Cutchogue, March 27, 1947, Box 51, Folder 7, Hertzog Papers, SSC.

27. Hertzog to Mrs. White, El Paso, April 10, 1947 (first quote); Mrs. White to Hertzog, Cutchogue, April 15, 1947 (second quote), Box 51, Folder 7, Hertzog Papers, SSC.

28. Mrs. White to Hertzog, Cutchogue, July 28, 1947 (first quote); Hertzog to Mrs. White, El Paso, August 20, 1947 (second quote), Box 51, Folder 7, Hertzog Papers, SSC.

29. Lowman, *Remembering Carl Hertzog*, 27, 45.

30. *El Paso Herald-Post*, July 7, 1961; December 2, 1962 (first quote); n.d., Box 1, Folder 6, White Papers, SSC (second quote); Metz, "Saga of Owen P. White."

Bibliography

DOCUMENTS

Congressional Record. January 15, 1934. Vol. 78.

Hertzog, Carl. Papers. C. L. Sonnichsen Special Collections Department, University of Texas at El Paso.

Jenness, B. F. Papers. C. L. Sonnichsen Special Collections Department, University of Texas at El Paso.

Population Schedules of the Ninth Census of the United States, 1870.

Population Schedules of the Twelfth Census of the United States, 1900.

Population Schedules of the Fifteenth Census of the United States, 1930.

White, Owen Payne. Papers. C. L. Sonnichsen Special Collections Department, University of Texas at El Paso.

———. Vertical files. Dolph Briscoe Center for American History, University of Texas at Austin.

———. Vertical files. El Paso Public Library, El Paso.

NEWSPAPERS

Boston Daily Globe
Chicago Sunday Tribune
Cleveland Call and Post
Dallas Morning News
Denton Herald
El Paso Herald-Post
El Paso Times
Frontier Times
Greensboro News Record
Houston Post

Long Island Traveler
New York Herald Tribune
New York Morning Telegram
New York Sun
New York Times
New York Times Sunday Magazine
Pasadena Star-News
San Antonio Light
St. Louis Post-Dispatch

BOOKS

Acheson, Sam Hanna. *Joe Bailey: The Last Democrat.* New York: Macmillan, 1932.

Anders, Evan. *Boss Rule in South Texas: The Progressive Era.* Austin: University of Texas Press, 1982.

Barkley, Roy, et. al., eds. *The Handbook of Texas Music.* Austin: Texas State Historical Association, 2003.

Barr, Alwyn. *Black Texans, 1528–1971.* Austin, TX: Pemberton Press, 1982.

Bass, Herbert J., ed. *America's Entry into World War I: Submarines, Sentiment, or Security?* New York: Holt, Rinehart and Winston, 1964.

Bazant, Jan. *A Concise History of Mexico.* Cambridge: Cambridge University Press, 1977.

Beals, Carlton. *The Story of Huey Long.* Westport, CT: Greenwood Press, 1935.

Berenbaum, Michael, and Fred Skolnik, eds. *Encyclopedia Judaica.* 2nd ed. Detroit, MI: Macmillan Reference USA, 2007.

Berg, Charles Ramirez. *The Latino Image in Film: Stereotypes, Subversion, and Resistance.* Austin: University of Texas Press, 2002.

Berkin, Carol, et al. *Making America.* Boston, MA: Houghton Mifflin, 1999.

Betz, Paul, and Mark C. Carnes, eds. *American National Biography.* New York: Oxford University Press. 2001.

Billington, Ray Allen, ed. *The Frontier Thesis, Valid Interpretation of American History?* New York: Holt, Rinehart and Winston, 1966.

Bode, Carl. *Mencken.* Carbondale: Southern Illinois University Press, 1969.

Boulard, Garry. *Huey Long Invades New Orleans: The Siege of a City, 1934–1936.* Gretna, LA: Pelican, 1998.

Bressler, Ann Lee. *The Universalist Movement in America, 1770–1880.* New York: Oxford University Press, 2001.

Brown, Norman D. *Hood, Bonnet, and Little Brown Jug: Texas Politics, 1921–1928*. College Station: Texas A&M University Press, 1984.

Buenger, Walter L. *The Path to a Modern South: Northeast Texas Between Reconstruction and the Great Depression*. Austin: University of Texas Press, 2001.

Burner, David. *Herbert Hoover: A Public Life*. New York: Alfred A. Knopf, 1979.

Burns, James MacGregor. *Roosevelt: The Lion and the Fox*. New York: Harcourt Brace, Jovanovich, 1956.

Burrough, Bryan. *The Big Rich: The Rise and Fall of the Greatest Texas Oil Fortunes*. New York: Penguin Press, 2009.

Campbell, Randolph B. *Gone to Texas: A History of the Lone Star State*. New York: Oxford University Press, 2012.

Carnes, Mark C., and John A. Garraty. *American Destiny: Narrative of a Nation*. New York: Longman, 2003.

Casdorph, Paul. *A History of the Republican Party of Texas, 1865–1965*. Austin, TX: Pemberton Press, 1965.

Chenery, William L. *Industry and Human Welfare*. New York: Macmillan, 1922.

Christian, Garna L. *Black Soldiers in Jim Crow, Texas, 1899–1917*. College Station: Texas A&M University Press, 1995.

Cole, Donald B. *Handbook of American History*. New York: Harcourt, Brace, and World, 1968.

Connery, Thomas B. *Journalism and Realism: Rendering American Life*. Evanston, IL: Northwestern University Press, 2011.

Cortner, Richard C. *The Kingfish and the Constitution*. Westport, CT: Greenwood Press, 1996.

Darity, William A., Jr., ed. *International Encyclopedia of the Social Sciences*. Detroit, MI: Macmillan Reference USA, 2008.

Degler, Carl N., Vincent P. De Santis, and Clarence L. Ver Steeg. *Introduction to American History*. 2 vols. Redding, CA: BVT Publishing, 2009.

Dillingham, William Pyrle. *Federal Aid to Veterans, 1917–1941*. Gainesville: University of Florida Press, 1952.

Donkin, Richard. *Blood, Sweat and Tears: The Evolution of Work*. New York: Texere, 2001.

Esler, Anthony. *The Human Venture, A World History: Prehistory to the Present*. Upper Saddle River, NJ: Prentice Hall, 2000.

Federal Bureau of Investigation. "Martin Dies." Washington, D.C.: FBI, 2000.

Fenberg, Steven. *Unprecedented Power: Jesse Jones, Capitalism, and the Common Good*. College Station: Texas A&M University Press, 2011.

Filler, Louis. *The Muckrakers.* University Park: Pennsylvania State University Press, 1976.

Fite, Gilbert, and Jim E. Reese. *An Economic History of the United States.* Boston, MA: Houghton Mifflin, 1965.

Frantz, Joe B. *Texas: A Bicentennial History.* New York: W.W. Norton, 1976.

Garcia, Mario T. *Desert Immigrants: The Mexicans of El Paso, 1880–1920.* New Haven, CT: Yale University Press, 1981.

Garner, Paul. *Porfirio Díaz.* Harlow, UK: Longman, 2001.

Gould, Lewis L. *Progressives and Prohibitionists: Texas Democrats in the Wilson Era.* Austin: University of Texas Press, 1973.

Graham, Hugh Davis, ed. *Huey Long.* Englewood Cliffs, NJ: Prentice Hall, 1970.

Grayzel, Susan R. *The First World War: A Brief History with Documents.* Boston, MA: Bedford/St. Martin's, 2013.

Hailman, John. *Thomas Jefferson on Wine.* Jackson: University Press of Mississippi, 2006.

Hair, William Ivey. *The Kingfish and His Realm: The Life and Times of Huey P. Long.* Baton Rouge: Louisiana State University Press, 1991.

Hamilton, Nancy. *Ben Dowell, El Paso's First Mayor.* El Paso: Texas Western Press, 1976.

Harris, Charles H., III, and Louis R. Sadler. *The Secret War in El Paso: Mexican Revolutionary Intrigue, 1906–1920.* Albuquerque: University of New Mexico Press, 2009.

Hinshaw, David. *Herbert Hoover: American Quaker.* New York: Farrar, Straus, 1950.

Jackson, Jack. *New Texas History Movies.* Austin: Texas State Historical Association, 2007.

James, Marquis. *Mr. Garner of Texas.* Indianapolis, IN: Bobbs-Merrill, 1939.

Kelly, Alfred H., and Winfred A. Harbison. *The American Constitution: Its Origins and Development.* New York: W. W. Norton, 1963.

Kobre, Sidney. *Development of American Journalism.* Dubuque, IA: William C. Brown, 1979.

Koertge, Noretta, ed. *Complete Dictionary of Scientific Biography.* Detroit, MI: Charles Scribner's Sons, 2008.

Kutler, Stanley I., ed. *Dictionary of American History.* New York: Charles Scribner's Sons, 2006.

Leuchtenburg, William E. *Franklin Delano Roosevelt and the New Deal, 1932–1940.* New York: Harper and Row, 1963.

Lorant, Steffan. *The Life and Times of Theodore Roosevelt.* Garden City, NY: Doubleday, 1959.

Lowman, Al. *Remembering Carl Hertzog: A Texas Printer and His Books*. Dallas, TX: Steel Point Press, 1985.

Malone, Bill C. *Country Music U.S.A.* Austin: University of Texas Press, 1985.

Malone, Dumas, ed. *Dictionary of American Biography*. New York: Charles Scribners Sons, 1961.

———. *Dictionary of American Biography, Supplement Five*. New York: Charles Scribners Sons, 1977.

Mayer, David N. *The Constitutional Thought of Thomas Jefferson*. Charlottesville: University of Virginia Press, 1994.

McComb, David G. *Houston, A History*. Austin: University of Texas Press, 1981.

McCullough, David. *John Adams*. New York: Simon and Schuster, 2001.

Metz, Leon Claire. *The Encyclopedia of Lawmen, Outlaws, and Gunfighters*. New York: Facts on File, 2003.

———. *John Wesley Hardin: Dark Angel of Texas*. El Paso, TX: Mangan Books, 1996.

Meyer, Michael C., William L. Sherman, and Susan M. Deeds. *The Course of Mexican History*. New York: Oxford University Press, 2003.

Mills, W. W. *Forty Years at El Paso, 1858–1898*. El Paso, TX: Carl Hertzog, 1961.

Murray, Joseph A. *Alexander Hamilton: America's Forgotten Founder*. New York: Algora, 2007.

Olien, Roger M. *From Token to Triumph: The Texas Republicans Since 1920*. Dallas, TX: Southern Methodist University Press. 1982.

Otteson, James R. *Adam Smith*. New York: Continuum International, 2011.

Richardson, Rupert N., et al. *Texas: The Lone Star State*. Boston, MA: Prentice Hall, 2010.

Rodgers, Marion Elizabeth. *Mencken: The American Iconoclast*. New York: Oxford University Press, 2005.

Rose, Al. *Storyville, New Orleans: Being an Authentic, Illustrated Account of the Notorious Red-Light District*. Tuscaloosa: University of Alabama Press, 1985.

Schaller, Michael, et. al., eds. *Reading American Horizons*. Vol. 2. New York: Oxford University Press, 2013.

Smith, Robert Barr. *Daltons! The Raid on Coffeyville, Kansas*. Norman: University of Oklahoma Press, 1996.

Sonnichsen, C. L. *Pass of the North: Four Centuries on the Rio Grande*. El Paso: Texas Western Press, 1968.

———. *Roy Bean, Law West of the Pecos*. New York: Devin Adair, 1958.

Stenerson, Douglas C. *H. L. Mencken: Iconoclast from Baltimore*. Chicago, IL: University of Chicago Press, 1971.

Stettner, Edward A. *Shaping Modern Liberalism: Herbert Croly and Progressive Thought*. Lawrence: University Press of Kansas, 1993.

Stratton, David H. *Tempest over Teapot Dome: The Story of Albert B. Fall.* Norman: University of Oklahoma Press, 1998.

Strickland, Rex W. *Six Who Came to El Paso: Pioneers of the 1840s.* El Paso: Texas Western College Press, 1963.

Timmons, Bascom M. *Garner of Texas: A Personal History.* New York: Harper & Brothers, 1948.

Timmons, W. H. *El Paso: A Borderlands History.* El Paso: Texas Western Press, 1990.

U.S. Congress. *Biographical Directory of the United States Congress, 1774–2005.* Washington, D.C.: U.S. GPO, 2005.

Vargas, Zaragosa. *Crucible of Struggle: A History of Mexican Americans from Colonial Times to the Present Era.* New York: Oxford University Press, 2011.

Walker, Henry P., and Don Bufkin. *Historical Atlas of Arizona.* Norman: University of Oklahoma Press, 1986.

White, Owen Payne. *The Autobiography of a Durable Sinner.* New York: G.P. Putnam's Sons, 1942.

———. *Lead and Likker.* New York: Minton, Balch, 1932.

———. *My Texas 'Tis of Thee.* New York: G.P. Putnam's Sons, 1936.

———. *Out of the Desert: The Historical Romance of El Paso.* El Paso, TX: McMath, 1923.

———. *Southwestern Milestones.* El Paso, TX: EPVF Writers, n.d.

———. *Texas: An Informal Biography.* New York: G.P. Putnam's Sons, 1945.

———. *Them Was the Days: From El Paso to Prohibition.* New York: Minton, Balch, 1925.

White, Richard D., Jr. *Kingfish: The Reign of Huey P. Long.* New York: Random House, 2006.

Williams, T. Harry. *Huey Long.* New York: Alfred A. Knopf, 1969.

ARTICLES AND DISSERTATIONS

Alcalde. 15, no. 2 (December 1926).

Christian, Garna L. "Always in His Heart: Owen Payne White and Old El Paso." *Southwestern Historical Quarterly* 92 (October 2008): 172–90.

———. "Sword and Plowshare: The Symbiotic Development of Fort Bliss and El Paso, Texas, 1849–1918." PhD diss., Texas Tech University, 1977.

Collier's. "Arizona, History." October 26, 1929.

Fernlund, Kevin J. "Senator Holm O. Bursum and the Mexican Ring, 1921–1924." *New Mexico Historical Review* 66, no. 4 (October 1991): 433–53.

Fry, Mervyn C. "The First Voice of Radio: Reginald Aubrey Fessenden." *Cat's*

Whisker 3, no. 1 (March 1973). Reprinted at Hammond Museum of Radio, www. hammondmuseumofradio.org/fessenden-bio.html.

Gambrell, Herbert. "Rattlesnake Pete." *Saturday Review of Literature* 5 (May 16, 1942).

Gibbs, Michael. "Carl Hertzog, Printer for the Southwest." *Pennsylvania Catalogue* no 10 (November 1938).

Humphrey, David C. "Prostitution and Public Policy in Austin, Texas, 1870–1915." *Southwestern Historical Quarterly* 86, no. 4: 473–516.

————. "Prostitution in Texas from the 1830s to the 1860s." *East Texas Historical Journal* 33 (1995): 27–43.

Knight, John Gordon. "Owen Payne White, El Paso's First Writer of Renown." *Password* (Summer 1965): 53–56.

Lugo, Mercedes. "El Paso's Own Señor, Cleofas Calleros." *Junior Historian* 29 (1968): 24–28.

Manzo, Fluornoy D. "Alfred Henry Lewis: Western Storyteller." *Arizona and the West* 10, no. 1 (Spring 1968): 5–24.

Osborn, Leigh White. "Scenes of My Childhood." *Password* (Winter 1994): 187–91.

Pringle, David F. "Oil and the Permanent University Fund: The Early Years." *Southwestern Historical Quarterly* 86 (October 1982): 277–82.

Richardson, D. A. "Judge Charles Bismark Ames." *Chronicles of Oklahoma* 13, no. 4 (December 1935): 391–98. digital.library.okstate.edu/Chronicles/vo13/vo13p391.html.

Sapon, Vladimir, and Sam Robino. "Right and Left Wings in Libertarianism." *Canadian Social Science* 5, no. 6 (2009): 135–42.

Time. "The Press: Comeback." March 30, 1931

White, Owen Payne. " Diatribe upon a Manly Theme." *American Mercury* 8, no. 9 (May 1926).

————. "El Paso." *American Mercury* 2, no. 8 (August 1924).

————. "Mobile." *American Mercury,* 43, no. 276 (December 1946).

————. "Reminiscences of Texas Divines." *American Mercury* 9, no. 33 September 1926): 95–100.

SELECTED ELECTRONIC SOURCES

Barnhart, James A. "Quin, Charles Kennon." *Handbook of Texas Online.* http://www.tshaonline.org/handbook/online/articles/fqu15.

Battle, William James. "University of Texas at Austin." *Handbook of Texas Online.* http://tshaonline.org/handbook/online/articles/kcu09.

Casdorph, Paul D. "Creager, Rentfro Banton." *Handbook of Texas Online.* http://www.tshaonline.org/handbook/online/articles/fcr15.

Farah, Cynthia. "White, Owen Payne." *Handbook of Texas Online.* www.tshaonline.org/handbook/online/articles/WW/fwh26.html.

Hulse, J. F. "Burges, William Henry." *Handbook of Texas Online.* http://www.tshaonline.org/handbook/online/articles/fbu72.

Mayer, Holly A. "Woman Wagoners: Camp Followers in the American War for Independence." *The American Revolution, 1763–1783.* Gilder Lehrman Institute of American History. www.gilderlehrman.org/history-by-era/american-revolution-1763–1783/war-for-independence/essays.

Melusin, Ronald W. "Bailey, Joseph Weldon, Jr." *Handbook of Texas Online.* http://www.tshaonline.org/handbook/online/articles/fba11.

Metz, Leon C. "Hardin, John Wesley." *Handbook of Texas Online.* http://www.tshaonline.org/handbook/online/articles/fha63.

———. "Mills, William Wallace." *Handbook of Texas Online.* http://www.tshaonline.org/handbook/online/articles/fmi41.

———. "The Saga of Owen P. White." El Paso County Historical Society. http://elpasohistory.com/component/content/article/2-uncategorized/76-owen-payne-white?highl.

———. "Selman, John Henry." *Handbook of Texas Online.* http://www.tshaonline.org/handbook/online/articles/fse10.

———. "Stoudenmire, Dallas." *Handbook of Texas Online.* http://www.tshaonline.org/handbook/online/articles/fstaw.

Newman, S. H. "Newman, Simeon Harrison." *Handbook of Texas Online.* http://www.tshaonline.org/handbook/online/articles/fne41.

Roosevelt, Theodore. "The Man with the Muckrake." Speech delivered April 14, 1906. Top 100 Speeches. American Rhetoric. www.americanrhetoric.com.

Smith, Julia Cauble. "Santa Rita Oil Well." *Handbook of Texas Online.* http://www.tshaonline.org/handbook/online/articles/dos01.

———. "Shafter, Tx." *Handbook of Texas Online.* http://www.tshaonline.org/handbook/online/articles/hns37.

UNPUBLISHED SOURCES

Baker, Rolin H. "A Boy's Life in Houston: Recollections, 1926–1931." 2006. Unpublished manuscript in possession of author.

"The Beloved Physician of Shafter—Dr. Alward Hamilton White." N.d. Unpublished manuscript in possession of author.

Osborn, Oliver. Correspondence with author.

Shatto, Mrs. Rebecca C. Family documents in possession of author.

Spence, Ruth Griffin. "The-Nickel-Plated-Highway-to-Hell: A Political History of Hidalgo County [Texas], 1952–1934." 1989. Unpublished manuscript. Available at http://www.scribd.com/doc/35951086/The-Nickel-Plated-Highway-to-Hell-Ruth-Griffin-Spence.

Index

Page numbers in italic text indicate illustrations.

Adams, Henry, 62
Adams, John, 8, 26
Adams, Samuel Hopkins, 5, 6, 80
Addams, Jane, 4
Adventure magazine, 62
Agricultural Adjustment Act, 118
Aikman, Duncan, 83
Alexanderson, Ernst F. W., 122
Alexander the Great, 54
Along the Rio Grande (Lewis), 40
Altgeld, John Peter, 4
American Federation of Labor, 3
American Magazine, 5
American Mercury, vii–viii, 61–62, 68, 79,
    145; free-thinking, 83
American Socialist Party, 3
Anderson, Sherwood, 83
Anthony, Susan B., 3
antireformer, 7
Anti-Saloon League, 81
Arena, 7
Arizona War, 19
Army and Navy Register, 43, 53
Atlantic Monthly, 4, 6
The Autobiography of a Durable Sinner
    (White, O. P.), 139–40, 151; Baily refer-
    ence in, 128–29; correspondence about,
    126–27, 130–31; dampened appeal for,
    128; Mencken on, 127–28; proposed

movie script, 135; radio interview, 140;
    reviews, 125–26; White, L., on, 126
awestruck observer prank, 77–78
Azuela, Mariano, 34

Bailey, Joseph Weldon, Jr., 128–30
Baker, Newton, 42, 44
Baker, Ray Stannard, 5, 6, 7, 8
Baker, Rollin H., 90
Baker, Yancy, 91–93, 95, 97–98, 109, 128
Balch, Earle II., 143–44
Baltimore Morning Herald, 61
Baltimore Sun, 61
banking reform, 7
Beach, Rex, 40
Beals, Carleton, 116
Bean, Roy, 23, 28
Beard, Charles, 4
Beatty, Bessie, 140
Beck, Thomas H., 113
Belfast Telegraph, 60
Bellamy, Edward, 3, 7
Bellinger, Charles, 120–21
Belsham, William, 8
Benson, C. A., 119
Bernhardt, Sarah, 22
Bible Belt, 91
Black, Loring M., 95
Black Legend, 58

Bonney, William ("Billy the Kid"), 18
Bonus Army, 49
Booth, Edwin, 22
Borajo, Antonio, 59
Boulard, Garry, 117
Boyd, Julian P., 132
Bradley, Edward, 82
Bradley, John, 82
Bratton, Sam Gilbert, 63–64
Brookhart, Smith W., 94, 97
Brown, Hendry, 110
Brown, Milton, 123
Brownsville Herald, 98
Bryan, William Jennings, 9, 114, 117
Buck, Gene, 116
Bullard, John, 18
Bunyan, John, 2
Burges, William H., 32–33, 140
Bursum, Holm Olaf, 63–64
Butte, George C., 65

Cabeza de Vaca, Álvar Núñez, 11, 59, 142
Cain, Ira, 126
Calleros, Cleofas, 29, 120
Calles, Elias, 84–87
"Camera Dick" (White, O. P.), 125
Capone, Al, 116
Cárdenas, Lázaro, 107, 123
Carnegie, Andrew, 3
Carranza, Venustiano, 36–37, 41, 84
Carter, Thomas, 33
Cathcart, Tom, 101–2
"Cattle Kings Pass with the Vivid West" (White, O. P.), 63
Chenery, William Ludlow, 8, 80–81, 93, 102, 124
Chicago Symphony Orchestra, 5
Chicago Tribune, 4
childhood, 15–20, 148
Childs, Marquis, 83
Chinblom, Carl R., 95
Choate, W. G., 32
Churchill, Winston, 101
class divisions, 5

Clayton, Frances, 147
Coles, A. P., 32
Collier, Peter Fenelon, 6
Collier's, 6, 151; assignments, 84–85; founding and early history, 6; hiring White, O. P., 81; introduction letter, 80; White, O. P., as staff editor, viii; White, O. P., increasing readership, 1, 81, 82; White, O. P., pulpit, 7–8; White, O. P., removed from masthead, 123–24
communism, 107
Connally, Tom, 112
consumption of wealthy, 4
Coolidge, Calvin, 85–86, 93–94
Corbett, Jim, 23
Corcoran, Hugh, 60
Coronado, Francisco Vásquez de, 11, 142
corporate power, 7, 9
Cortner, Richard C., 117
Cosmopolitan, 40
Coughlin, Charles E., 114
counterfeiting, 86
Country Home, 101
Crane, Stephen, 3
Creager, R. B., 91–94, 96–98, 121, 128
Croly, Herbert, 9
Culberson, Charles, 23
Custer, George, 148
Cutting, Bronson, 91, 109
"Cutting Free" (White, O. P.), 109

Dallas News, 76–77, 119
Daniels, Josephus, 43–44
Darwinism, 2, 4, 58
Davidson, Lynch, 83
Davis, Britton, 32–33
Davis, Charles, 42
death threats, viii, 2, 82
Dejacque, Joseph, 8
Democratic Party convention of 1928, 89–91
Denton Herald, 68
De Zayas, George, 115–16

Díaz, Porfirio, 32–36, 51, 85–86, 116
Dies, Martin, 107
Dobie, J. Frank, 68, 88
Doolittle, James H., 134
Douglass, Frederick, 16
Dowell, Ben, 12, 52, 78
Doyle, Arthur Conan, 5
Dreiser, Theodore, 3, 40

Earp, Morgan, 19
Earp, Wyatt, 19
Easter, Henry, 30–31
economic liberalism, 9
economic panics, 2
Eddy, J. A., 32
Edison, Thomas, 122
Eighteenth Amendment, 50, 100
Einstein, Albert, 133
Elephant Butte Dam project, 33, 35, 87–88
El Paso, 69; culture and society, 22; eco-
    nomic growth, 21–22, 37, 50; gunsling-
    ers, 13–14; history and settlement,
    11–12; KKK in, 50–51; during Mexican
    Revolution, 37; National Guard
    headquarters, 42–43; during
    Prohibition, 50, 100; railroads, 12–13,
    56; reform movement, 29–30, 41–42,
    57; settlers, 17–18; as sporting town,
    22–23; White, A. M., medical prac-
    tice, 20, 23–24; White, O. P., return
    visit, 140–41
El Paso County Historical Society, 147
El Paso Herald, 21, 29–30, 39, 51, 57
El Paso Times, 29–30, 50–51, 57, 119, 123, 138
Ely, Richard, 4
Emerson, Ralph Waldo, 6
Estes, W. Lee, 97
ethnic judgments, 59

Fall, Albert B., 25, 36, 63, 99, 112
Farmers' Alliance movement, 9
farming, 39–40
Fascists, 2
Favor, Milton, 103

federal aid to schools, 7
Federal Farm Loan Board, 104–5
Federalist Party, 8
Ferguson, James Edward, 64–67, 83, 92
Ferguson, Miriam Amanda ("Ma"), 64–
    67, 79, 82–83
Ferguson Farm Tenant Act, 64
Fessenden, Helen M., 122
Fessenden, Reginald Aubrey, 122
Fitzgerald, F. Scott, 115
Fitzsimmons, Bob, 23, 30
Flood Control Act of 1928, 88
Flower, Benjamin, 7
Following the Color Line (Baker), 5
Forti, F. G., 119
Forty Years at El Paso (Mills), 55–56
Fountain, A. J., 55
Frank, George, 13
Franz Ferdinand, 40–41
Freeland, F. B., 95–96
free trade, 10
frontier individualism, 11
"A Frontier Mother" (White, O. P.), 99–
    100, 125
Frontier Times, 145

Gard, Wayne, 119, 138
Garibaldi, Giuseppi, 35
Garland, Hamlin, 3
Garner, John Nance, 105–6, 121, 123, 125
gas industry, 112–13
Gellhorn, Martha, 101
George, Henry, 4, 7, 9–11
Georgism, 11
Geronimo, 33
Gibson, Randall L., 87
Gladden, Washington, 3
Gonzalez, Abraham, 35
Good Housekeeping, 88
government regulation, 4
G. P. Putnam's Sons, 125, 128–29, 135, 140–
    41, 143, 147
Grangers, 9
"The Great American Fraud" (Adams), 5

Great Depression, 49, 99; Hoover during, 103–5

The Great Gatsby (Fitzgerald), 115

Great Western, 13

Greenback Party, 3

"Growth of Caste in America" (Russell), 5

gunslingers: El Paso, 13–14; White, O. P., and, 24–25, 87, 101

Haardt, Sara, 61

Hair, William Ivey, 117

Hamilton, A. J., 55

Hamilton, Alexander, 8

Hamiltonian model, 9

Hapgood, Norman, 6, 80

Hardin, John Wesley, 13–14, 24–25, 30, 62, 149

Harding, Warren G., 92

Hare, Jimmy, 38

Harper's, 6–7

Harris, Frank, 40

Hart, Juan, 29

Hart, Simeon, 55

Harte, Bret, 61

Hays, John Coffee, 101

Hemingway, Ernest, 101

Hepburn Act, 7

Herald, 29–30

Hertzog, Carl, 88, 141, 145–47

Hidalgo, Miguel, 142

Hidalgo County, Texas, 93–98, 127

"High Handed and Hell Bent" (White, O. P.), 91–98

Hill, George, Jr., 97

The History of the Standard Oil Company (Tarbell), 5

Hitzinger, J. G., 32

Hobby, William P., 37

Hoffman, Arthur Sullivant, 62

Holden, H. M., 94

"The Holy Ghost Takes Texas" (White, O. P.), 119

Hoover, Herbert, 49, 64, 91; during Great Depression, 103–5; White, O. P., unease, 105

Houston, Sam, 28, 119, 138

Houston Chronicle, 90

Houston Post, 119

Howard, Charles, 59

Howard, Tillie, 13

Howe, Marian, 138

Howells, William Dean, 3, 6

Huckleberry Finn (Twain), 61

Huddart, John James, 33

Huerta, Victoriano, 36, 39, 51

Hughes, Ann Leigh, 31

Hylan, John F., 78

Ickes, Harold, 107, 110, 111, 149

illness, 101–2, 124

Indian sympathizer, 20, 107

Industry and Human Welfare (Chenery), 80

Interstate Commerce Commission, 7

"In the Nature of Prophecy" (White, O. P.), 106

James, Henry, 6

James, Jesse, 82

Jefferson, Thomas, 8, 26

Jeffersonian Reform, 8–9

Jenks, Ed, 43

Jenness, J. F., 89

"A Job for Jack" (Shepherd), 94

Johnson, Burges, 141

Johnson, Hugh ("Iron Pants"), 107

Johnson, Nunnally, 83

Jones, Jesse H., 89–90

Jones, Wesley, 33

The Jungle (Sinclair), 5

Just Me and Other Poems (White, O. P.), 61

Kansas City Star, 126, 139

Kelly, Henry, 16

Kendrick, C. W., 32

Kimbrough, B. D., 94

King, Richard, 113

Kipling, Rudyard, 5

Knights of Labor, 3
Krupp, Haymon, 79
Ku Klux Klan (KKK), 65, 67, 82, 91, 94; in
    El Paso, 50–51; opposition, 83, 97

La Follette, Robert M., 94
Lamar, L. Q. C., 87
Lamar, Mirabeau B., 79
Landon, Alfred, 98, 128
land value, 4
Langtry, Lily, 22
law practice, 38
lawsuits, viii, 2, 100, 113, 128, 150
Lea, Tom, 145–46
Lead and Likker (White, O. P.), 101
Lehlback, Frederick R., 95
Lewis, Tracy Hammond, 40
libertarianism, 1; beliefs, 8; free trade, 10;
    White, O. P., frontier, 51, 131, 149, 151
Liberty, 81
Light Crust Doughboys, 123
Lincoln, Abraham, 55
Lindbergh, Charles, 86
Lloyd, Henry Demarest, 4, 6
London, Jack, 3, 5, 6
Lone Star, 29
Long, Huey: background, 113–14; down-
    ward spiral, 116–17; White, O. P., and,
    115–17, 150
Longfellow, Henry Wadsworth, 6
Los de abajo (Azuela), 34
Lowell, James Russell, 6
lower classes, 3

MacArthur, Douglas, 49
Madero, Francisco, 33–36, 39, 60
Madison, John, 8
Magoffin, James Wiley, 12, 29
Magoffin, Joseph, 29, 57
Magón, Ricardo Flores, 34
Maher, Peter, 23, 30
Manning, James, 13
Markel, Lester, 62–63, 66–67, 75; White,
    O. P., fired by, 79–80

marriage, 53
Marsh, Benjamin C., 85
Martin, R. L., 119
Martinez, Feliz, 32
Masters, Edgar Lee, 83
Masterson, Bat, 149
Maverick, Fontaine Maury, 121
Mayfield, Earle B., 50
McAllen Daily Press, 95
McCarthy, Joseph R., 107
McClure, Samuel, 5–6
McClure's Magazine, 5–6
McCormick, Cyrus, 3
McCutcheon, Frances Dunn, 31
McCutcheon, W. S., 31
McKinley, William, 9
McManus, Maureen, 140
McMath, William S., 54–55, 60–61, 88,
    100, 126–27
Meat Inspection Act, 5
Mencken, H. L., 1, 6, 54, 68, 83; on *The
    Autobiography of a Durable Sinner*, 127–
    28; background, 61; encouragement
    from, 100–101; on Holy Ghost, 110;
    *Out of the Desert: The Historical
    Romance of El Paso* review, 61–62; on
    Roosevelt, F. D., 106; on Smith A. E.,
    91; on *Texas: An Informal Biography*,
    139; White, O. P., discovered by, 132;
    White, O. P., friendship, vii, 100–101;
    White, O. P., on health, 131–32
Mexican culture, 58–59
Mexican Revolution, viii, 34–35; El Paso
    during, 37; films, 58; White, L., photos,
    38; White, O. P., on, 51–52; Wilson
    mishandling, 51
Mexico City, 32–34
Mexico government representative pro-
    posal, 135
Mills, William Wallace, 55–57
Milwaukee Journal, 94
Mississippi River Commission, 87–88
Montgomery, W. R., 96
Moody, Dan, 83, 95, 97

moral code, vii
Morehead, Charles R., 30
Morrill Land Grant Act, 79
Morrow, Dwight, 86–87
M'Rose, Martin, 24
muckraking, 1; decline, 7; early writers, 2–7; Lloyd's role, 4; Roosevelt, T., originating term, 2; White, O. P., career, 75–98
Mullen, Frank, 124, 135
Munsey's, 40
My Texas Tis of Thee (White, O. P.), 101, 118–20

Nast, Thomas, 7
National Arts Club honors, 137
National Industrial Recovery Act, 112, 118
National Labor Union, 3
National Prohibition Party, 3
National Recovery Administration, 108
natural resources, 109–10
Nelson, John E., 95
New Deal, 9, 108–9, 121; criticism, 123; White, O. P., on, 117–18, 149
Newlands, Francis G., 33
Newman, Simeon Harrison, 29
New York Morning Telegram, 60
New York Sun, 77
New York Telegraph, 40
New York Times, 1, 64–65, 93, 119, 145, 151
New York Times Sunday Magazine, 62–63; White, O. P., agreement, 75–76
Nolan, Philip, 142
"No Man's Land" (White, O. P.), 107
Norris, Frank, 3
Northern Securities, 7
nullification doctrine, 9

Obregón, Álvaro, 37, 85–87, 93
O'Daniel, W. Lee, 122–23
oil industry, 111–12; Santa Rita oil well, 79; Standard Oil, 4, 5, 6; White, O. P., business, 53
Oñate, Juan de, 11

Orozco, Pascual, 35–36
Osborn, O. S., 31, 102
Outlaw, Baz, 24
Out of the Desert: The Historical Romance of El Paso (White, O. P.), vii, 1, 50, 54–58, 123; Dobie saluting, 68; Mencken review, 61–62; regional success, 60; as solid history, 150
Overton, John H., 116

Pace, Eliza Ann, 16
Palm Beach gambling, 82
Parr, Archer, 92
Pasadena Star-News, 139
patent medicine, 5
Patton, George, 44
Payne, David Hamilton, 16
Payne, David Monroe, 31
Payne, Frank Hamilton, 31
Payne, Jesse Bignal, 31
Payne, Walker Floyd, 31
People's Party, 9
People's Reconstruction League, 87
Pershing, John J., 33, 37, 39, 44, 60, 142
Phillips, David Graham, 1, 4, 6
Phillips, John Sanborn, 5
Phillips, Moses Dresser, 6
Pickrell, Frank T., 79
Pilgrim's Progress (Bunyan), 2
Poe, Floyd, 53
poetry, 32, 44–45, 52, 143, 150–51
Poincaré, Raymond, 46
Polk, Baxter, 147
Populist Party, 3
poverty, 3–4, 10
Powell, Robert, 90
Progress and Poverty (George), 10
prohibition, 94; El Paso during, 50, 100; White, O. P., on, 100–101, 151
Promise of American Life (Croly), 9
prostitution, 27, 57, 120
protest tradition, 2
public health, 5
Pullman, George M., 3

Pulsifer, Herbert, 138
Pure Food and Drug Act, 5, 7

Quetzalcoatl, 54
Quin, Charles Kennon, 121

racial segregation, 9
Radio, the Voice of the World, 124
railroads, 12–13, 56
ranch owner, 38–39
"Rattlesnake Pete," 2, 47, 118, 131, 149
Rauschenbusch, Walter, 3
Rayburn, Sam, 112
reform movement, 4; banking reform, 7;
    El Paso, 29–30, 41–42, 57; *El Paso
    Herald* as voice, 57; Jeffersonian
    Reform, 8–9; White, O. P., as anti-
    reformer, 7
Regeneración, 34
Reid, John, 38
"Reminiscences of Texas Divines"
    (White, O. P.), 83–84
Reyes, Bernardo, 36
Reynolds, Horace, 138
Riis, Jacob, 4
Riley, James Whitcomb, 61
Robertson, Felix D., 65
Rockefeller, John D., 4
Rockefeller, John D., Jr., 43
Rogers, Will, 117
Roosevelt, Franklin Delano, 44, 90–91,
    105; Bonus Army and, 49–50;
    Mencken on, 106; White, O. P., and,
    106, 125
Roosevelt, Theodore, 4, 32, 92, 110; Meat
    Inspection Act and, 5, 7; muckraking
    term originated, 2; Pure Food and
    Drug Act and, 7; at Toltec Club, 33
Russell, Charles Edward, 5

saloons, 27–28
Salt War, 120
Santa Rita oil well, 79
Saturday Evening Post, 6, 81

"Scalping the Indian" (White, O. P.), 107
Scarborough, George, 13, 24
Schechter v. United States, 112
Schlesinger, Arthur M., 116
schooling, 20–21, 148
Scientific American, 6
Scopes Monkey Trial, 61
Sedition Act, 8
self-deprecation, 82
Selman, John ("Uncle John"), 13–14, 24–
    25, 29–30, 149
Service, Robert, 61
"Setting Them Up in Ohio" (White,
    O. P.), 100–101
Seventeenth Amendment, 7
Shame of the Cities (Steffens), 4
Sharp, T. F., 54–55
shell-shocked veterans, 49
Shepherd, Morris, 131, 149
Shepherd, William G., 94, 98
Sherman Antitrust Act, 7
"The Significance of the Frontier in
    American History" (Turner), vii
"The Silver Mirage" (White, O. P.), 118
Sinclair, Harry F., 112
Sinclair, Upton, 1, 3, 5, 6, 8
single tax, 10
Sixteenth Amendment, 7
Slater, Hughes Decourcy, 30
slavery, 9
The Smart Set, 6
Smith, Adam, 8
Smith, Alfred E., 78, 90–91
Smith, J. A., 29
Smoot-Hawley Tariff, 104
Social Gospel movement, 3
Socialists, 5
Sonnichsen, C. L., 125–26
Sons of Temperance, 28
Southwestern Ballads (White, O. P.), 52
Southwestern Milestones (White, O. P.),
    52, 147
Spaulding, H. J., 142
Standard Oil, 4, 5, 6

Stanton, Elizabeth Cady, 3
Starr, Belle, 110
state's rights, 9
Steffens, Lincoln, 4, 5, 7, 8
Stephenson, Hugh, 12
Stewart, U. S., 32
Stilwell, Frank, 19
St. Louis Post-Dispatch, 77
Stoudenmire, Dallas, 13, 25, 81
Stowe, Harriet Beecher, 6
Street, Julian, 80
Strickland, Rex, 55–56
strikes, 3
suffrage, 4, 27
Sullivan, Mark, 80

Taft, Robert A., 98
Taft, William Howard, 34–35, 92, 114
Tammany Hall, 7, 109
Tarbell, Ida, 1, 5, 6, 8
Teapot Dome scandal, 25, 87, 99, 112
temperance movement, 27–28
Texans, 113
Texas, 83–84, 101, 118–20, 119; frontier
    towns, 28; mores, 76; saloons, 28. *See
    also* El Paso; Hidalgo County, Texas;
    University of Texas
Texas: An Informal Biography (White,
    O. P.): Mencken on, 139; panoramic
    sweep, 137–38; reviews, 138–40
Texas Rangers, 13, 23, 67–68, 95, 145
Them Was the Days (White, O. P.), 76–77,
    139
Thomas, Theodore, 5
Thompson, Howard, 24
Tibbits, C. N., 32
Toltec Club, 32–33, 35, 148
Toltecs, 52, 58
Townsend, Francis E., 114
"The Treason of the Senate" (Phillips), 4
Treaty of Guadalupe Hidalgo, 12
Triangle Shirtwaist Factory fire, 94, 109
Turner, Frederick Jackson, vii, 4, 11
Turner, Timothy, 38

Turney, W. W., 32
Twain, Mark, 6, 61, 127
Tweed, William ("Boss"), 4, 7

United States Government Advertiser, 43
University of Texas, 25–26, 79, 82

Veblen, Thorstein, 4
Vestal, Stanley, 139
Villa, Francisco ("Pancho"), 35–37, 39, 51
Virginia Pilot, 61
Volker Act, 91

Wagner, Robert F., 108–9
Wainwright, Jonathan, 134
Walker, Stanley, 76, 126, 139–40
Wallace, Henry, 135
Ward, Artemus, 61
Ward, Lester Frank, 4
Warren, Francis, 33
Wealth Against Commonwealth (Lloyd), 4
Wealth of Nations (Smith), 8
weapon buying, 81–82
Weiss, Carl, 115
Wells, James B., 92
"Western Trails" last book, 141–43, 145–47,
    150
Westinghouse, George, 122
Wharton, Edith, 6
"When the Public Needs a Friend"
    (White, O. P.), 108
White, Alward, Jr., 15, 18, 31; acting out
    plays, 19; christening, 20; death of,
    101–3; marriage, 103; medical practice,
    38–39; medical school, 30
White, Alward McKeel, 15; cattle-rustlers
    and, 18; death of, 26; El Paso medical
    practice, 20, 23–24, 148; frontiersman,
    18–19; ranching, 16–17
White, Hazel Harvey ("Mike"), viii, 97,
    103; attracting, 52–53; driving of, 131;
    marriage, 53; move to New York City,
    75; at Peconic Bay, 133–34; "Western
    Trails" last book and, 145–47

White, Kathryn, 15–16; cyanide tablets and, 18; death of, 30–31, 101; El Paso society and, 22; frontier experience, 18–19; ranching, 17

White, Leigh (Osborn), 15, 19, 45, 103; on *The Autobiography of a Durable Sinner*, 126; christening, 20; on El Paso society, 22; marriage, 31; Mexican Revolution photos, 38; papers donated, 147; visits to, 89, 123, 140; wedding attendant, 53

White, Owen Payne, *70, 73*; acting out plays, 19; antireformer, 7; on Anti-Saloon League, 81; army enlistment, 44–45; attracting Mike, 52–53; awestruck observer prank, 77–78; on Bailey, 128–29; on Bellinger, 120–21; birth, 1, 11; breezy style, 125; at brother's funeral, 103; as businessman, 30–31; on Calles, 84–86; childhood, 15–20, 148; christening, 20; *Collier's* as pulpit for, 7–8; Collier's hiring, 81; *Collier's* readership increase, 1, 81, 82; *Collier's* staff editor, viii; on communism, 107; correspondence, 126–27, 130–31; on counterfeiting, 86; death of, 144; on Democratic Party convention of 1928, 89–91; on elections, 63–65; El Paso return, 140–41; ethnic judgments, 59; failing health, 141, 143–44; farming and, 39–40; on Federal Farm Loan Board, 104–5; on Ferguson, M., 66–67, 79, 82–83; on Fessenden, R. A., 122; first bout of intoxication, 24; in France, 45–46; frontier libertarianism, 51, 131, 149, 151; Garner and, 105–6; on gas industry, 112–13; gunslingers and, 24–25, 87, 101; Hoover unease, 105; hospital unit assignment, 46–47, *72*; on Hylan, 78; illness, 101–2, 124; Indian sympathizer, 20, 107; jewelry store job, 25; legacy, 147; Long and, 115–17, 150; lower-octane material, 82; making of, 1–14; Markel firing, 79–80;

Markel reviewing, 63; marriage, 53; Mencken discovering, 132; Mencken friendship, vii, 100–101; on Mencken's health, 131–32; Mexican culture and, 58–59; on Mexican Revolution, 51–52; in Mexico City, 32–34; Mexico government representative proposal, 135; Mills and, 56–57; on Mississippi River Commission, 87–88; moral code, vii; move to New York City, 75, 149; muckraking career, 75–98; National Arts Club honors, 137; national career, 49–68; on National Recovery Administration, 108; on natural resources, 109–10; on New Deal, 117–18, 149; as news reporter, 40; as new veteran, 52; *New York Times Sunday Magazine* agreement, 75–76; obituaries, 145; on O'Daniel, 122–23; oil business, 53; on oil industry, 111–12; on Palm Beach gambling, 82; at Peconic Bay, 133–34; poetry, 32, 44–45, 52, 143, 150–51; potboiler articles, 110; practicing law, 38; on prohibition, 100–101, 151; protest tradition, 2; public schooling, 20–21, 148; ranch owner, 38–39; Rattlesnake Pete, 2, 47, 118, 131, 149; Roosevelt, F. D., and, 106, 125; on Santa Rita oil well, 79; sarcasm, 51; self-deprecation, 82; as serious writer, 53–55; social life, *71*; solid historian, 150; on Texans, 113; on Texas Rangers, 67–68; threats to, 97; Toltec Club and, 32–33, 35, 148; on Toltecs, 52, 58; tongue-in-cheek style, 149; at University of Texas, 25–26; on University of Texas, 79, 82; on Wagner, 108–9; on war bonds, 136; on weapon buying, 81–82; "Western Trails" last book, 141–43, 145–47, 150; Wilson as target, 60; wit, viii, 1; world view, 106–7; on World War I atrocities, 46–47; World War I reporter, 43; World War II patriotic

White, Owen Payne (*continued*)
    efforts, 2, *74*, 137; on World War II
    war bonds, 136; writers encouraged
    by, 88–89. *See also specific topics*
White, Richard D., Jr., 117
Whitman, Marcus A., 142
Whittier, John Greenleaf, 6
Wilkinson, James, 142
Williams, Al, 117
Williams, T. Harry, 116–17
Wills, Bob, 123
Wilson, Woodrow, 7, 36–37, 39, 41, 104;
    Mexican Revolution mishandling, 51;
    toasts to, 46; as White, O. P., target, 60
Wing, Andrew S., 102
Wingo, T. M., 32
wireless communication system, 122
Wise, William D., 30
wit, viii, 1

Woman's Home Companion, 88
Women's Christian Temperance Union, 3,
    28
Wood, Leonard, 33
Woodful, Walter, 111
World War I: reporter, 43; shell-shocked
    veterans, 49; start of, 40–41; White,
    O. P., on atrocities, 46–47
World War II: onset, 124; patriotic efforts
    on home front, 2, *74*, 137; White, O. P.,
    on war bonds, 136
Wurzbach, Harry, 97

Yeats, John W., 119

Zapata, Emiliano, 36
Zimany, Alexander, 126
Zimmerman telegram, 41